Metonymy

'Metonymy' is a type of figurative language used in everyday conversation, a form of shorthand that allows us to use our shared knowledge to communicate with fewer words than we would otherwise need. 'I'll pencil you in' and 'let me give you a hand' are both examples of metonymic language. Metonymy serves a wide range of communicative functions such as textual cohesion, humour, irony, euphemism and hyperbole – all of which play a key role in the development of language and discourse communities. Using authentic data throughout, this book shows how metonymy operates, not just in language, but also in gesture, sign language, art, music, film and advertising. It explores the role of metonymy in cross-cultural communication, along with the challenges it presents to language learners and translators. Ideal for researchers and students in linguistics and literature, as well as teachers and general readers interested in the art of communication.

JEANNETTE LITTLEMORE is a Reader in Applied Linguistics and Head of the Department of English Language and Applied Linguistics at the University of Birmingham.

Metonymy: Hidden Shortcuts in Language, Thought and Communication

Jeannette Littlemore

CAMBRIDGE
UNIVERSITY PRESS

University Printing House, Cambridge CB2 8BS, United Kingdom

One Liberty Plaza, 20th Floor, New York, NY 10006, USA

477 Williamstown Road, Port Melbourne, VIC 3207, Australia

314-321, 3rd Floor, Plot 3, Splendor Forum, Jasola District Centre, New Delhi-110025, India

79 Anson Road, #06-04/06, Singapore 079906

Cambridge University Press is part of the University of Cambridge.

It furthers the University's mission by disseminating knowledge in the pursuit of education, learning and research at the highest international levels of excellence.

www.cambridge.org
Information on this title: www.cambridge.org/9781108454162

First published 2015
First paperback edition 2018

A catalogue record for this publication is available from the British Library

ISBN 978-1-107-04362-6 Hardback
ISBN 978-1-108-45416-2 Paperback

For Dan, Joe and Oscar

Contents

Figures

Acknowledgements

First and foremost I would like to thank Andrew Winnard at Cambridge University Press for his constant support and encouragement throughout the writing of this book and for having believed in the project from the outset. I would also like to thank Joanna Breeze, also at Cambridge University Press, for leading the production process. I am also indebted to a number of people who have provided valuable feedback and who have had very interesting things to say about the contents of this book. These include: Satomi Arizono, Antonio Barcelona, John Barnden, Tony Berber Sardinha, Ewa Biernacka, Lynne Cameron, Alan Cienki, Alice Deignan, Pilar Durán Escribano, Charles Forceville, Ray Gibbs, Nicholas Groom, Robert Holland, Joseph Holloway, Susan Hunston, Almut Koester, Tina Krennmayr, Graham Low, Fiona MacArthur, Khalid Mahmood, Daniel Malt, Joe Malt, Oscar Malt, Alice May, Rosamund Moon, Lee Oakley, Daphne Papadoudi, Paula Pérez-Sobrino, Peter Richardson, Ana Roldan Riejos, Francisco Ruiz de Mendoza, Wendy Scase, Elena Semino, Gerard Steen, Rachel Sutton-Spence, Caroline Tagg, John Taylor, Paul Thompson and Tong Xiaoqiong. I would also like to thank the anonymous reviewers, especially the writer of the clearance review who provided particularly valuable feedback which shaped the final version of the book. My final thanks go to Sara Peacock, who was much, much more than an editor, and to Helen Bitton, who has created a first-class index, and who 'has now started to spot Metonymy everywhere!'

Introduction

Metonymy is a cognitive and linguistic process through which we use one thing to refer to another. For example, we might use the word 'Hollywood' to refer to mainstream American films, or the word 'Shakespeare' to refer to plays and poetry by Shakespeare. In these examples, a place and a person are used to refer to things that are strongly related to that particular place and that particular person. Metonymy often involves using a simple or concrete concept to refer to something that is more complex or more abstract, or even sensitive, so in American history the terms '9/11' and 'Pearl Harbor' are used to refer to the events that took place on that date and in that place respectively. As we will see in this book, metonymic thinking is extremely widespread. We think metonymically all the time in order to put the large amount of information that is available about the world into a manageable form. The presence of metonymy in our everyday thinking means that it leaves traces in language and in other forms of expression.

Metonymy is often discussed in relation to metaphor but the two are quite different. Whereas metaphor usually involves some sort of comparison between largely unrelated entities (or entities that are construed as being unrelated in that particular context), in metonymy, the relationship between a term and its referent is usually much closer. From the point of view of the analyst, this makes it harder to spot, but from the point of view of the user, the nature of metonymy renders it a much more subtle way of conveying nuance, evaluation and perspective.

Since the 1990s we have seen a proliferation of books on metaphor, but there are no extensive book-length treatments of metonymy that discuss its role in authentic discourse and other forms of communication. This is surprising given the ubiquity of metonymy and the key functions that it performs. As well as its referential function, which is well documented, metonymy is used, for example, to build identity within discourse communities and to facilitate speedy communication. It helps build relationships through appeals to shared knowledge and through these same processes it can facilitate social 'distancing'. Metonymy involves indirectness, which means that it underlies a great deal of euphemism, hedging and vague language. It serves important evaluative purposes and is often used for positioning oneself within a debate. The potential that metonymy offers for 'language play' means that it underpins a significant amount of humour and irony, and other ludic and creative uses of language. Moreover, as this book will show, the presence of metonymy in all modes of expression reflects the key role that it plays in the formulation and communication of ideas.

Because metonymy is so subtle and so nuanced, it is easily missed or misinterpreted. The most common misinterpretations occur when a metonymically intended meaning is taken literally or metaphorically, or alternatively when a literal or metaphorical meaning is understood as a metonymy. Misunderstandings such as these can occur even between people who know each other well and who have sufficient shared knowledge to facilitate the extensive use of metonymy. They can also occur in professional or academic contexts when, for example, researchers from different disciplines communicate with one another on interdisciplinary projects. As we will see in Chapter 8, misinterpretations also occur in global geopolitical settings, and these can contribute to political conflict both nationally and internationally. Misinterpretations are even more likely to occur in communication between people who have different cultural and linguistic backgrounds. Because metonymy is so subtle, the reasons for these misinterpretations are often missed, and misunderstandings continue.

The aim of this book is to present a full discussion of the different types of metonymy that have been identified in the literature, the different functions that metonymy performs, the contribution that it makes to successful communication in language and other forms of expression, the role that it plays in intercultural communication, and the types of misinterpretations that can occur in these contexts. Real-world data are used throughout. The book's primary focus is on metonymy in language but it also considers the role played by metonymy in different modes of expression, such as art, music, film and advertising. I examine current theories of metonymy, most of which have been developed within the cognitive linguistic paradigm, and assess the extent to which these theories could usefully be extended to account for the complex, multi-layered nature of metonymy as it occurs 'in the wild'. I also look at how metonymy is processed in the mind and at how the ability to understand and produce metonymy develops over time in both typically developing individuals and individuals with linguistic impairments.

Contextualised examples of metonymy are analysed in depth to show how metonymy operates in spoken and written language as well as in sign language, and other forms of expression. When discussing the role played by metonymy in spoken language, I focus on the interactive, dynamic role played by metonymy in two-way communication. This allows for an exploration of the role played by metonymy in the gestures that accompany speech. I look at exchanges involving adults and children, and native and non-native speakers of English, in everyday, academic and workplace settings. The discussions of metonymy in written language adopt a very broad definition of 'written language' to allow for a consideration of the use of metonymy in modern media, such as text messaging, as well as in different written genres, taken from sources ranging from journalism, through business correspondence, to literature, narrative and academic writing. The data include extracts of written language produced by native and non-native speakers of English. Many of the examples used in this book are taken from authentic language corpora, such as the Bank of English (BofE), the British National Corpus (BNC), the Corpus of Contemporary American English (COCA) and Webcorp. No artificial examples are used. There are also discussions of the ways in which metonymy is used in other media, which illustrate its multimodal and dynamic nature. The book thus aims to provide an analysis of metonymy as it is really used, in order to produce a theoretical and practical account of its role in language and other forms of communication.[1]

Before beginning the book, we need a note on terminology. In the literature on metonymy, individual instances of metonymy are sometimes referred to as 'metonyms' and sometimes as 'metonymies'. This difference generally reflects the perspective of the writer. People looking at metonymy from a purely lexical perspective generally prefer the term 'metonym', whereas people studying the phenomenon from a cognitive linguistic perspective generally prefer the term 'metonymy'. Because the approach taken in this volume is broadly in line with a cognitive linguistic perspective, and because the scope of the volume extends well beyond language, the term 'metonymy' is used throughout.

[1] All instances of metonymy that are discussed in this book were identified as such by at least two speakers of the language in which they occurred. In order to code instances as 'metonymy', Biernacka's (2013) metonymy identification procedure was employed. As we will see in Section 6.2, this identification procedure is not unproblematic. Where problems were encountered, these are elucidated in the text. In order to extrapolate from a single instance of metonymy to a 'metonymy type', an adapted version of Steen's (1999) procedure for conceptual metaphor identification was employed. This is also explained in Section 6.2.

1 'What those boys need is a good handbagging'

What is metonymy?

1.1 Introduction

Metonymy is a figure of language and thought in which one entity is used to refer to, or in cognitive linguistic terms 'provide access to', another entity to which it is somehow related. In order to illustrate this, let us look at an example:

The trains are on strike. (BofE)

In order to understand this sentence, we use our knowledge of trains, including the fact that they have drivers, and that without these drivers no trains will run, to infer that it is not the actual trains that are on strike, but the drivers of those trains.

Let us look at another example:

The kettle boiled and bubbled. (BofE)

Here we use our common-sense or everyday knowledge of what kettles are for to infer that it was of course not the kettle that 'boiled and bubbled', but the water inside it. In these particular examples, we draw on our knowledge of the relationships between trains and their drivers and between kettles and their contents in order to understand what is actually meant. In a very basic sense, therefore, metonymy is a process which allows us to use one well-understood aspect of something to stand for the thing as a whole, or for some other aspect of it, or for something to which it is very closely related (Gibbs, 1994). It is most appropriately seen as a tool that we use to think about things and to communicate our thoughts, and, as such, it is a property of both our conceptual and our linguistic system (Gibbs, 1999).

One of the reasons why we need metonymy is that it is impossible to encapsulate all aspects of our intended meaning in the language that we use. In other words, language always 'underspecifies' meaning in that it cannot possibly express everything that is relevant to its interpretation (Radden *et al.*, 2007), and inferences are needed to work out what is meant (Frisson, 2009). Related to this is the fact that we think 'metonymically' because it is physically impossible to consciously activate all the knowledge that we have of a particular concept at once, so we tend to focus on a salient aspect of that concept, and use this as point of access to the whole concept. For example, when asked to picture a computer, most people will picture just the screen, rather than the hard disk, the tower, the mouse and so on. When asked to think of 'France', people might picture a place in France that they visited, or a rough map of France, or an iconic representation of France such as the Eiffel Tower. It is impossible to picture the whole of France at once as this information could not be held in one's working memory, even if one had travelled extensively in France. To a large extent, therefore, it can be said that metonymy is prevalent in language simply because it is a property of our everyday thought processes (Langacker, 1993).

Metonymy is often discussed alongside metaphor and, as we will see in subsequent chapters, is occasionally confused with metaphor. However, as we can see from the above examples, unlike metaphor, which usually involves some sort of comparison between two unrelated entities, metonymy is a cognitive and linguistic process whereby one thing is used to refer to something else, to which it is closely related in some way. The relationship does not involve comparison. To illustrate, let us look at another example:

Do you want me to *pencil you in* for the time being? (BofE)

In this example, 'pencil you in' is used metonymically to mean 'make a provisional appointment'. The secretary offers to write the appointment in pencil rather than pen so that the customer can make last-minute changes if necessary. 'Pencil in' thus stands metonymically for what one might do with a pencil (i.e. write something down which can subsequently be rubbed out). The word 'you' is also used metonymically in this example to refer to 'your name'. This example is typical of the way in which metonymy is used in everyday language as a kind of communicative shorthand, allowing people to use their shared knowledge of the world to communicate with fewer words than they would otherwise need.

Although in the above example metonymy serves a mainly referential purpose, it can be used for a wide variety of communicative functions, such as relationship-building, humour, irony and euphemism (Deignan *et al.*, 2013; Panther and Thornburg, 2007; Ruiz de Mendoza Ibáñez and Otal Campo, 2002). One of its key functions is to provide a subtle form of evaluation of people or things (Levin and Lindquist, 2007). In the following example, the word 'suits' is a metonymy which refers in a negative way, to accountants and managers:

The best part of working at night is that *the suits* have gone home. (BofE)

By referring to accountants and managers via the suits that they wear, the writer manages to portray them as being somewhat characterless, conventional but powerful individuals who could simply be replaced with another 'suit' if anything unfortunate should happen to them. Metonymy is also used in order to be deliberately vague (see Channell, 1994 for a discussion of the functions of vague language). For example, if we ask 'What are you doing at Christmas?', 'Christmas' most probably refers to the holiday period around the Christmas time of year, and not to Christmas Day specifically. It would sound unnecessarily pedantic to ask 'What are you doing on Christmas Day itself and in the days immediately before and after Christmas?'

A common type of metonymy involves the use of a producer to refer to a product, as in:

The kind of character we often find in *Dickens*. (BofE)

In this example, the 'producer' (Dickens) refers metonymically to his 'product' (i.e. books written by Charles Dickens). In the literature on metonymy, this would be referred to as an example of a PRODUCER FOR PRODUCT metonymy. It is conventional in the literature to indicate these 'over-arching' metonymy types using of small capitals, as has been done here. Other metonymies involving the PRODUCER FOR PRODUCT relationship include the following:

I softened to a mere fortissimo, trudging through *the Mozart.* (BofE)

A fifty-year-old *Steinway* that has been reconditioned. (BofE)

Another type of metonymy involves PART FOR WHOLE relationships, as in:

The perfect *set of wheels* for the young racer. (BofE)

In this example, 'set of wheels' refers to the whole car. Corpus evidence suggests that when the expression 'set of wheels' is used to refer to the whole car, it is nearly always in the context of a young man purchasing a car, or of positively evaluating a car. This positive evaluation may come from the fact that the focus is on *the wheels* and these are the key part of the car that moves; the expression may thus evoke an image in which there is nothing on the wheels to slow them down. This example shows how metonymy can be used to highlight some features of a phenomenon and leave others in the shade (Langacker, 1993). It also shows how the meaning of metonymy often depends heavily on the context in which it occurs.

At times, a single action is used to refer metonymically to a complex event, as in:

Put the kettle on. I'll be home by five o'clock. (BofE)

Here, 'put the kettle on' refers to the whole process of making a cup of tea (or coffee). It would be very odd to list all the actions involved in making a cup of tea so the use of metonymy here is necessary to allow communication to take place in an appropriate time period. In some contexts, 'put the kettle on' can have an additional pragmatic meaning of 'let's sit down and talk about it' when someone tells a friend of a problem, as we can see in the following example from British English:

Now dry your eyes and *we'll put the kettle on.* (BofE)

This is an instance of 'metonymic chaining' (Dirven, 2003), where one metonymy (in this case, 'put the kettle on' for 'make a cup of tea') leads to another ('drink tea together' for 'drink tea together while sharing one's problems'). It could also be seen as 'metaphoreme', which Cameron and Deignan (2006: 674) define as non-literal expression which 'combine[s] specific lexical and grammatical form with specific conceptual content and with specific affective value and pragmatics'. Both of these phenomena (metonymic chaining and metaphoreme) are explored later in the book.

In yet another type of metonymy, a person's salient feature (or the one that is most relevant to the situation at hand) can be used to refer to the person as a whole, as in:

But the brothers needed *muscle*, which is where Frankie Fraser came in. (BofE)

In this example, 'muscle' is a metonymy for a strong (and, in this particular case, violent) person. The most interesting or relevant *characteristic* of someone or something is used to refer to the *person or thing*. Frankie Fraser was a notoriously violent London gang member and criminal. The 'muscle' here is presumably going to be used to beat someone up or to provide a threat to do so, so we have another possible case of metonymic chaining here involving an OBJECT FOR ACTION metonymy (the muscle stands for what it is going to be used for) and an ACTUAL FOR POTENTIAL metonymy (the actual beating up represents the potential threat of a beating). Other metonymies involving body parts can involve the brain, as in 'Ayyad may have been *the brains behind* the making of the bomb' (BofE), or the mouth, as in '*so many mouths to feed* and jobs to find' (BofE), or just about any other part of the body. Metonymies such as these can have a depersonalising effect and therefore can convey subtle (often negative) evaluations of the people being talked about.

We can see from this short list of examples that metonymy is used to communicate fairly complex ideas relatively efficiently and that it can serve as shorthand for much longer events or ideas. It is so prevalent that our language would sound odd without it. Successful communication involving metonymy requires a large amount of shared knowledge between speakers, concerning their worldview and their expectations of 'how things should be' (Durán Escribano and Roldan Riejos, 2008). This means that despite being an efficient communicative device, metonymy has the potential to cause serious misunderstandings if the shared knowledge and expectations on which it relies are not perfectly matched. It is often difficult to pinpoint the source of such misunderstandings, as both metonymy and metonymic inferences can be very difficult to detect. As we will see in Chapter 8, the problem can become even more noticeable when metonymy is used in exchanges between people from different cultural or linguistic backgrounds.

Although all of the above examples have involved language, metonymy is first and foremost a *cognitive* phenomenon, and refers to any instance (regardless of whether language is involved or not) where a salient aspect of a particular entity is used to access the entity as a whole, or to a related entity (Langacker, 1993). For instance, when asked to recall the place where we grew up, we are more likely to picture a particular street rather than the whole town, and when asked to think of a friend, we are more likely to picture their face than any other part of their body. Metonymic *thinking* is what connects a part to a whole or to a related entity in our minds. This can be illustrated through an interesting series of metonymies that surrounded Margaret Thatcher during her period as the British Prime Minister (1979–90). Margaret Thatcher had a reputation for being a fierce and uncompromising leader who inspired both fear and respect among her followers. Anecdotally, members of Margaret Thatcher's inner Cabinet claimed that when she was temporarily called away from Cabinet meetings, she would often leave her handbag on the table and that its presence made them feel as if she were very much still in the room, so they would behave accordingly (Norton, 1990). Thus the handbag became a metonymy for Margaret Thatcher's presence and for her powerful personality. The image of Margaret Thatcher holding her handbag subsequently came to represent her particular (right-wing) views of politics and economics, her political persona as a shrewd and thrifty housewife, and her particular (negative) attitude towards the European Union, where she sought value for money at all costs. All of these connotations result from extended metonymic thinking processes. Linking back to language, Margaret Thatcher's handbag also lies behind the meaning of the term 'handbagging', which is used to refer to the process of receiving a stern telling-off, usually from a woman, as in the noun phrase 'a good handbagging' in the following example:

What those boys need is *a good handbagging.* (BofE)

The term 'handbagging' tends to have negative, ironic (and somewhat sexist) overtones, because of its strong associations with Margaret Thatcher and 'bossy women' in general.

The fact that metonymy is a cognitive phenomenon, not just a linguistic one, means that it appears in a range of other modalities besides language (Müller, 2008). Metonymy has been found to play a role in a wide variety of different modes of communication and meaning creation, such as art, music, film and advertising. For instance, in Japanese 'manga' cartoons, the absence of hands (and sometimes feet) in the picture of a character can metonymically represent loss of control by that character (Abbott and Forceville, 2011). Metonymy is also prevalent in sculpture and architecture, particularly religious architecture, where various metonymic devices are exploited in several modalities at once in order to create desired 'iconic' effects. In music, repeated extracts, or more recently, sampling, can provide metonymic (often ironic) references to other pieces of music or even whole styles of music. Conducting also involves metonymy, as do the gestures employed by music teachers when teaching musical concepts (Chuang, 2010). Metonymy can also be found in forms of media that are intrinsically *multimodal*, such as film and advertising. The role of metonymy in film is well attested, reflecting the enormous potential for metonymy afforded by changes in angle and camera focus. For example, to continue with the theme of 'hands', Forceville (2009) shows how in Robert Bresson's film *Un condamné à mort s'est échappé* (A Man Escaped) close-ups of hands are used repeatedly throughout the film to metonymically represent phenomena that either aid or impede the protagonist's escape from a Nazi prisoner-of-war camp. In advertising, sought-after lifestyles and other aspirations can be hinted at through a variety of metonymic devices. One might catch a glimpse of a designer handbag, an attractive man, or the edge of an 'infinity pool', and use these to build up an image of a particular lifestyle and then picture oneself living that life. In both film and advertising, complementary metonymic messages can be conveyed in a single scene through the language, camera angle, actor movement and music. As we will see in later chapters, the ways in which metonymy works in these art forms can, at times, be different from the ways in which it works in language, although there are substantial areas of overlap.

1.2 Metonymy from a cognitive linguistic perspective

There have been two broad approaches to the study of metonymy: the cognitive approach, which is mostly concerned with the conceptual properties of metonymy, and the linguistic approach, which has tended to focus on how metonymy operates in language. These approaches generally complement one another, although there are occasional inconsistencies between them. Most of the recent work on metonymy has been carried out in cognitive linguistics, a field of study which focuses on the relationship between language and thought. The most widely agreed upon cognitive linguistic definition of metonymy is as follows:

> Metonymy is a cognitive process in which one conceptual element or entity (thing, event, property), the vehicle, provides mental access to another conceptual entity (thing, event, property), the target, within the same frame, domain or idealized cognitive model (ICM). (Kövecses, 2006: 99)

As we can see from this definition, a key idea for cognitive linguists is that metonymy draws on the relationship that exists between the two items within a particular knowledge network. Some of the terminology in this definition needs unpacking. Early work in cognitive linguistics (e.g. Fillmore, 1982) referred to these networks of knowledge as 'frames'. These are 'static or dynamic representations of typical situations in life and their typical elements' which are formed via a process of 'inductive generalisations from our everyday experiences' (Blank, 1999: 173). Blank distinguishes between 'static frames' and 'dynamic scenarios'. PRODUCER FOR PRODUCT metonymies, such as the 'Steinway' and 'Mozart' examples listed above, involve 'static frames', as there is no time element involved. In contrast, the 'put the kettle on' metonymies mentioned above involve 'dynamic scenarios' as they make reference to a series of actions including, for example, putting the teabags in the teapot, pouring the water on top of them then pouring the tea into a cup and drinking it. These actions come together to form a dynamic process, of which 'putting the kettle on' is only the start.

In reality there can never really be a cut-and-dried distinction between 'static' and 'dynamic' knowledge. To illustrate, the British Sign Language (BSL) sign for 'taxi' involves clicking one's fingers, and thus refers to a static phenomenon (the taxi) via a reference to the beginning of a dynamic process (the summoning of a taxi). Similarly, one possible BSL sign for 'bus' involves showing an imaginary bus pass, which again evokes knowledge of a dynamic nature, such as knowledge of the fact that some people have bus passes that they have to show to the driver in order to be allowed onto the bus. We can therefore conclude that the division between 'static frames' and 'dynamic scenarios' is somewhat artificial in practice.

For these reasons, it is more appropriate to talk about 'idealised cognitive models' (ICMs), as these emphasise the encyclopaedic, flexible, slightly idiosyncratic nature of the knowledge networks that we have in our heads (Lakoff, 1987; Radden and Kövecses, 1999).[1] Idealised cognitive models encompass the cultural knowledge that people have and are not restricted to the 'real world'. That is to say, they also encompass people's subjective views of a particular concept and can be highly idiosyncratic as they are an abstraction from people's encounters with that particular concept. They are highly schematic and flexible, and can be static or dynamic, or both. They are 'idealised' in the sense that they are not necessarily 'real'.

A possible ICM for 'cars' is shown in Figure 1.1. As we saw above, metonymy allows us to use one part of an ICM to refer, or 'gain access' to another. Within this driving ICM, metonymies might include:

[1] Lakoff (1987) lists five types of ICM: propositional ICMs, image schema ICMs, metaphoric ICMs, metonymic ICMs and symbolic ICMs. What I am referring to here are propositional ICMs. The fact that Lakoff includes metaphor and metonymy in his list is somewhat infelicitous as these are best seen as operational or 'dynamic' cognitive processes rather than non-operational cognitive models. This view is also expounded by Ruiz de Mendoza Ibáñez, 1998.

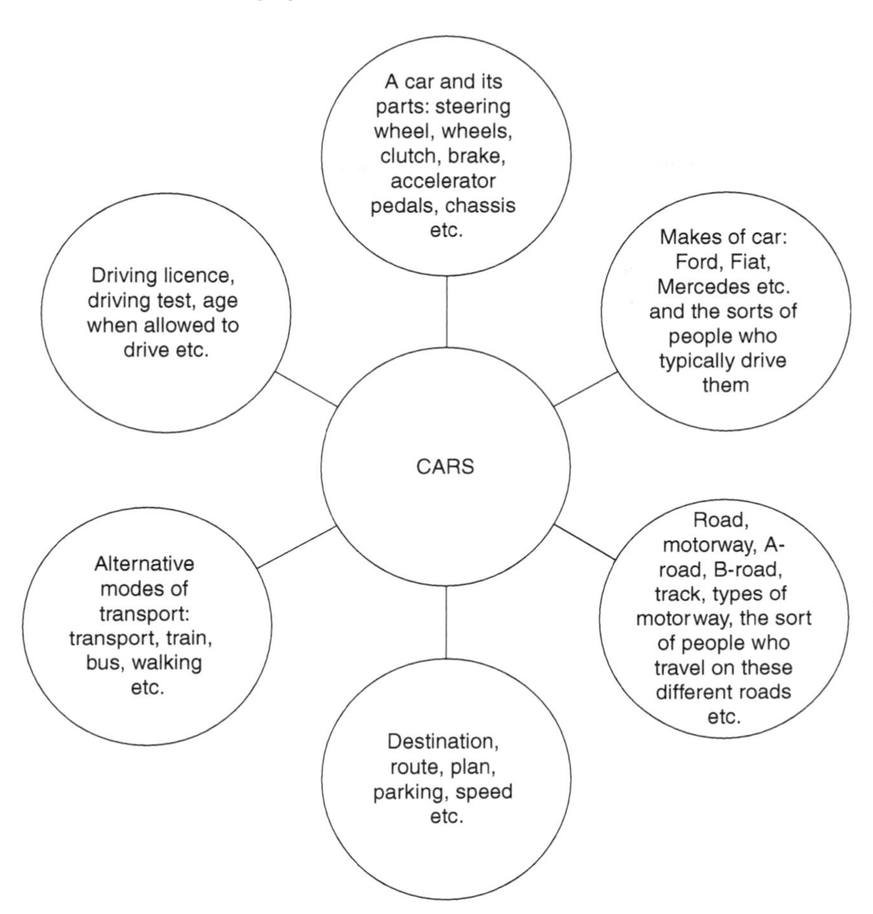

Figure 1.1 A possible idealised cognitive model for 'cars'

He falls asleep *at the wheel* at 5.30. (BofE)

Low quality junk food typical of *the M25 commuter.* (BofE)

Businessmen and women rush to work in *Mercedes and Jaguars.* (BofE)

Steve *floored the accelerator*, the *tyres screeched* and I smelled *burning.* (BofE)

New Labour has long sought to appeal to *Mondeo Man.* (BofE)

Webb wove his way between the leisurely *Sunday drivers*, curbing his impatience. (BofE)

At the wheel, which is metonymic shorthand for 'while driving' tends to collocate with 'falling asleep', presumably because the idea of being 'at the wheel' is construed as being somehow less active than simply 'driving'. The *M25 commuter* is portrayed as someone who leads a very busy lifestyle, rushing to and from work, and often doesn't have time to eat properly. The fact that the M25 is a circular road possibly underscores the monotony and repetitiveness of their life, and the fact that it is a popular road round London, used by many thousands of drivers a day emphasises the banality and everydayness of the M25 commuter. The Mercedes and Jaguars in which the businessmen and women 'rush to work' connote busy and affluent lifestyles. The three metonymies *floored the accelerator*, the *tyres screeched* and *I smelled burning* work together to invoke an image of excessive speed. *Mondeo Man* is an expression that was popular in Britain in the 1980s and 1990s. It is metonymic shorthand for an 'average' family man who likes his car, lives in the suburbs, and possibly spends his weekends cleaning his car and pottering in his garage (a *Mondeo* is an example of the sort of 'sensible' car that such a man might own). *Mondeo Man* is, by definition, not an 'exciting' man. *Sunday drivers* are people who like to drive at a slow, leisurely pace, as if they were on a 'Sunday outing', much to the annoyance of other drivers. The British Sign Language (BSL) sign for 'car' involves a person turning a steering wheel, which is also a metonymy.

This ICM also gives rise to non-linguistic metonymies. The Mini driven by the comic character Mr Bean is a kind of metonymic shorthand for his character. It is a rather sickly yellow-coloured British car, which is much too small for him, with different coloured panels where he has had it repaired on the cheap. The fact that he drives this car links him to it, meaning that it could be seen as a metonymy for his character. On the other hand, the fact that cars and people constitute different 'conceptual domains' means that Mr Bean's Mini could also be viewed as a metaphor. The difficulties involved in distinguishing metonymy from metaphor are discussed below and in Chapter 6.

We ought, at this point, to think a bit more about what ICMs are and how they come to exist. The best way to describe them is as a series of embodied, encyclopaedic, abstract, loosely connected and somewhat idiosyncratic knowledge networks that we have in our minds. But how do they get there? The explanation usually given is that ICMs build up gradually over time as a result of our interactions with the world and the people in the world. In other words, they are largely 'usage-based'. So, for example, the 'driving' ICM that we have just referred to arises as a result of our experiences with cars, which explains why ICMs are sometimes somewhat idiosyncratic: a person who knows how to drive a car will have a slightly different 'car' ICM from a child who is only ever a passenger, and a car mechanic will have a different, more detailed 'car' ICM than either of these groups. These 'specialist' ICMs underlie the development of much of the (often metonymic) specialised terminology that is used by experts in various fields. As well as an individual's own interaction with cars, a 'car' ICM will also be shaped by other people's views of cars and is therefore, to a large extent, socially constructed and culturally specific: we do not need to have had first-hand experience of 'Sunday drivers', 'M25 commuters' or 'Mondeo men' to understand who or what these terms are referring to. To sum up, ICMs are shaped by our own experiences of the world and by the experiences of others who share the world that we inhabit. This is why their content is largely shared across discourse communities while also displaying idiosyncratic tendencies. They also evolve, as individual experiences develop and cultural attitudes change over time. It is of course important to note that no instance of metonymy is ever understood in relation to just one ICM. Comprehension of the car-related examples mentioned above would probably involve the activation of several ICMs at once, including, perhaps, a 'driving' ICM, a 'types of drivers' ICM, 'Sunday' ICM, a 'motorways' ICM and so on. The number and type of ICMs that are activated at any one time will depend largely on context.

Finally, it is useful to consider another important concept in cognitive linguistics, that of the 'image schema'. Image schemas are one of the most basic building blocks of cognition and constitute another type of ICM. Image schemas are the first and most fundamental mental representations of knowledge that we develop as children. They arise from our first encounters with objects and the ways in which our bodies interact with those objects, and are thus 'embodied'. They include, for example, the fact that objects can be contained (the CONTAINER schema), objects can form part of other objects (the PART–WHOLE schema) and things can be central or peripheral (the CENTRE–PERIPHERY schema); that objects can be countable or uncountable (the MASS–COUNT schema) and that objects and people can move from one place to another along a sequence of continuous locations (the SOURCE–PATH–GOAL schema). As we will see throughout this book, image schemas such as these are heavily involved in metonymy production and comprehension.

Metonymy can therefore be seen as a cognitive process which we use all the time when we use language or, as we will see later in the book, any form of symbolic communication. When metonymic thinking is active, new metonymies may emerge, but more often than not, the metonymies that we use are so conventional that we may not recognise them as such. Metonymic thinking becomes more apparent when novel metonymies are produced, or when we encounter metonymies that are new to us, such as when we are exposed to new languages or enter new discourse communities.

1.3 The differences between metonymy and metaphor

One of the most popular and enduring ways of explaining metonymy is to compare and contrast it with metaphor. Since Jakobson's influential paper (1956) in which he postulated that metaphor and metonymy constitute two distinct ways of perceiving and processing information about the world, linguists have identified a number of ways in which metonymy contrasts with metaphor. However, as we will see later in this book, the dividing line between metaphor and metonymy is by no means clear cut, with some researchers (Dirven, 2003) arguing that literal language, metonymy and metaphor are best viewed as sitting along a continuum ranging from literal language through to metaphor, with metonymy sitting in the middle. There is by no means a consensus regarding the nature of the difference between metaphor and metonymy.

In an attempt to explain the differences between metaphor and metonymy, some cognitive linguists (e.g. Lakoff, 1987) have employed the concept of 'domains', which was originally proposed by Langacker (1987). Domains are similar to ICMs in that they constitute the coherent and relatively stable knowledge structure that we have about any particular entity. The difference is that domains are in some ways less idealised and abstract. According to these linguists, the most practical way of contrasting metaphor with metonymy is to say that metaphor involves a *mapping across domains.* So, for example, we might think of moving forward in time as being like moving forward in space, hence the conceptual metaphor LOVE IS A JOURNEY, which gives rise to linguistic instantiations, such as:

Their slowly evolving relationship *reached a turning point.* (BofE)

In this metaphor, TIME, SPACE, LOVE and JOURNEY could all be considered as domains, with time and space being seen as more primary than love and journey. In both cases there is mapping from the domain of TIME to the domain of SPACE, or from the domain of LOVE to the domain of JOURNEY.

In contrast to this, in metonymy the mapping is thought to take place *within a single domain*, so in the following extract, part of the journey (in this case the beginning) is used to refer to the whole journey:

Her son, the king, *set out* to Africa to wage war. (BofE)

Also of relevance here is Croft's (2002) 'Domain Highlighting Model'. Croft argues that any given entity forms part of a 'domain matrix' and different parts of this 'domain matrix' are highlighted or 'triggered' in different contexts. A domain matrix is 'the range of possible domains to which a lexical item serves as a point of access (Evans, 2007: 63). For instance, if we talk about Shakespeare being 'in bed', then we trigger the 'Shakespeare as a person' part of the matrix, whereas if we comment that 'Shakespeare is difficult to read', then we trigger the 'Shakespeare as a writer' part of the matrix.

Another approach to metonymy, advocated by Peirsman and Geeraerts (2006a), involves the notion of similarity versus contiguity, which constitutes the second way in which metaphor and metonymy are thought to differ. Whereas metaphor involves *similarity* (in a very crude sense, love affairs are compared to journeys), metonymy involves *contiguity* (the start of a journey is contiguously related to, or 'adjacent to' the rest of the journey; they are not separate entities). However, as we will see at several points in this book, 'contiguity' is a difficult concept to capture as the extent to which entities can be said to be contiguous varies enormously according to the context and one's own point of view. Peirsman and Geeraerts' work is discussed in more detail in Chapter 3, and the similarities and differences between metonymy and metaphor are elaborated on in Chapter 6.

1.4 Aims and overview of the book

In this chapter, I have provided a definition of metonymy and illustrated it with a number of examples. I have also provided a brief discussion of cognitive linguistic approaches to metonymy, and introduced some of the terminology that is used in the analysis of metonymy, by discussing concepts such as 'frames', 'domains' and 'idealised cognitive models'.

As we saw in the introduction, this book aims to present a full discussion of the different types of metonymy, the different functions that metonymy performs, the contribution that metonymy makes to successful communication in language and other forms of expression, and the types of misinterpretations that can occur. In the subsequent chapters, I will show that metonymy is present in both language and thought as well as in a range of other modalities, that it performs a wide range of crucial functions, and that it presents both excellent opportunities for expression and potential pitfalls in all forms of communication. I will do this by exploring the use of metonymy in a wide range of data. As well as looking at metonymy in written and spoken language I also consider the role that it plays in more multimodal forms of expression. I examine current theories of metonymy, most of which have been developed within the cognitive linguistic paradigm, and test these theories out on real-world data. I suggest ways in which existing cognitive linguistic approaches to metonymy could usefully be extended and adapted to account for the complex, dynamic, nuanced, culturally resonant and multi-layered nature of metonymy in language and other modes of expression. The book closes with a set of proposed real-world applications of metonymy.

Chapter 2 provides a foundation to the book by outlining the taxonomies of key metonymy-producing relationships that have been identified in the cognitive linguistic literature. One taxonomy is focused on in detail, and components of this taxonomy are tested out on real-world data. Key findings in this chapter are that the pragmatic functions of metonymy, its strong dependence on context, and its complex relationship with metaphor are sometimes underplayed in the cognitive linguistic taxonomies, and that both context and linguistic form play key roles in determining the meanings of metonymic expressions.

Chapter 3 explores a number of models that have been proposed in order to explore and analyse metonymy. These models will be used in subsequent chapters as a basis for the analysis of metonymy in real-world data. The chapter begins with some of the more traditional approaches that have attempted to classify metonymy into two or three discrete categories, and then moves on to models that are based on corpus data and which take a 'radial category' approach to the categorisation of metonymy. Finally, three models are presented that treat metonymy as a dynamic phenomenon whose meanings emerge in context and over time. I suggest ways in which parts of some of these models might be adapted to account for metonymy in real-world contexts.

Chapters 4 and 5 focus on the functions of metonymy. As we will see, metonymies often have specific semantic and pragmatic meanings that cannot always be predicted by the metonymy-producing relationships discussed in Chapter 2. Chapter 4 looks at some of the well-attested functions of metonymy that have been identified, mainly in the linguistics literature. These include its referential functions as well as its role in highlighting and construal, anaphoric reference and cohesion, its illocutionary functions, and the role that it plays in relationship-building and in the establishment and maintenance of discourse communities.

Chapter 5 focuses on the less widely explored, creative, evaluative and attitudinal functions of metonymy, and extends the discussion to other forms of expression and communication, such as art and music. In particular, it analyses the contributions that are made by metonymy to euphemism, dysphemism and hyperbole, irony and vagueness, and looks at how metonymy is used to convey evaluation, ideology and positioning. It also explores the creative use of metonymy in language, art, music, film and advertising. It shows how a consideration of these different functions of metonymy in these different forms of expression can be used to develop existing theories of metonymy, and discusses the ways in which a consideration of metonymy in other forms of expression relates to existing work on semiotics. In the section on ideology and positioning I look at how deliberate use is sometimes made of metonymy to reinforce the process of 'otherisation' in texts where 'alien' cultures are being discussed.

Chapter 6 discusses the difficulties involved in identifying metonymy in both language and other forms of expression. The difficulties involved in metonymy identification derive largely from the fact that it is an extremely difficult concept to define, and that notions such as 'contiguity' and 'ICMs' are often difficult to pin down when faced with real-life examples of metonymy. It can sometimes be very difficult to see where metonymies begin and end and it is therefore not always clear whether metonymy should be studied at the level of the word or the phrase. Similar problems arise with the identification of metonymy in different modes of expression, where it can also shade into metaphor or become so general that it is no longer a concept that is of use to analysts. In this chapter, as well as discussing problems in its identification, I look at attempts that have been made to automatically identify metonymy in language corpora. Significant progress has been made in this area, and reliable and consistent approaches to the automatic identification of metonymy are being proposed and tested. This is an exciting development as large-scale systematic studies of metonymy will allow researchers to make much more robust, empirically based claims about how it works and what it is used for.

In Chapter 7, the focus is on metonymy in the mind. The chapter begins with a meta-analysis of studies that have been made of metonymy comprehension and production in children and adults, with and without linguistic impairments, as well as developmental studies of metonymy. From this meta-analysis, I draw conclusions about the neurological and psychological nature of metonymic processing and attempt to identify the underlying cognitive processes that drive metonymy comprehension and production. This is a very active and fast-moving area of research, and I suggest future studies that could usefully be conducted in order to identify the neurological and psychological substrates of metonymy. The discussion then turns to patients with schizophrenia and related disorders, and explores the role played by metonymy in the formation and expression of their delusions. Schizophrenic delusions often result from a merging of the real and imagined worlds, and metonymic thinking plays a key role in this process. The chapter closes with a number of proposals for ways in which a more explicit focus on metonymic thinking might usefully be incorporated into psychological counselling.

Chapter 8 discusses cross-linguistic and cross-cultural variation in metonymy and the challenges that this presents to language learners and translators. I look, for example, at cross-linguistic variation in lexical metonymy, such as the use of body parts to indicate actions and character traits, the use of place names to refer to events that took place there, and the use of personification. I then move on to explore variation in the ways in which metonymy is used in pragmatic inferencing and indirect speech acts. After having discussed cross-linguistic variation in metonymy and its link to cross-cultural variation, I report the findings from a small number of studies that have explored the challenges that it presents to language learners and translators. The chapter looks at how learners sometimes 'under-interpret' metonymy, seeing it as literal language, or 'over-interpret' it, seeing it as metaphor. It also looks at the impact of first language influence on metonymy production as well as at other influences such as over- and under-extension, contingency learning and the role of input, and shows how errors involving metonymy tend to result in the sort of learner language that sounds not necessarily 'wrong' but somehow 'marked'. I then consider the ways in which metonymy (in both language and gesture) might be taught most effectively to learners of different languages, and report on findings from studies that have attempted to use language corpora for metonymy awareness-raising purposes. Finally, I move on to the challenges that metonymy presents to translators, particularly where humour is involved, and suggest ways in which these challenges might be addressed. The chapter ends with a discussion of the idea that metonymic thinking constitutes a translation strategy in its own right.

Chapter 9 provides a conclusion to the book, summing up the main characteristics of metonymy that have been identified. These include the fact that metonymy is found in many other forms of expression besides language, the fact that metonymy serves a very wide range of rhetorical functions, the fact that metonymy is often used playfully and creatively and for humorous effect, the fact that metonymy can be found in many different parts of speech, and the fact that metonymy is subtle, flexible, dynamic and contextually determined. The chapter then closes with a forward-looking perspective, outlining ways in which metonymy can be used in the real world. The focus is on potential real-world applications of metonymy research in the areas of psychotherapy, education, advertising, inter-cultural communication (in its broadest sense), second language teaching and translator training.

2 'He coughed and spluttered a lot and sneezed his lunch all over the place'

Types of metonymy and their behaviour in real-world data

2.1 Introduction

In Chapter 1, we looked at what metonymy is, how it works and what it does. We also saw that there are over-arching metonymy types, such as, for example, PLACE FOR PRODUCT, which sanctions the use of the word 'Bordeaux' to refer to a type of wine, or OBJECT FOR ACTION, which sanctions the use of the word 'handbagging' to refer to the act of hitting someone with a handbag. In this chapter, I look in detail at a selection of these metonymy types and illustrate them with examples from real-world data. I then use these examples to show how, by looking at metonymy 'in the wild', it is possible to identify further characteristics, and even, in some cases, new types of metonymy that are not covered in the original taxonomy. I provide evidence for the pragmatic and/or evaluative import of many apparently 'innocuous'-sounding metonymies and for the importance of phraseology in determining metonymic meaning.

A large number of taxonomies of metonymy types[1] have been proposed in the literature (Lakoff and Johnson, 1980/2003; Norrick, 1981; Radden and Kövecses, 1999[2]; Ruiz de Mendoza Ibáñez and Mairal Uson, 2007; Sappan, 1987; Seto, 1999; Ullmann, 1951; Yamanashi, 1987). These taxonomies are useful to the analyst as they provide a way of categorizing different types of metonymy, and of seeing how they relate to one another. They also help in the

[1] Metonymy types are also referred to as 'metonymy-producing relationships', 'high-level metonymies' or 'conceptual metonymies'. Some of these terms are problematic. The term 'metonymy-producing relationships' downplays the role of metonymy in the actual relationship, the term 'high-level metonymy' is associated with one particular model of metonymy, and the term 'conceptual metonymy' implies that the relationships are relatively fixed and static, and there is no psycholinguistic research to date that shows for certain that people access conceptual metonymies when they are attempting to understand metonymic utterances (Gibbs, 2007). For these reasons, I use the term 'metonymy types' as it allows for flexibility with respect to the metonymy types themselves and the ways in which they are discussed.

[2] This taxonomy is also reproduced in Kövecses (2010).

identification process, and help researchers explore the universal/language-specific nature of metonymy. At times, however, these taxonomies have been illustrated with artificial examples, which do not always provide strong support for the claims that are being made. Moreover, the authors of these taxonomies have little to say about the evaluative or pragmatic functions of the types of metonymy that they list. In this chapter examples from real-world data are used to explore these features.[3] The focus in this chapter will be on a taxonomy proposed by Radden and Kövecses (1999). This is the most exhaustive and influential taxonomy to have been proposed to date and is the most widely cited. As well as proposing a number of metonymy types, Radden and Kövecses also suggest a number of principles determining vehicle selection. I look at these too, in relation to real-world data.

2.2 Metonymy types and their manifestations in real-world data

The taxonomy proposed by Radden and Kövecses is hierarchical. They divide metonymy types into two over-arching categories: WHOLE AND PART and PART AND PART. Each of these categories contains a number of ICMs, which in turn sanction a range of metonymy types.

WHOLE AND PART metonymies involve situations where part of something stands for a whole (e.g. when 'America' is used simply to refer to the United States of America) or situations where the whole of something is used to refer to a part of it (e.g. when a 'head count' is used to refer to a 'people count'). Radden and Kövecses identify six ICMs within this over-arching category, which in turn give rise to twenty-one metonymy types. These involve physical entities (where one part of an entity can represent the whole or vice versa), scales (where the end of the scale can be used to refer to the whole scale), constitution (where, for example, the material that an object is made of can be used to refer to the object itself), events (where a part of an event can stand for a whole event), category membership (where one member of a category can be used to represent the category as a whole) and properties of categories (where a salient property of a category can be used to refer to a category as a whole).

In PART AND PART metonymies, something is used to refer to a concept to which it is simply related (e.g. one might say that that someone 'married money', where money is simply something that belongs to the spouse rather than being 'part' of them). Within this over-arching category, Radden and Kövecses identify ten ICMs which give rise to forty-three types of metonymy-producing relationship. These involve action (where for example an object used in an action, or the manner in which an action is performed, can be used to refer

[3] Any claims about 'patterns' of behaviour are based on a minimum of forty instances in the BofE, the BNC or WebCorp.

to the action itself), perception (where an actual entity can be used to refer to one's emotional or physical experience of that entity, as in 'there goes my knee'), causation (where for example a particular cause may be used to refer to its effect, or vice versa), production (where for example the producer of an object might be used to represent the object itself), control (where the controller of an entity or of group of people may stand for the entity or the people themselves), possession (where an object represents the person who owns that object, as we saw in Chapter 1 with Margaret Thatcher's handbag), containment (where a container stands for its contents, or vice versa), location (where for example a place might stand for a particular event that took place there), sign (where words stand for the concepts they express), and modification of form (where a modified form of a word might stand for the word itself). In this book all of these metonymy types will be explored at some point, with the exception of 'sign', as this is too broad a conception of the notion of metonymy to be useful. An overview of Radden and Kövecses' taxonomy is shown in Figure 2.1, along with an example of a metonymy type corresponding to each ICM.

Radden and Kövecses' taxonomy has made a significant contribution to the metonymy literature as it has provided researchers with a common language with which to share their knowledge of, and insights into, metonymy. However, the examples that Radden and Kövecses use to illustrate the different metonymy types are, for the most part, decontextualised, which prevents them from making observations that go beyond the semantic level. In this section, I take a number of metonymy types from their taxonomy and look at how they work in real data. This will allow us to see, for example, how metonymy often has strong pragmatic content, how the meaning of the same metonymy varies across different contexts, and how metonymic meaning is often closely related to form. The chapter begins by looking at a selection of metonymy types that involve whole–part relationships and then moves on to consider a number that involve part–part relationships.

Examples of whole–part metonymy types and their manifestations in real-world data

My aim in this section is not to cover every ICM in this taxonomy, but to draw attention to a selection of ICMs that give rise to metonymy types which, when explored using real-world data, exhibit further characteristics that are not discussed in the literature. Three ICMs are chosen: the 'thing and its part' ICM, the 'category and property' ICM and the 'constitution' ICM.

Metonymy types involving the 'thing and its part' ICM. The first type of WHOLE FOR PART metonymy to be discussed by Radden and Kövecses is the

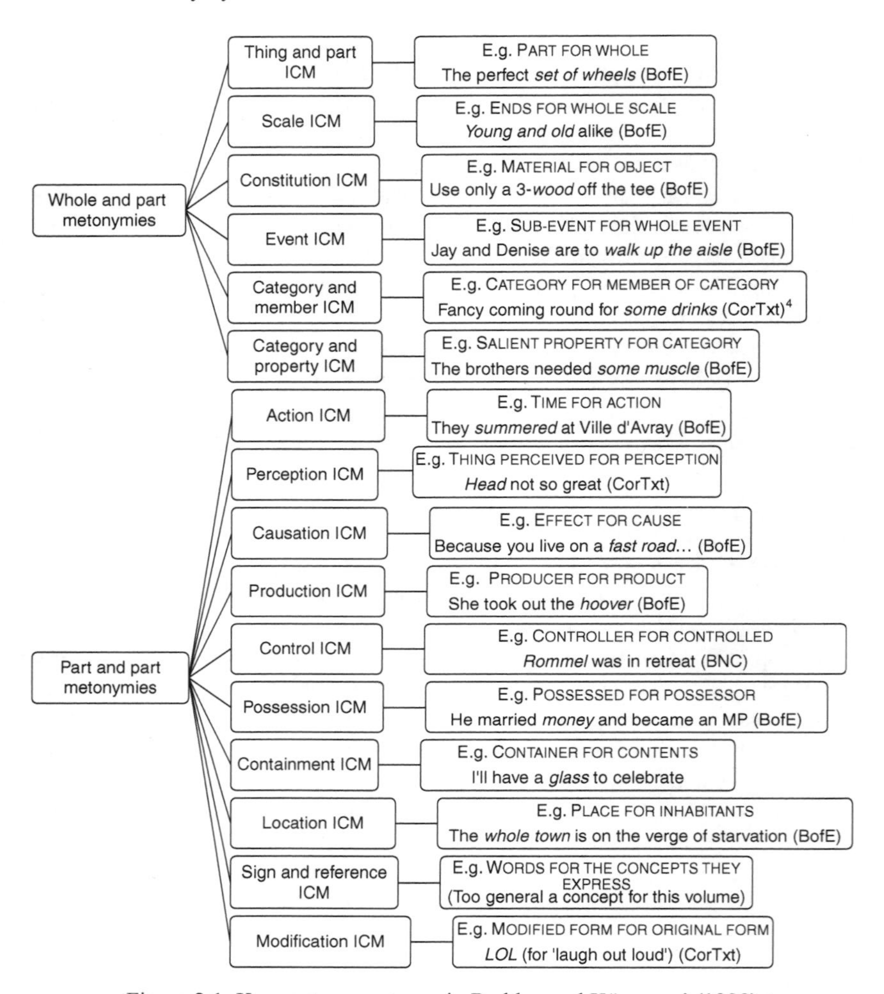

Figure 2.1 Key metonymy types in Radden and Kövecses' (1999) taxonomy

PHYSICAL WHOLE FOR PART metonymy. Corpus-based examples of this type of metonymy include the following:

The *university* will change its mind next week. (BofE)

The *police* turned up at about 5.30. (BofE)

[4] CorTxt is a 190,000-word corpus of 11,067 text messages sent by friends and family, collected in the UK between 2004 and 2007 by Caroline Tagg (Tagg, 2012).

In these examples, the whole university is used as shorthand for members of the University Council or Governing Committee, and 'the police' refers to some members of the police force. These cases of metonymy are so subtle that some readers may question their status as metonymy, and see them simply as a literal use of language. However, their status as metonymies is supported by the fact that expressions such as these are not possible in all languages. For example, in Greek the second sentence would sound very odd, as the normal way of expressing this idea in Greek is to say something along the lines of: 'some members of the police force turned up' (Littlemore *et al.*, 2011b).

PHYSICAL WHOLE FOR PART metonymies tend to be somewhat rare in real-world data. Indeed, in their study of metonymy in text messaging, which involved the close analysis of 1,000 text messages, Littlemore and Tagg (in preparation) found no instances of them, though they found numerous examples of metonymy involving other types of PART FOR WHOLE relationship.

In contrast, PHYSICAL PART FOR WHOLE metonymy are more common, They often involve body parts, such as those in the following examples:

The *hired hands* are here. (BofE)

A simple *count of heads* in and out of Britain. (BofE)

There is some controversy surrounding the idea of PART FOR WHOLE relationships. Seto (1999) argues that it is important to make the distinction between what he calls 'partonomy' relationships (for example, the relationship between a hand and a body) and what he calls 'taxonomy' relationships (for example, the relationship between 'fir' and 'tree'). He argues that the former give rise to metonymy (such as when we offer to give someone a hand) but the latter are best described as 'synecdoche', which he argues is a different sort of relationship and should not be included under the heading of 'metonymy'. His main reason for drawing this distinction is that partonomy is based on the perception of contiguity in the real world, whereas taxonomy is based on the conception of a categorical hierarchy in the mind. However, as we will see throughout this book, it is often difficult to make a distinction between 'real' contiguity and contiguity 'in the mind'. All of the information that we have about 'the real world' is filtered through mental models that reflect our world views, and this is reflected in our language. This is why, when we look at examples of PART FOR WHOLE relationships in real-world linguistic data, the distinction between metonymy and 'synecdoche' becomes very blurred. For these reasons, many cognitive linguists, such as Lakoff and Johnson (1980/2003) include synecdoche within the term metonymy. This is the line that will be followed in this book. PART FOR WHOLE metonymies are particularly productive in non-linguistic forms of expression, such as art and music. This issue is discussed in Chapter 5, whereas here the focus is on their manifestation in language.

A pragmatic feature of PART FOR WHOLE metonymies that is not discussed in the literature is that when they are used to talk about people, they tend to have a strong depersonalising effect as they reduce the person to their most relevant attribute. The *hired hands* example above refers to the workers' fitness for work and the *count of heads* example simply refers to whether or not they are here. Part for whole metonymies are prevalent in sexism and other forms of prejudice, as we can see in this woman's testimony:

I couldn't bear the way men regarded me as just a *pair of legs*. (BofE)

One reason why these 'body part' metonymies sound particularly offensive may relate to the imagery that they evoke. As we will see in Chapter 7, the way in which metonymic language is processed in the mind is similar to the way in which literal language is processed. This means that in order to understand the above examples, people are almost literally reduced to an image of their hands, heads and legs, which is, by definition, reductive and dehumanising.

Metonymy types involving the 'category and property' ICM. One reason for the depersonalising effect of the above example is that, when applied to people, the PHYSICAL PART FOR WHOLE relationship is closely related to another type of PART FOR WHOLE metonymy, in which the DEFINING PROPERTY OF A CATEGORY STANDS FOR THE WHOLE CATEGORY. In Radden and Kövecses' taxonomy, this is said to evoke the 'category and property' ICM. We can see this relationship at work in the following examples:

Society treats *blacks* differently. (BofE)

Kenneth Branagh is a *ginge*. (BofE)

When this type of metonymy is applied to people it is often particularly offensive. This is because it can serve to artificially create a category of people who coincidentally share a feature. Other implicit (and often negative) attributes are then sometimes added to the category. The whole idea of a group of people having a 'defining property' is itself offensive, and in many ways it would be more appropriate to talk about 'salient' properties. SALIENT PROPERTY OF A CATEGORY FOR THE WHOLE CATEGORY is another metonymy type within Radden and Kövecses' taxonomy. This metonymy type provides a better account of examples such as these, as 'salience' is very much in the eye of the beholder and it is not objective. There is increasing recognition of the offensive nature of DEFINING PROPERTY OF A CATEGORY FOR THE WHOLE CATEGORY metonymies when labelling people with illnesses or syndromes by referring to the syndrome itself, such as 'dyslexics', 'schizophrenics' and 'epileptics'. It is now seen as more appropriate to label people who suffer from these syndromes as 'a person with dyslexia' and so on. On the other hand, in some contexts, when speakers want to create distance from a particular group of people, they will deliberately evoke the depersonalising effects of PART FOR WHOLE/DEFINING PROPERTY OF A CATEGORY FOR THE WHOLE CATEGORY metonymy in their strategy of 'otherisation'. This is discussed in depth in Chapter 5.

Another type of metonymy that relies on PART FOR WHOLE relationships is the SUB-EVENT FOR THE WHOLE EVENT, metonymy, which we can see in the following examples.

He *ordered a pizza* and we drank loads of red wine. (BofE)

Jay and Denise are expected to *walk up the aisle* in the summer. (BofE)

It's Venus, as *a trip to the library* would have told you. (BofE)

In these examples, one part of an event or process (usually the beginning or the end, or the most salient part of the event) represents the whole event or process. We use metonymies such as these because it would be too lengthy and pedantic to describe the whole process. In the examples listed here, we use our knowledge of the world to infer that the pizza arrived and was eaten, the couple took part in a wedding ceremony when they reached the end of the aisle, and that in the library, books were read. The third example shows how metonymy can co-occur with personification (trips to libraries do not literally 'tell' people things). This characteristic of metonymy sometimes makes it difficult to distinguish from metaphor, a point which is discussed at length in Chapter 6, which looks at issues relating to the identification of metonymy. Another interesting thing to note about these examples is that they have differing degrees of salience. The first is barely recognisable as a metonymy as it refers to an extremely common event schema (that of ordering and eating a meal). The second example is slightly more noticeable as it draws on a specific and less mundane event schema and the third example draws on a much looser event schema, combining this with an apparent case of personification.

Metonymy types involving the 'constitution' ICM. Another type of metonymy identified by Radden and Kövecses that involves a PART FOR WHOLE relationship is the MATERIAL CONSTITUTING AN OBJECT FOR THE OBJECT metonymy, which involves the 'constitution' ICM. We can see this relationship at work in the following examples:

Beginners at golf should use only a *3-wood* off the tee. (BofE)

He presented *a paper* to the Cambridge Philosophical Society. (BofE)

In these examples, the material that an object is made of is used to refer to the object itself. Both are conventional metonymies. However, they also illustrate how knowledge of the particular meanings attached to language by different discourse communities is an important prerequisite to metonymy comprehension. In the Bank of English, 'wood' in the context of golf only appeared as part of a name of a golf club (a golfer can choose between a '1-wood', a '2-wood' or a '3-wood'). Presenting a paper refers to the act of speaking at a conference. However the actual details of what is involved in 'presenting a paper' vary significantly across different academic disciplines. In some disciplines, the meaning is quite close to the literal meaning in that presenters will read from a printed text, and they may even hand out (i.e. literally 'present') paper copies of their talk to members of the audience. In other disciplines, this would be unheard of, and the speaker would be expected to speak more naturally, perhaps using PowerPoint, or simply talk without notes. No actual paper would be present. In these latter cases the use of the term 'paper' shades into metaphor as there is no actual paper. Thus the metonymic meaning of this sentence sits on a sliding scale, and varies according to the academic community of which one is a member.

At times, MATERIAL FOR OBJECT metonymies carry an extra meaning that is not listed in Radden and Körecses' taxonomy. We can see this in the following example:

I'll have a *glass* to celebrate. (BofE)

In this example, the MATERIAL FOR OBJECT metonymy combines with the CONTAINER FOR CONTAINED metonymy to refer to the contents of the glass. But this is not the whole story, as it refers specifically to an *alcoholic* drink. In fact, when 'a glass' is used on its own like this, it rarely means anything other than an alcoholic drink and the speaker who uttered the sentence above would be surprised to be offered a glass of orange juice. Thus the meaning is narrowed further via a CATEGORY FOR MEMBER OF CATEGORY metonymy. This phenomenon is also present in the widespread use in English of the word 'drinks' to refer specifically to alcoholic drinks when used in the context of social engagements. We can see this in the following example that is taken from a corpus of text messages that was explored by Littlemore and Tagg (in preparation):

Fancy coming round for a peek and *some drinks* this eve before going on to somewhere nicer? (CorTxt)

As well as involving a CATEGORY FOR MEMBER OF CATEGORY metonymy, this text message also involves a SUB-EVENT FOR WHOLE EVENT metonymy, as *some drinks* refers to a social event, including conversation, perhaps some 'nibbles' and possibly a party atmosphere. Thus this example involves both a WHOLE FOR PART relationship and a PART FOR WHOLE relationship. The fact that a single instance of metonymy can involve more than one relationship challenges the view, which can be inferred from some accounts in the literature, that metonymy is a relatively straightforward and simple trope, in comparison with metaphor. As we will see throughout this book, when we look at metonymy in real-life data we see that, like metaphor, it is often messy and difficult to categorise, and that it can convey several different meanings at once.

Another feature of metonymy that is revealed by a focus on real-world data is that word form and syntax can change their connotation quite significantly. We can see this in the following examples:

Yoko had a separate closet just for her *furs*. (BofE)

I went in to see the head master wearing *furs* and diamonds. (BofE)

someone so much in the public eye should want to be seen wearing *fur* (BofE)

Politically-correct women can no longer wear *fur*. (BofE)

Although all of these examples involve a MATERIAL FOR OBJECT metonymic relationship, the choice of the singular or plural word form reflects different attitudes towards the garments. The use of the plural form: 'furs' in the first two examples emphasises the fact that the wearing of fur indicates wealth, or at least a desire to appear wealthy. This is reflected in the fact that among the most popular collocates to the left and right of 'furs' in the Bank of English corpus are words such as: 'diamonds', 'jewellery', 'satins', 'spices' and 'accessories'. The use of the singular form 'fur' in the second two examples does not carry this connotation, and tends instead to be used in slightly disapproving contexts and is evaluated negatively. This meaning is reflected in the types of words that appear among the most popular collocates to the left and right of the word fur, which include words such as fake, animals and seals.

The same sort of meaning shift can be found in the plural and singular metonymic uses of the word 'leather' when it is used to refer to particular types of clothing, as we can see in the following examples:

Even the waitresses wear *leather* and carry whips. (BofE)

Jennifer was wearing *leathers*, having arrived as usual on her motorbike. (BofE)

Again, although both examples involve a MATERIAL FOR OBJECT metonymic relationship, in the first example, the word *leather* clearly relates to the wearing of sexually provocative clothes, whereas in the second the words *leathers* relates to the protective clothing that is worn by motor cyclists. A corpus search for the lemmas 'wear + leather' and 'wear + leathers' respectively reveals that these meanings are conventionalised. We can therefore see that the MATERIAL FOR OBJECT metonymy is productive in English but that the actual meanings of what is said extend well beyond that of 'things made from this material'. The presence of a singular or plural word form indicates which reading is intended.

Examples of part–part metonymy types and their manifestations in real-world data

As we saw above, Radden and Kövecses also outline a large number of PART FOR PART metonymy types in their taxonomy, and in this section we look at some of these in real-world data. As with the whole–part metonymies, the intention is not to cover every ICM, but rather to look at a selection of ICMs and some of their associated metonymy types, and to explore how they work in real-world data. The focus will be on metonymy types involving the 'action' ICM, the 'causation' ICM, the 'production' ICM, the 'possession' ICM and the 'location' ICM.

Metonymy types involving the 'action' ICM. A particularly productive sub-group of PART FOR PART metonymies consists of those involving action. For example, there are a number of MANNER FOR ACTION metonymies, which are exemplified as follows:

I rose to my feet and *tiptoed* through the hall. (BofE)

A man from a different company *sprang out* of his office. (BofE)

These types of metonymy are fairly common in English but are virtually non-existent in many other languages. This is because different languages have been found to encode information about the manner of movement in different ways. Talmy (1985) categorises languages into two types, in terms of the way in which they habitually construe movement. In 'satellite-framed' languages (such as English), the focus is on the manner. The manner of movement is expressed within the verb, and the direction of movement is expressed through a preposition, as in 'to dash in', 'to slip out', 'to creep up' and 'to eat away'. In 'verb-framed' languages (such as Spanish), only the actual direction of movement is expressed in the verb, and the manner of movement is expressed as a non-finite verb as in 'entro en la casa corriendo' (he entered the house running) and 'sali corriendo a la calle' (I exited running into the street). The focus in Spanish is thus very much on the direction of movement, rather than the manner. Research suggests that speakers of satellite-framed language are predisposed to cognitively encode motion events in a different way from speakers of verb-framed languages (Slobin, 2000). I will return to the issue of cross-linguistic variation in metonymy use in Chapter 8, where I will discuss the implications that this has for cross-linguistic communication, translation and language teaching.

Within the 'action' ICM, we also have a number of AGENT FOR ACTION metonymies, such as:

Anti-aircraft guns were *manned* and firing. (BofE)

Thousands were *butchered* to feed the gangs of labourers. (BofE)

Another type of 'action' metonymy in Radden and Kövecses' taxonomy is OBJECT INVOLVED IN AN ACTION FOR THE ACTION, which can be seen in the following examples.

Leaving Mrs Howard all alone to do the *shampooing.* (BofE)

You can *carpet* the same size room for under £35. (BofE)

This particular type of metonymy is particularly productive in Japanese, where, as we will see in Chapter 6, it plays a major role in creative borrowings from other languages.

A closely related metonymic relationship to this is the INSTRUMENT FOR ACTION metonymy, which we saw in Chapter 1 when we looked at the term 'handbagging'. A corpus search for examples such as these reveals a pattern which carries a particular meaning in English. This pattern can be seen in the following examples.

A good handbagging (BofE)

They'll let you off with *a light birching.* (BofE)

Next time he encounters a monster he'll give it *a good shoeing.* (Webcorp)

This pattern, which consists of a + adjective + metonymic gerund, appears to convey a complex mix of pragmatic information in that all the expressions are vaguely ironic and tongue in cheek as well as being mildly aggressive and threatening. We will see in Chapter 6 that grammatical patterns such as these can play a key role in metonymy identification.

Within the action ICM, we also have MEANS FOR ACTION metonymies, which are exemplified in the following citations:

He wouldn't get to page two before the producer *laughed him out of the office.* (BofE)

They *booed him off the stage.* (BofE)

He coughed and spluttered a lot and *sneezed his lunch all over the place.* (BofE)

These last three examples illustrate the role of phraseology in meaning construction. They all involve what Goldberg (2006) refers to as a 'caused motion' construction. A literal example of a 'caused motion' construction would be 'Jeannette threw the metonymy book out of the window'. The use of this construction indicates that the fact that the book went out of the window was a direct result of Jeannette having thrown it – that is to say, 'threw' is a transitive verb. In Table 2.1, we can see how when 'laughing', 'booing' and 'sneezing' appear in this construction, they start to behave like transitive verbs, although there is nothing intrinsically transitive about them. If one were asked to describe these verbs out of context, one would probably describe them as being 'intransitive'.

Table 2.1 *The caused motion construction*

CAUSE	MOTION	FIGURE	PATH	GROUND
Jeannette	threw	the metonymy book	out of	the window
The producer	laughed	him	out of	the office
They	booed	her	off	the stage
He	sneezed	his lunch	all over	the table

The fact that the words 'laughed' 'booed' and 'sneezed' are being used in this construction allows the reader to infer that as a result of the laughing, booing or sneezing, some sort of movement took place. In order to understand these examples, one must have some sort of background knowledge of the meaning of the construction. Research suggests that constructions carry their own meanings and that they are stored in the long-term memory. This reflects the mutually dependent relationship that can exist between phraseology and metonymy. Because these words are used within this particular construction, their meanings are shaped and squeezed into something different from what might be seen as their 'basic' senses. The technical term for this process is 'coercion', and, as we can see in these examples, it often involves metonymy.

MEANS FOR ACTION metonymies that occur within the caused motion construction can be extended metaphorically to refer to situations where people change their minds:

Who could have *talked her out of* that? (BofE)

The ease with which metonymy can be turned into metaphor when an abstract context is introduced is a theme that will recur through this book as we see it not only in language but also in gesture and other non-linguistic forms of communication.

Another action-based metonymy type is TIME FOR ACTION, where the time when an action was completed can be used to represent the action itself. A corpus search using the Bank of English suggests that this metonymy type is somewhat rare in English. It is only used for seasons and those examples that can be found tend to sound either archaic or pretentious when used about humans, although they do not sound quite so marked when used about animals:

In 1861 they *summered* at Ville d'Avray. (BofE)

The wealthy who '*summered*' in the expensive hotels. (BofE)

She has *wintered* in Dubai after showing top-class form in England last season. (BofE)

As expected, no examples were found for metonymic uses of 'autumned' or 'springed', which reflects one of the principles underlying vehicle choice that we will look at in more detail in the next section.

Metonymy types involving the 'causation' ICM. Another set of PART FOR PART metonymy types proposed by Radden and Kövecses involves causal relationships and are thought to evoke the 'causation' ICM. Of these, the most prototypical are CAUSE FOR EFFECT metonymies, such as:

The owners of lustrous, shining, *healthy* hair. (BofE)

Hair itself can be neither healthy nor unhealthy as it is dead matter. However, it can reflect the general health of the person who has it: healthy people are more likely than unhealthy people to have hair that is shiny and bouncy.

The inverse relationship results in EFFECT FOR CAUSE metonymies, such as the following:

A good *healthy* diet might include lots of fruits. (BofE)

Because you live on a *fast road* . . . (BofE)

In the first of these examples, it is not the diet itself that is 'healthy', but the diet does lead to the person being healthy. The terms 'healthy diet' and 'healthy hair' represent metonymic relationships that are diametrically opposed to one another. Whereas 'healthy hair' is the result of good health, a healthy diet is a cause of good health. A study of the most frequent collocates immediately following search term 'healthy' reveals the most frequent collocates involving metonymy to be 'healthy diet', 'healthy food', 'healthy lifestyle' and 'healthy living'. The only metonymy-based collocate to appear in the top twenty is 'healthy skin', which appears after the four that have just been mentioned. This finding suggests that, for this particular word, the EFFECT FOR CAUSE relationship is more productive than the CAUSE FOR EFFECT relationship. The fact that we can switch so readily between these different readings is testimony to the flexible nature of metonymy and of the human mind.

In the second example, it is not the road itself that is fast, but the cars that travel along it. Certain qualities of the road (its width, its location, perhaps even the quality of the road surface) make certain drivers deem it suitable for speedy driving. Here, the meaning slides easily from the road to the cars because of the contiguous relationship between them. Again, this highlights the underspecified nature of language and the flexible metonymic thinking that the human mind has to engage in, in order to understand it.

Metonymy types involving the 'production' ICM. Another type of PART FOR PART metonymy identified by Radden and Kövecses is the PRODUCER

FOR PRODUCT metonymy, which involves the 'production' ICM. Examples of this metonymy are:

If she had been wearing *Dior* and diamonds . . . (BofE)

He decided to buy himself a *Rolex.* (BofE)

An interesting feature of metonymies such as these is that they tend to be used for expensive, high-quality products. It would sound strange (or even ironic) to say that she was 'wearing Primark' or that he decided to 'buy himself a Timex'. As we can see in these examples, at their most basic level, PRODUCER FOR PRODUCT metonymies involve using the name of a producer to refer to the product that has been produced. However, they can be extended via a second metonymic process (MEMBER OF A CATEGORY FOR A CATEGORY) to refer to all products of that type, regardless of whether they have actually been produced by that particular producer, as we can see in the following examples:

She took out the *hoover*, meaning to clean the house. (BofE)

I even tried taping it down with *sellotape.* (BofE)

It's got 'rock 'n' roll' written all over it in *biro.* (BofE)

Although these seem relatively unmarked when taken individually, when we look at several examples together in a corpus we can see that they often convey a feeling of everydayness or 'banality'. The fact that biros are cheap, made of plastic and easily replaceable can be contrasted with more 'serious' entities such as 'artefacts' or even 'God', to achieve ironic or humorous effect, as we can see in the following two examples:

The artefact turned out to be a plastic *Biro* with the words 'Barclays Bank' down the side. (BofE)

No doubt the hand of God is directing her *Biro* as she writes the Gospel According to Eileen. (BofE)

Closely related to PRODUCER FOR PRODUCT metonymies are PLACE FOR PRODUCT MADE THERE metonymies, such as:

Cheryl brought out the best *china.* (BofE)

A bed of salad greens surrounded by *Cheddar.* (BofE)

Again, these particular metonymies tend to be used for prestige items, and are more common in cultures that place a particularly high value on regional produce, such as wine, as we can see in the following examples:

It's quite definitely a *Loire.* (BofE)

This wine has the depth of character of a *Gigondas.* (BofE)

The population of Gigondas is just over 600, but such is the popularity of its wine that it is known all over the world.

Metonymy types involving the 'possession' ICM. Radden and Kövecses list another type of PART FOR PART metonymy: the POSSESSOR FOR POSSESSED metonymy, which evokes the 'possession' ICM. An example often given in the literature for this metonymy-producing relationship is 'that's me', which Radden and Köreczes argue might be uttered by a customer in a restaurant when two dinners are delivered. It was impossible to find any instances of 'that's me/you/him' with this exact meaning in the British National Corpus, although several English-speaking informants attested to having heard this expression or something similar either when pointing at dinners in restaurants, as Radden and Kövecses suggest, or when pointing to chairs that have been temporarily vacated by someone, who has perhaps gone to the bar. The same string can also refer to other types of PART FOR PART metonymic relationship. It is most often used to refer metonymically to a photograph of the speaker, as in the following example:

That's me with hair. (BNC)

It can also be used to indicate a TRAIT FOR PERSON metonymy:

That's me all over isn't it? (BNC)

In this last example, 'that's me' appears to carry negative and ironic overtones.

The inverse of the POSSESSOR FOR POSSESSED metonymy is the POSSESSED FOR POSSESSOR metonymy, which can be seen in the following example:

Then he married *money* and became an MP. (BofE)

The negative connotations of this last example derive from the fact that the person is reduced to something that they possess and is thus to a large extent dehumanised. Here, the POSSESSED FOR POSSESSOR relationship appears to be shading into a TRAIT FOR PERSON relationship, which as we saw above can convey strong negative evaluation.

Metonymy types involving the 'location' ICM. Another type of metonymy that is rarely 'neutral' is the PLACE FOR INHABITANTS metonymy, which evokes the 'location' ICM. As we can see in the following examples, PLACE FOR INHABITANTS metonymies often have a strong hyperbolic feel to them:

The *entire village* is expected to give samples at a local blood unit. (BofE)

The *whole town* is on the verge of starvation. (BofE)

Your *country* needs you. (BofE)

The hyperbole derives from the fact that it is virtually impossible for *every* resident of a particular village, town or country would fit the description that is being made of them. The expressions also have a strong emotive element to them, emphasising the fact that people are united by, or that they need to 'pull together' in times of adversity. For example, the first extract is taken from the 21 October 1999 edition of *The Sun*, a popular tabloid newspaper, which often runs somewhat sentimental, 'feel-good' stories. The full extract is:

And neighbours in Glenfary, Perthshire, have been quick to offer support for their local hero. The *entire village* is expected to give samples at a local blood unit in a desperate bid to find a bone marrow match that could help cure Ian. (BoE)

A metonymic relationship that is closely related to the PLACE FOR INHABITANTS relationship is the PLACE FOR INSTITUTION metonymy, which, as we can see in the following examples, can also serve an important pragmatic function:

Number 10 refused to comment. (BofE)

Not worthy of further *White House* comment. (BofE)

These metonymies refer respectively to the British Prime Minister (and his government) and the American President (and his government). They serve the dual function of hiding the protagonist, while at the same time endowing him with more status. The tradition and heritage associated with the 'Number 10' and the 'White House' are partly transferred to the individuals themselves, and their agency is partly, but not entirely, hidden. We can see another example of this in the following example, where 'the City' is used metonymically to refer to bankers and financiers who work there:

'Never has *the City* been as powerful or its influence as pervasive', they say. While the rest of the economy, and in particular manufacturing, has struggled. (BofE)

Again, the fact that 'the City' is a long-established, historical part of London endows the people who work there with a degree of respectability, which some would argue they do not deserve.

In this section, we have looked at a variety of metonymic relationships and have seen that in many cases certain types of relationship appear to be associated with particular types of pragmatic content. Some types of metonymy have strong evaluative overtones, some typically co-occur with other kinds of figurative language, some attach themselves to particular constructions reflecting the close relationship between form and function, and some like to form chains with other metonymies. In addition to this, some metonymy types appear to be much more productive than others. This list is by no means exhaustive but it should serve to illustrate the wide variety of ways in which one concept can be used metonymically to refer to another, the ubiquity of metonymy in everyday language, and the close relationship between different types of metonymy and their associated pragmatic overtones. Even by looking at small amounts of data such as these, we can see how the definitions of metonymy types discussed in the literature can be enriched by the use of corpus data. In the next section, we turn our attention to another important contribution made by Radden and Kövecses, that there is a limited set of principles governing the process by which metonymic vehicles are selected. Again, their ideas are illustrated with real-life examples, and these examples are used to further develop their original proposals.

2.3 Principles determining vehicle choice and their manifestations in real-world data

In addition to their taxonomy of metonymy types, Radden and Kövecses (1999) provide a useful list of principles that explain why certain types of words and phrases tend to get selected as metonymic vehicles and others do not. For example, they propose that concrete items are more likely to be chosen than abstract items because they are easier to perceive. This explains why someone is more likely to say that they have a 'desk job' than, for example, a 'data analysis' job. We find it easier to picture a desk than 'data analysis'.

Another principle, which results from cultural preferences, dictates that events occurring at the beginning or the end of a process are more likely to be selected to represent the overall process than events occurring in the middle. Radden and Kövecses refer to this as the INITIAL OR FINAL OVER MIDDLE principle. This principle can be seen in expressions such as:

Neither managed to get on a bike from *January* to *December.* (BofE)

In this example, it would be very odd to replace the months with say 'March' and 'November', or any other arbitrary months. The principle is often at work in metonymies where a part of a complex event is chosen to represent the whole event; it tends to be the beginning or the end of the event that is chosen, rather than the things that happen in the middle. Thus, as we saw in Chapter 1, when people refer metonymically to the process of making a cup of tea, they refer to 'putting the kettle on', which occurs at the beginning of the process, rather than, for example, 'putting tea bags in the pot', which occurs towards the middle of the process.

The same principle also applies to extremes, where extreme cases are more likely than cases to be found in the middle of a scale to represent the scale as a whole. This explains why, as we saw above in Section 2.2, and as Panther and Thornburg (1998) point out, in travel brochures, we often read that resorts are open 'to both summer and winter visitors' (BofE), meaning that they are open year-round. It would be very odd to read that such resorts are open to 'spring and autumn visitors' because this contravenes the principle; summer and winter have more marked characteristics (at least in Europe) and are more noticeably different from each other than spring and autumn.

A further principle, which also reflects cultural preferences, is the BASIC OVER NON-BASIC principle determining vehicle selection. This principle is often at work when vague approximations are being used, as we can see in the following examples:

I have heard about a *dozen* stories like this. (BofE)

They had around *twenty* survivors on board. (BofE)

Vague language serves a range of useful communicative functions, and as such is far from being an example of 'poor communication' (Cutting, 2007). The communicative functions of vague language and the role that metonymy plays in these functions are discussed in more depth in Chapter 5, which looks at the functions of metonymy in different modes of expression.

Many of the principles determining vehicle selection correspond to people's everyday experiences with the world, which illustrates an underlying cognitive linguistic premise that language is by and large both a reflection and product of our everyday interactions with the real world. In this section I discuss some of these principles, using corpus data to illustrate both the particular pragmatic and formal features that they display in addition to the information provided in Radden and Kövecses' model.

The principles proposed by Radden and Kövecses fall into three broad categories. These are 'human experience' (our everyday interactions with the world), 'perceptual selectivity' (things that we are more likely to notice because of the way our brains work) and 'cultural preferences' (things that we have learned to notice because of the culture in which we have been brought up). In addition to this, our preference for certain vehicle types is also influenced by our need to be clear and relevant (these are referred to as 'communicative principles'). There can also be overriding factors, such as the desire to produce certain rhetorical effects, or to speak euphemistically. In these situations, the speaker may want to be deliberately vague, which means that the principle of clarity will be overridden. These principles and factors are illustrated in Figure 2.2.

As with the metonymy types discussed above, interesting pragmatic and formal features associated with these principles can be revealed when we look at authentic data. Here I take just a few of the principles and explore them in more depth using real-life examples.

A principle that has been identified by Radden and Kövecses and that relates to cultural preferences is the idea that stereotypical ideas are more likely to be selected as metonymic vehicles than non-stereotypical ideas. This makes sense, as stereotypical concepts are arguably more accessible or cognitively available than less stereotypical ones and are thus more likely to be used as a point of access to other ideas. An example of this relationship is:

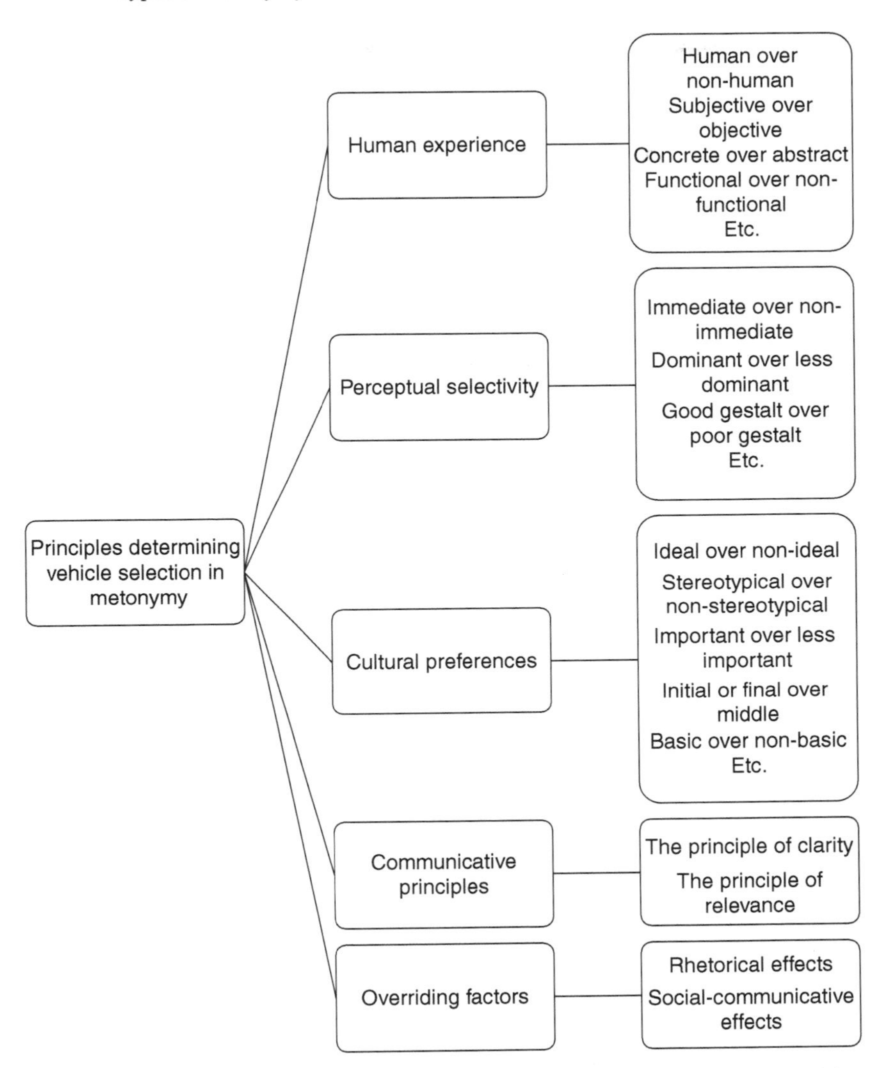

Figure 2.2 Principles determining vehicle selection in metonymy (Radden and Kövecses, 1999)

STEREOTYPICAL OVER NON-STEREOTYPICAL:

Sure, *boys will be boys* won't they Val? (BofE)

This example relies on stereotypical knowledge concerning the ways in which 'boys' behave, which may include, for example, the fact that they are a bit naughty, somewhat irresponsible, and most importantly that this is natural. Both parts of the expression are metonymic to some extent. The first use of 'boys' in the expression refers simply to men. The metonymic element here is the idea that most men still have elements of the 'boy' that they used to be within them. The second use of 'boys' in the expression refers to behaviour that is stereotypical of both men and boys when they get together in a group (i.e. rowdy, a bit naughty) and the implication is that people should be tolerant of that behaviour because 'that's just how men are'. This metonymy is heavily loaded with cultural presuppositions. The examples of this phrase in the Bank of English nearly always refer to men, not boys, and there is a covert message that bad behaviour should be tolerated in men in a way that it would not be tolerated in women. This reflects a widespread, stereotypical view of gender roles, which involves a restriction on the range of 'appropriate behaviours' that are available to women. Unsurprisingly, the string 'girls will be girls' occurs only once in the 550 million-word BofE.

This evaluative function of metonymy is particularly prominent when it is used to refer to groups of people of a certain nationality. For instance, in his discussion of the ways in which metonymy contributes to generic reference, Radden (2005: 21) distinguishes between four types of reference:

a. (?) The Italian is fond of children [definite singular generic].
b. (?) An Italian is fond of children [indefinite singular generic].
c. Italians are fond of children [indefinite plural generic].
d. The Italians are fond of children [definite plural generic].

He argues that the first of these, the 'definite singular generic', involves the metonymy REPRESENTATIVE MEMBER OF A CLASS FOR THE CLASS, pointing out that the reason why (a) sounds marked is that one member of the class is taken as representative while the others recede into the background. This emphasises the homogeneity of the species and makes the reference appropriate for animals but not for people. We can see this in examples such as:

The natterjack toad is a toad native to sandy and heathland areas of Europe. (Webcorp)

The Black-winged Pratincole is a wader in the pratincole bird family. (Webcorp)

The giant African land snail is the largest species of snail found on land. (Webcorp)

In English, it is possible to use this construction about people, but because it is more usually used to describe animals, it has acquired a negative semantic prosody (Louw, 1993), which makes it insulting. In the Bank of English, constructions such as this are most likely to appear in the right-wing popular press and reflect racist attitudes:

The Italian is far more bothered with how *he* looks. (BofE)

According to Radden's analysis, the use of this particular metonymy would put Italians on the same level as animals, which explains why it comes across as sounding bigoted. Corpus data reveals that this sort of metonymy is sometimes signalled by the use of 'your' instead of 'the', as we can see in this extract from the novel *Staring at the Sun*, by Julian Barnes:

> Once they had stopped on the short twelfth (an unprecedented act on a par three) while Leslie gravely explained, 'Besides, *your Jew* doesn't really *enjoy* golf.' (Barnes, 1986: 8)

This utterance, combined with the fact that Leslie is, in this scene, playing golf at a club where Jewish and Black people are not allowed to be members, contributes to the reader's view of Leslie as a bigot who holds somewhat outdated, racist views.

Radden's second type of generic, the 'indefinite singular generic' can also be used to convey prejudicial views. This involves the metonymy of A RANDOM MEMBER OF THE CLASS FOR THE WHOLE CLASS and as such needs the whole class to be seen as identical. Again, this undermines the individuality of human beings. Indeed, there is only one instance of this particular usage with reference to Italians in the Bank of English, and here the writer is clearly aware of the effect that he or she is creating:

> Strangled by a spaghetti stereotype, *an Italian* is supposed to lay bricks. (BofE)

The third and fourth generics do not really involve any kind of linguistic metonymy but they do reflect underlying conceptual metonymies whereby a stereotypical member of a class stands for the class as a whole. Such vague impressionistic stereotypes allow for the generalisation of properties across a whole set of individuals, which can lead to racism.

Radden and Kövecses point out that the principles determining vehicle selection can be overridden when a speaker or writer wants to achieve a particular rhetorical effect, although they do not go into detail about how these overriding effects actually operate. A focus on real-world data can be illuminating as it shows how this can work in practice. For example, discourse analysis has shown that particular terms are chosen for vehicle selection simply because they have been used at previous points in the text, sometimes in a literal and sometimes in a metaphorical form. Consider, for example, the following extract from the *Sun* newspaper, which appears in the Bank of English:

> They took a *hand* each and took a lap of honour for officialdom . . . ending with Reed leaping into the *arms* of a startled Gerard Houllier. Now that WOULD have been a gesture of lasting significance. The *hired hands* in the TV studio could have had a field day – after checking the slow-mo to make sure it was Houllier and not David O'Leary who caught him. (BofE)

In this example, the use of the term *hired hands* is preceded by a literal use of the word hand, which is unlikely to be a coincidence. Studies in psycholinguistics show that psychological priming effects can operate across the literal/figurative divide (Giora and Fein, 1999), which suggests that the literal use of the word 'hand' at the beginning of this extract may, to some extent, have 'primed' its subsequent metonymic use.

Another way in which the desire to achieve particular rhetorical effects influences metonymic vehicle selection relates to the human preference for phonological similarity. In his study of multi-word units in the British National Corpus, many of which involved metonymy, Gries (2011) found a statistically significant degree of alliteration. Alliterative examples included 'bread and butter' (to refer to basic needs) and 'black and blue' (to refer to bruising). This finding was replicated by Benczes (2013), who investigated the role of alliteration in the formation of creative metaphoric and metonymic phrases. He argues that alliteration is particularly common in these phrases because it acts as an attention-attracting device, it helps the reader to decipher the meanings of the figurative expressions, it aids a novel expression's acceptability and long-term retention, it signals informality and it helps the creation of social bonds. Thus phonological similarity cannot be ruled out as a possible motivating factor behind vehicle choice in metonymy. This is in line with early cognitive linguistic predictions, which suggest that phonological features can be as important as semantic ones in determining the way language is used (Langacker, 1987).

Studies of corpus data also reveal further principles determining vehicle selection that have not been observed by Radden and Kövecses. For instance, Handl (2011) found a competing principle to the HUMAN OVER NON-HUMAN principle in her corpus study of metonymy. She used the British National Corpus to explore a widely cited example in the metonymy literature whereby a musical instrument is used to refer to the player of that instrument, as in 'the sax has the flu'. This example has been used in the literature to illustrate the principle of HUMAN OVER NON-HUMAN in vehicle selection. However, she found it to be very rare in the British National Corpus. The name of an instrument was more likely to be used metonymically to refer to the sound that it produces rather than to the person who plays it. She thus proposed a further principle for metonymic vehicle selection, which she labelled the 'salience of the target within the vehicle' principle. The sound that a musical instrument makes is a far more salient, or 'central' aspect of a musical instrument than the person who plays it, so in this example SALIENCE OF THE TARGET WITHIN THE VEHICLE trumps the HUMAN OVER NON-HUMAN principle.

Many of the key metonymy-producing relationships and the principles determining vehicle selection in Radden and Kövecses' taxonomy are relatively easy to explain in cognitive terms. As we saw in Chapter 1, one of the key tenets in cognitive linguistics is that our understanding of the world around us is *embodied* – that is to say, we understand things in terms of what they mean to us and how we can best make use of them or interact with them in some way. Another way of putting this is to say that, as humans, we have a somewhat 'self-centred' view of the world. Thus, when we encounter an object, one of our first (automatic) responses is to think about what that object means to us and what we (or other humans) can do with it. Thus, if we see a chair we perceive of it first and foremost as something that we can sit on; if we see a glass, we understand it first and foremost as something that we can put liquid in, and drink from; if we see a messy high chair, covered in food, we are immediately able to picture the toddler sitting in the high chair, making the mess. This is why we are so readily able to access, for example, OBJECT FOR ACTION, CONTAINER FOR CONTAINED, and EFFECT FOR CAUSE metonymic relationships. Work in neurolinguistics is even beginning to indicate that certain clusters of neurons are specifically designed to relate the physical properties of objects to the most suitable cognitive motor programmes that will allow us to interact with them manually in a purposeful way (Gallese and Lakoff, 2005). In other words, when we see a teapot, or even a picture of a teapot, in our minds we automatically prepare to take hold of the handle and pour the tea. Thus the metonymic relationships discussed in this chapter, which involve a link between action and perception, have a clear neurological substrate. Future work in this area may well reveal other neural substrates that account for some of the other common metonymic relationships that have been identified in the literature. Radden and Kövecses also point out that contextual factors may override some of the principles of vehicle selection that they have identified. When we look at the functions of metonymy in language and multimodal communication in Chapters 4 and 5, we will see that this is indeed the case. Both vehicle selection and the meanings of the metonymies themselves are highly dependent on genre and register features, such as the relationships between the speakers, their field of discourse, their overall communicative aims, and the mode of communication.

2.4 Conclusion

This chapter has explored a range of metonymy-producing relationships and has looked at a number of principles guiding vehicle selection. We have seen that the use of authentic data reveals important information about the evaluative and pragmatic import of certain types of metonymy, the ways in which different metonymies combine with each other and with other types of figurative language, and the types of phraseologies that typically accompany different types of metonymy. We have seen, for example, how different types of metonymy sometimes work in pairs, often shade into metaphor, and sometimes have particularly narrow meanings that are conventional for certain speakers in certain discourse communities. This use of authentic data will continue throughout the book, combined with a continued focus on the cognitive basis of metonymy, gradually building up a picture of metonymy that emphasises its richness and complexity.

3 'He's only bowin' to his passport'

Theoretical models of metonymy: uses and drawbacks

3.1 Introduction

So far, we have looked at a number of metonymy-producing relationships and principles determining vehicle selection, and have used authentic language data to explore the pragmatic and formal features of metonymy that accompany these relationships and principles. The focus so far has been mainly on Radden and Kövecses' taxonomy. In this chapter, I extend the coverage to look at a range of other models of metonymy, again seeing how these models might be elaborated through the use of authentic language data. Some of the models involve concepts that were discussed in Chapter 2, but develop more sophisticated classifications of the types of metonymy that emerge from these concepts. Other models emphasise the role of various psychological processes that are thought to be involved in metonymy comprehension and production and use these as a basis for metonymy description and classification.

The aim of this chapter is to present and evaluate these models, and in particular to consider how useful they are for the analysis of metonymy in real-world data. I begin with an introduction to, and evaluation of, four models of metonymy that have made significant contributions to the field, but which may need to be adapted slightly in order to deal effectively with some types of real-world data. These are Warren's (1999, 2004) model of 'referential' and 'propositional' metonymy, Panther and Thornburg's (1998) model of 'referential', 'predicational' and 'illocutionary' metonymy, Ruiz de Mendoza Ibáñez and Diez Velasco's (2002) model of 'source in target' and 'target in source' metonymy, and Peirsman and Geeraerts' (2006a) 'varying strengths of contiguity' model. I then move on to look at Langacker's work on 'active zones, profiling and reference point ability'. Langacker sees metonymy as part of a more general cognitive process through which different parts of a word's meaning are foregrounded or backgrounded in different contexts. This is problematic for metonymy scholars as it suggests that all instances of language involve metonymy to some extent, thus making it too broad a phenomenon to study meaningfully. An attempt to respond to this challenge is Barcelona's (2003b) 'progressive membership constraint' model, which views the different types of metonymy as sitting along a cline from typical 'referential metonymies' of the type discussed in Chapter 1 to the more schematic 'reference point' metonymies discussed by Langacker. After introducing this model, I discuss subsequent work that has been conducted by Handl (2011), who has used corpus data to highlight the role of 'underspecified meaning'. The chapter closes with an exploration of three other approaches to language study that are starting to be used to analyse metonymy, although they were not designed exclusively for this purpose. These are blending theory, relevance theory, and complex systems theory. I outline the contribution that each of these theories has made to our understanding of metonymy, and assess the benefits and drawbacks of using them to study metonymy in the real world.

3.2 Established models of metonymy: uses and drawbacks

As was said above, this section begins with an exploration and an evaluation of four well-established models of metonymy, each of which has made an important contribution to the literature. We will see how, when confronted with real-world data, parts of these models stand up well, whereas others tend not to work so well. The first two of these models (Warren's distinction between referential and propositional metonymy and Panther and Thornburg's distinction between referential, predicational and illocutionary metonymy) categorise metonymy according to what it is used for. The third model (Ruiz de Mendoza Ibáñez and Diez Velasco's distinction between 'source in target' and 'target in source' metonymy) focuses on the relationship between the source and target domain. The fourth model, Peirsman and Geeraerts' (2006a) 'varying strengths of contiguity' model, foregrounds the different types of contiguity that operate within metonymy.

Referential and propositional metonymy (Warren, 1999, 2003, 2006)

One of the most influential models of metonymy is Warren's (1999, 2003, 2006) model, which distinguishes between 'referential' metonymy and 'propositional' metonymy. Of the two types, 'referential' metonymy is the most typical form of metonymy. An example of a referential metonymy is as follows:

People are hungry for *Shakespeare* in America. (BofE)

In this example, the noun 'Shakespeare' refers metonymically to 'plays written by Shakespeare'. Warren postulates a distinction between 'referential metonymy' (where one *entity* is related to another) and 'propositional metonymy' (where one *proposition* is related to another). An example of a propositional metonymy is:

Rosalind *raised her eyebrows* and held out her hand. (BofE)

In this example, the fact that Rosalind 'raised her eyebrows' triggers the proposition that she was surprised. Superficially, referential metonymies tend to violate truth conditions (it is not possible to 'eat' Shakespeare), whereas propositional metonymies relate one proposition to another via an 'if-then' relationship (*if* she raised her eyebrows *then* she must be surprised). Furthermore, referential metonymies are nouns (with a few rare exceptions) whereas propositional metonymies can suggest notions represented by adjectives, such as *surprised* in the example here, but may also involve other parts of speech.

The focus of Warren's work is on referential metonymy. She provides a detailed account of the phenomenon, based on the analysis of a large number of examples taken from the literature on metonymy. In this analysis, she discusses the rationale for the use of referential metonymy, along with an account of its semantics and its syntactic behaviour. She contends that the interpretation of referential metonymies reveals a modifier-head construction, in which the modifier is the explicit noun and the head the inferred element. For instance, *the* ***potatoes*** *are boiling* is understood to mean 'the water which contains the potatoes is boiling'. In other words, the interpreter amends the expression so that it harmonises with the predicate and the non-literacy is dissolved. She also contends that, like the other modifier-head combinations, referential metonymies express a limited number of 'semantic patterns'. These patterns correspond, in nature, to the 'metonymy types' proposed by Radden and Kövecses, but are described at a much more general level. They comprise: causation, location in space and time, possession, composition, and representation.

One observation she makes is that while in metaphor there is thought to be more than one possible mapping between the vehicle and its referent, in referential metonymy there is usually only one, although the reader or listener can use their world knowledge to access more complex meanings. So, for example, in the metaphor LOVE IS A JOURNEY there are many ways in which a love affair might be like a journey (i.e. both have a beginning and an end; they are both often thought to be purposeful, or 'going somewhere'; in both it is possible to take a wrong turning, and so on), whereas in metonymy there is usually only one mapping. We can see how this contrasts with metonymy by looking at the following sentence:

Andy [. . .] was delighted that so many *anoraks* had come out to see the ship. (Webcorp)

Here, Warren would argue that linguistic knowledge gives us 'people with anoraks', exemplifying a PART-WHOLE metonymic link, and the fact that they are 'geeky' depends on world knowledge. This account differs slightly from the account that a cognitive linguist would give, as in cognitive linguistics no distinction is drawn between denotative and connotative knowledge; both types of knowledge are thought to be subsumed within the broader concept of 'encyclopaedic knowledge', which involves the activation of relevant ICMs (see Chapter 1). This example illustrates the ways in which metonymic mappings can be complex and highly context dependent. This will become even more apparent in subsequent chapters, which explore metonymy in different types of data.

A further difference between metaphor and referential metonymy, according to Warren, is that metaphor can be involved in a form of language play called 'zeugma', where two contrasting readings are activated at once, as in, for example, 'the colonel took his hat and his leave'. Here there is incongruity in the fact that a literal and metaphorical reading of the same source item appear in the same phrase, and this incongruity leads to a humorous interpretation. In contrast, if literal and metonymic readings of the same source term appear in the same phrase, this does not lead to zeugma. For example, it is not incongruous, or even particularly marked, to say something like 'I found the Metonymy book quite heavy-going so I put it down for a bit and watched TV'.

In both metaphor and metonymy, these 'double framings' can be exploited for rhetorical effect. In metonymy however, because of the reduced role of incongruity (i.e. zeugma), the effect tends to be more subtle than in metaphor. Here is one of Warren's (2003) examples illustrating how double-framing in metonymy is involved in language play:

the hand . . . that rocks the cradle will rule the land (Warren, 2003; 127)

Here, Warren argues that the image of 'the gentle hand of a loving mother' is contrasted with 'the firm grip of a strong-willed, ambitious person' (ibid.; 31). She goes on to point out that the mother of a ruler will, as a result of the care that she has given him (or her) as a baby, exert influence over the way in which he (or she) rules the country.

Warren argues that metaphor can operate above the phrasal level while referential metonymy does not. Metaphorical expressions from the same source domain can work together to form 'themes' which extend across large sections of text, whereas this does not generally happen with metonymy (Warren, 2003: 117). However, as we will see in subsequent chapters, when we take a broader definition of metonymy we see that it can operate at the level of the text where it can form themes that contribute to the overall coherence of the text.

According to Warren, the vast majority of referential metonymies are noun phrases, although there are some examples of adjectives functioning as referential metonymies. This occurs when a metonymy is a modifier. We can see this in the following example:

Have you got a *red pen*? (BNC)

Here, the term 'red pen' refers metonymically to a pen that has red ink in it. The pen itself may be any colour.

It is possible for a single phrase to be both referential and propositional, as we can see in the following excerpt, from Act 1 of Arthur Miller's 1955 play *A View from the*

Bridge. In this play, Eddie, Catherine's uncle, is deeply suspicious of Catherine's boyfriend, who he thinks is simply using her to gain American citizenship:

CATHERINE: No, Eddie, he's got all kinds of respect for me. And you too! We walk across the street he takes my arm – he almost bows to me! You got him all wrong, Eddie; I mean it, you –

EDDIE : *He's only bowin' to his passport.*

CATHERINE: His passport?

EDDIE: That's right. He marries you he's got the right to be an American citizen. That's what's goin' on here. (*She is puzzled and surprised.*) You understand what I'm tellin' you? The guy is lookin' for his break, that's all he's lookin' for.

(Miller, 1995: 28; emphasis added)

Here, Eddie refers to Catherine as her boyfriend's 'passport', and goes on to explain that the boyfriend is only interested in marrying her so that he can remain in America. At first sight, this use of the word 'passport' appears to constitute an example of Warren's 'referential' metonymy (one would not normally bow to a passport). However, an if-then relationship is also implied (*if* he marries her *then* he will obtain an American passport), which suggests that it also has elements of propositional metonymy.

Warren's position represents the traditional view of metonymy, and before the 1990s, this restrictive view of what constitutes metonymy was widely shared amongst linguists. However, since the 1990s, with the increasing attention that cognitive linguists have paid to metonymy, broader, more encompassing definitions have been proposed. It is in this broader, more encompassing framework that this book is situated, as such a view is helpful in explaining the complex, and sometimes contradictory characteristics that metonymy can exhibit when it is found 'in the wild'. All of the subsequent models discussed in this chapter adopt this broader view of metonymy.

Referential, predicational and illocutionary metonymy (Panther and Thornburg, 1998)

Panther and Thornburg (1998) offer a slightly more fine-grained distinction than Warren, and identify two broad types of metonymy: 'propositional' and 'illocutionary'. 'Propositional' metonymies are further broken down into the two sub-types: 'referential' and 'predicational'.

To a large extent, referential metonymies are identical to those identified by Warren in that they involve relationships between entities, as in the following example, where 'the buses' refer to the drivers of those buses:

The growing list of countries where *the buses are on strike*. (BofE)

Predicational metonymies mostly involve relationships between events. An example of a predicational metonymy is:

He was *able to tell me* that it had merely gone into spasm. (BofE)

Here the term 'able to tell me' metonymically stands for the fact that 'he did tell me'. In these sorts of metonymies, a potential event expressed through a form of modality (e.g. the ability, possibility, permission or obligation to undertake an action) is metonymically linked to its occurrence in reality. Metonymies such as these would be classed as POTENTIAL FOR ACTUAL in Radden and Kövecses' framework.

Illocutionary metonymy involves pragmatic inferencing. For example, in the following example, the question 'Have you got a fiver?' is linked through an illocutionary metonymy to the question 'Please can you lend or give me five pounds?'

Have you got a fiver? I want to pay the boy for his petrol. (BofE)

Rather than relying on frame or ICM-based relationships, illocutionary metonymies rely on scenario-based relationships. That is to say, they rely on the speaker and hearer's knowledge of a 'typical scenario' (in the above example the 'typical scenario' would involve lending a friend some money in order to help him or her pay for something). One part of the scenario is used to refer to other parts of it. These might include the necessary preconditions for an event, the event itself and the consequences of the event. Thus, in the above example, a precondition (i.e. that the hearer is in possession of a five-pound note) is used metonymically by the speaker to ask if he or she can borrow it. According to Panther and Thornburg, the 'literal' meaning of a metonymy is always relevant to the interpretation of a metonymic expression; it is not the case that metonymy simply involves the substitution of one word for another.

Panther and Thornburg's model makes two key contributions to the field of metonymy studies. These are its focus on illocutionary metonymy and the attention that it pays to the role played by metonymy in grammar. These mark metonymy out as something far more encompassing than a lexical phenomenon. Their model shows how typical metonymic relations (such as CAUSE FOR EFFECT, RESULT FOR ACTION, PRODUCER FOR PRODUCT and so on) operate as *natural inference schemas* within our long-term memory, and that they can be rapidly retrieved to help us access the intended meaning of the utterances that we hear. This is an important contribution as it allows for a more systematic study of the role of metonymy in pragmatics and grammar, allowing analysts to investigate different metonymic relationships that are involved in different kinds of pragmatic inferencing. Their model will be referred to frequently in subsequent chapters.

'Source in target' metonymy and 'target in source' metonymy (Ruiz de Mendoza Ibáñez and Diez Velasco, 2002)

Another model of metonymy which, like those discussed above, has made a key contribution to the metonymy literature, but which may need to be developed to account for some types of real-world data, is that proposed by Ruiz de Mendoza Ibáñez and Diez Velasco (2002). They believe the distinction between referential and propositional metonymy to be irrelevant, and focus instead on the relationship between the metonymic expression and its referent. They argue that all instances of metonymy can be described as one of two types: either as a 'target in source' metonymy, where the metonymic term is part of its referent, or as a 'source in target' metonymy, where the referent is part of the metonymic term.

The example that they give of a 'target in source' metonymy is the Pill to refer specifically to the contraceptive pill, as in:

The great contribution that *the Pill* has made to personal choice. (BofE)

Here, the word Pill is used to refer to a specific type of pill, which means that the target of the metonymy (the contraceptive pill) is a subset of the domain covered by the general word 'pill'.

The example that they give of a 'source in target' metonymy is the use of 'hand' in expressions such as:

All *hands* on deck. (BofE)

In this example, the 'hands' refer to the sailors who are doing hard physical work so the hands are simply part of the domain.

Another way of describing their approach is to say that in 'target in source' metonymies the referent is a sub-domain of the metonymic vehicle, whereas in 'source in target' metonymies the metonymic vehicle is a sub-domain of the referent. Ruiz de Mendoza Ibáñez and Diez Velasco argue that 'source-in-target' metonymies involve 'domain expansion', while 'target-in-source' metonymies involve 'domain reduction', and that these are two fundamental processes. They adopt a very broad definition of what is meant by the 'source' and 'target', which allows them to classify a wide range of metonymies as 'target-in-source' metonymies. For example, in their model, the following would be classified as a 'target-in-source' metonymy:

IBM hired Jerry Hawk. (BofE)

This is because the source domain (IBM) includes everything that a speaker might know about this domain, including the fact that it has managers and that those managers have the capacity to hire and fire. The fact that IBM as a whole is used to refer to this particular aspect of the company means that the metonymy involves 'domain reduction'.

If we think back to the taxonomy of metonymy types proposed by Radden and Kövecses (1999) which we saw in Chapter 2, we will notice a marked difference between their approach and the approach employed by Ruiz de Mendoza Ibáñez and Diez Velasco. Whereas Radden and Kövecses distinguish between part/whole and part/part metonymies, Ruiz de Mendoza Ibáñez and Diez Velasco group *all* metonymies under the first of these headings. They do this by extending the notion of the ICM. So for example, the sentence 'she married money' would be a TRAIT FOR PERSON metonymy under Radden and Kövecses' approach, whereas it would simply be a PART FOR WHOLE metonymy under Ruiz de Mendoza Ibáñez and Diez Velasco's approach, as wealth would be seen as a possible part of the ICM for an 'ideal spouse'.

Ruiz de Mendoza Ibáñez and Diez Velasco's approach constitutes a useful tool for metonymy analysis, especially when we look at the role of metonymy in genres and registers that are specific to particular discourse communities. The process of 'domain reduction' appears to be particularly productive in the meaning-making processes in which individual discourse communities engage. As we will see in Chapter 4, discourse communities often take fairly commonly used words and give them their own particular, much more specific meanings, thus creating a feeling of in-group membership. For example, Deignan *et al.* (2013) show how in the language used by a group of supporters at a children's football club, the instruction to 'kick it' has a narrowed-down, metonymic meaning of 'kick it really hard, with conviction'. It does not simply mean 'kick it'. The concept of domain reduction is also useful when speakers wish to be deliberately vague, for example when they want to avoid singling out a particular individual within an organisation who may have been responsible for a particular action. The very broad definition of domains that they adopt is also useful in explaining anaphoric reference and textual cohesion involving metonymy. For these reasons, I will make regular references to their model when discussing the functions of metonymy in real-world data.

Some metonymic expressions can involve both a source in target mapping and a target in source mapping. Ruiz de Mendoza Ibáñez and Diez Velasco illustrate this with the sentence:

Shakespeare is on the top shelf. (Ruiz de Mendoza Ibáñez and Diez Velasco, 2002: 517).

They point out that this sentence involves both a TARGET IN SOURCE relationship (where 'Shakespeare' is used to refer to 'books written by Shakespeare') and a SOURCE IN TARGET relationship (where Shakespeare's work is used to refer to the actual books in which this work appears).

When we look at examples of metonymy in real-world data and take contextual and pragmatic meanings into account, we see that this combination of TARGET IN SOURCE and SOURCE IN TARGET relationship within a single metonymy is arguably more widespread than Ruiz de Mendoza Ibáñez and Diez Velasco suggest. Let us begin by exploring their two earlier examples that were used to illustrate the different relationships. As we saw above, they point out that the use of the term 'the Pill' to refer only to the contraceptive pill is clearly a TARGET IN SOURCE metonymy as it refers only to a specific pill. However, on a more general level, it could also be said to be a SOURCE IN TARGET metonymy as it provides metonymic shorthand to a much wider set of events, including the taking of the Pill, and the set of societal changes that occurred because of the Pill, as we can see in these examples:

The Pill is much safer than abortion. (BofE)

The Pill genuinely liberated married women. (BofE)

The Pill gave them sexual equality. (BofE)

The example 'all hands on deck', which they provide as an example of a SOURCE IN TARGET metonymy, can also be said to involve both types of relationship. In their model, the hands stand for the bodies of the sailors but it could be re-analysed as a TARGET IN SOURCE metonymy, as the hands stand for one just particular thing that we do with our hands (i.e. work). Indeed, in the Bank of English, the expression 'all hands on deck' occurs forty-three times, and not once is it used to refer to sailors. It refers in nearly all cases to the idea of working together and 'mucking in', and the hands do not stand for sailors, but what people do with hands (i.e. work). We do not know whether the expression ever did refer to sailors or whether it was ever used by sailors. The fact that we do all sorts of things with our hands besides working suggests that the referent is narrower than the metonymic vehicle, 'hands'.

These examples show that it can be very difficult to decide whether a particular metonymic expression is a 'target in source' metonymy or a 'source in target' metonymy, and that when we look at the contextual meanings of metonymic expressions, we find evidence of both relationships occurring at once. This is probably due to the broad definition of ICMs that Ruiz de Mendoza Ibáñez and Diez Velasco adopt. The more broadly we define an ICM, the more difficult it becomes to say whether one is part of another or vice versa. This, however, does not detract from the usefulness of the model when accounting for the functions played by metonymy in real-world data. As mentioned above, we will see in Chapters 4 and 5 how the notion of domain reduction helps to explain the ways in which particular discourse communities metonymically narrow down the meaning of word until it means something very specific to that community. It is also useful in accounting for metonymy-based textual cohesion. We will also see how the notion of domain expansion is useful for showing how metonymy can be used to discriminate against large groups of people who happen to share a single characteristic.

Peirsman and Geeraerts' (2006a) varying strengths of contiguity

Peirsman and Geeraerts' model of metonymy constitutes a radical departure from the preceding models as it treats metonymy as a radial category. The basic idea of a 'radial category' is that whenever we put things into categories, we are able to identify those which are core 'prototypical' members of the category, and those which are less central. So if we were to set up the category of 'pets', a cat or a dog might be seen as 'prototypical' (at least in the UK). Other animals, such as snakes and rats would be seen as less prototypical, and lions and tigers even less so. The latter would probably shade into the category of 'zoo animals' though they might also be seen as pets at a stretch. Thus at this point the category of 'pets' shades into the category of 'zoo animals' and the boundary between them is fuzzy. So radial categories can be said to have prototypical and less prototypical members and fuzzy boundaries between them. There are very few things in life that exist in discrete categories with clear boundaries, and it would be wrong to try and categorise language in this way too. The idea that language exists with radial categories is a fundamental tenet of cognitive linguistics, and radial category approaches have been applied to word senses, phonological features, intonation patterns, linguistic constructions and grammar rules (Taylor, 2003). It thus makes sense to see metonymy as a phenomenon which exists within a radial category.

In their radial category model of metonymy, Peirsman and Geeraerts emphasise the importance of contiguity between the vehicle and its referent; in other words, they are interested in how close the term used is to its intended meaning. For them, prototypical metonymies involve cases where the term is part of its metonymic meaning, or vice versa. An example of such a metonymy would be:

I'll be able to eat every day and *have a roof over my head.* (BofE)

Here, *a roof over my head* is part of its intended meaning, *a house*, so the example would be classed as prototypical. An example of a metonymy that lies between the core and periphery of the category would be:

The whole theatre fell ill. (BofE)

Here *the theatre* refers to the people who were sitting in the theatre. There is a contiguous relationship between them (as the people were actually in the theatre at some point) so the metonymy would be classed as being midway between the core and the periphery of the category. An example of a highly peripheral metonymy would be as follows:

Clinton plans a *round table* discussion. (BofE)

Here there may not be an actual 'round table' in the room. The metonymy is based on the idea that people 'might' be sitting round a round table and thus all participating equally in the discussion, but they might not. Because there is not necessarily a round table in the room, the term and its referent cannot be said to be contiguous in any way, so it is a peripheral example of metonymy.

Peirsman and Geeraerts also argue that metonymies lying towards the edge of the category are less 'bounded' than those at the centre. Bounded entities have a clear cut-off point, whereas unbounded entities do not. A metonymy involving two bounded entities, which would thus be seen as prototypical, is:

I couldn't bear the way men regarded me as just a *pair of legs*. (BofE)

The metonymy *pair of legs* would be described by Peirsman and Geeraerts as prototypical as both the term (a pair of legs) and its referent (a woman) are bounded entities. Metonymies where either the term or its referent (or both) are unbounded, would be seen as lying towards the periphery of the category. An example of such a metonymy would be:

The classic *Hollywood* narrative. (BNC)

Here, although Hollywood is bounded (there is probably a city line somewhere in the suburbs) its intended referent is not. It is difficult to say exactly what it means and the concept of a Hollywood film is probably itself a radial category that has fuzzy boundaries with other genres.

Finally, Peirsman and Geeraerts see concrete metonymies as lying at the centre of the category and more abstract metonymies lying towards the periphery, so for example the following would be seen as prototypical:

Fancy a new *set of wheels*? (BofE)

Here both a set of wheels and its referent, a car, are concrete entities. Lying towards the periphery are metonymies involving more temporal or abstract entities, such as:

Jay and Denise are expected to *walk up the aisle* in the summer. (BofE)

The referent of this metonymy, 'getting married' is less concrete than 'a car' because you cannot see it, get in it or be run over by it.

To sum up, according to Peirsman and Geeraerts, metonymy types radiate out from prototypical instantiations in three different ways: they gradually become less contiguous, less bounded and less concrete. This model is useful as it shows that metonymies can differ from one another in more than one way. However, one problem with the model is that, when faced with metonymies from real-world data, it is sometimes difficult to see which category they fit into. We can see this by looking more closely at some of the examples discussed above. The expression 'have a roof over my head' refers, in very basic terms, to the idea of actually having a house, so at first sight there appears to be a high degree of contiguity between the vehicle term and its referent. However, the expression also carries an extra meaning of having enough money to provide for one's basic needs, and here we start to see less continguity between the vehicle and its referent. The exact degree of contiguity between a vehicle and its referent can therefore be very difficult to identify when metonymies are used in context, as there can be more than one referent. Moreoever, it is not always clear which referent(s) is/are intended as they are often vague and underspecified. The same can be said for boundedness. We have already seen, in Chapter 2, that 'a pair of legs' does much more than simply refer to a woman, and that it carries all sorts of connotations about a woman's sexuality and availability. These connotations are not easily covered by the notion of a 'bounded entity'. Again, because the metonymy does not have a clear, single referent, it is difficult to measure the extent to which this referent is 'bounded'. Finally, it can be difficult to determine the level of concreteness of some metonymic expressions. We saw this in Chapter 1 with the 'brothers needed some muscle' example. Here, we could say that 'some muscle' simply refers to a strong man, in which case the referent is highly concrete, or it could refer to a build-up of forces prior to a fight, which is a slightly less concrete phenomenon. The main problem with this model is that it assumes a one-to-one correspondence between the vehicle term and its referent, and in reality this is not always the case. Having said that, it is useful to see metonymy as a radial category, and Peirsman and Geeraerts are right to say that different types of metonymy can radiate out from the centre along different axes. For this reason, the model is useful when analysing the different senses of ambiguous metonymies in context.

Langacker's (1993) focus on active zones and what this means for models of metonymy

One of the most influential cognitive linguistic theories of metonymy is that proposed by Langacker (1993). He argues that metonymy is involved virtually every time a different aspect of word's meaning (or the domain that it represents) is highlighted by its use in a different context. This, he argues, is because a shift in profile is generally involved. For example, there is a metonymic relationship between the use of the word 'university' to refer to the actual buildings and the use of the word to refer to the institution or a university sports team, as shown in the following three examples:

[. . .] former students living closer to *the university.* (BofE)

The university currently offers degree programmes in Pharmacy, Occupational Therapy, Midwifery [. . .] (BofE)

[. . .] they played a friendly against *the university.* (BofE)

Each of these senses 'profiles' a different aspect of the university and therefore involves metonymy. His argument is based on the premise that words alone are incapable of fully specifying the meaning intended by the speaker and that there is always a degree of indeterminacy. The information that is provided in the actual words that we read or hear does not itself establish the precise connections that are understood by the speaker and hearer. In Langacker's words:

'explicit linguistic coding gets us into the right neighbourhood [. . .] but from there we have to find the right address by some other means' (Langacker, 2009: 46).

These 'other means' frequently involve metonymy. In each case, a different part (or 'facet') of our knowledge of the referent is brought to the fore. In other words, it becomes the focus of our attention. This facet is then 'profiled' and becomes an 'active zone'. Individual words can only ever point to a broad area of meaning, and different facets of that meaning become active in different contexts. Metonymy is therefore a reflection of our fundamental 'reference point ability', which refers to our capacity to decide which facet is being profiled in any particular instance of language use. To illustrate further, each of the following sentences profiles a different understanding of the word 'town':

They had to go into *town* shopping. (BofE)

This *town* has been trying to change me. (BofE)

The next *town* to Ashburton. (BofE)

A promotion-relegation play-off against Omagh *Town*. (BofE)

These examples refer respectively to the town centre, the people who live in the town, the physical location of the town and the town football club. The metonymic 'work' that needs to be done to interpret these examples involves drawing on the various ICMs that are triggered by the word 'town'. Equally, different meanings of the word 'film' are profiled in each of these examples:

Anyway, I loathe that entire *film* world. (BofE)

The *film* cost 3 million dollars. (BofE)

A *film* projector, a slide projector and . . . (BofE)

The meaning of the word 'film' that is being profiled in each of these three examples gradually becomes more concrete, reflecting the context in which it occurs. Langacker (2009: 54) suggests that another way to help us understand metonymy is to look at compound nouns, such as 'butterfly net' and 'mosquito net', which can be seen in the following examples:

I take my *butterfly net* and walk in the jungle. (BofE)

I set up my *mosquito net* under the bridge. (BofE)

In each case, a different facet of the word 'net' is profiled by the noun that it compounds with. The first is talking about a net that is used to catch butterflies, whereas the second is talking about a net that is used to protect the user from mosquitoes. The relationship between the two nouns is different in each compound even though the grammatical structure is the same. The reason for these different interpretations is that different ICMs are invoked in each case: in the case of the butterfly net, the idea is that we like to catch butterflies because they are pretty and in the case of mosquitoes, the idea is that we need to protect ourselves from them because they bite and carry diseases such as malaria. These examples are of course, highly conventional so we do not need to engage in active metonymic thinking in order to understand them. In other words, they are 'conventional' metonymies. When faced with novel metonymies, we need to engage in 'metonymic thinking' in order to understand them. Langacker (2009: 54) illustrates this nicely with his example of a made-up compound: 'elephant table'. This could be a table made out of an elephant's foot, a table covered in elephant ornaments, a table shaped like an elephant, and so on. Because the metonymic connection is not fixed we are free to form our own connections and therefore understand the term in different ways. Metonymy can therefore be described as a thinking process that allows us to make sense of utterances by profiling a particular facet of a given phenomenon. The active zone is different in each of these cases. Empirical support for Langacker's theory is provided by Onysko and Degani (2012), who presented participants with a range of entirely novel English compounds (such as 'voice canoe', 'bucket philosopher' and 'word truck') and asked them to make sense of them. They found that the meanings produced always involved metonymic links between the constituents of the compounds, although they sometimes interacted with metaphor too.

Langacker's notion of active zones is by no means limited to language. It is equally relevant to other forms of communication and is particularly common in the medium of cinema, which is inherently metonymic because of the way in which different camera angles can be used to change the angle, perspective and focus of the 'shots'. This idea is discussed in depth in Chapter 5, which looks in detail at the different functions served by metonymy in multimodal forms of expression. The notion of active zones has also been used by researchers to show how metonymy is central to grammar and what might loosely be described as grammar 'rules' as well as to language change. A whole volume of papers has been dedicated to this idea (Panther *et al.*, 2009), and this work will be explored in Chapter 6.

Langacker's view of metonymy presents a serious challenge to metonymy scholars as it suggests that, in some respects, just about all instances of meaning and communication are metonymic, as meaning comprehension nearly always involves highlighting some aspects of a phenomenon and putting others in the shade. Although this is interesting from a philosophical perspective, it presents a practical problem to those interested in defining and investigating metonymy, as it implies that there is nothing 'special' about examples such as those discussed in the Introduction, and that they are no different from any other form of language. However, there clearly is something interesting and different about metonymy that makes it worthy of investigation. The fact that a great deal of humour derives from the contrast between metonymic readings of words and their more basic senses means that humans do recognise it as a discrete phenomenon, albeit subconsciously. Metonymy scholars have therefore sought to reconcile the apparently contradictory views of 'metonymy as a pervasive unremarkable phenomenon' and 'metonymy as something special'. Even Langacker agrees that there is something of a cline from prototypical 'stands for' metonymy and the more nebulous 'active zone' metonymy discussed in his work.

Barcelona's (2003b) progressive membership constraint model and Handl's (2012) radial category approach to metonymy

Barcelona (2003b, 2011) rises to the challenge presented by Langacker's work by proposing a radial category approach to metonymy that accounts for both the prototypical examples of metonymy that are based on contiguity, and instances of metonymy that simply involve domain highlighting. Prototypical metonymies at the centre of the category are the sorts of referential metonymies discussed in Chapter 1 that could, in some cases, be described as reflecting 'stands for' relationships. Those at the periphery of the category involve domain highlighting, of the type discussed by Langacker. Metonymies in the 'half way' category are referred to as 'typical'. The model is shown in Figure 3.1.

Barcelona's prototypical model of metonymy is a useful development in metonymy theory but it is not without its problems: it does not provide much detail about the exact nature of 'typical' metonymies that lie between prototypical and peripheral examples, and it is difficult to see why it gives such preferential treatment to referential metonymies.

Handl (2011) improves upon Barcelona's model of metonymy by bringing in the notion of 'underspecified meaning'. Her study of metonymy in the British National Corpus led her to conclude that a very large number of metonymies have a meaning that is in fact 'underspecified'. In these metonymies, the basic sense of the vehicle term is retained and contributes to the contextual meaning of the expression, meaning that both the basic meaning and the contextual meaning are present. In order to illustrate this type of metonymy, she uses two examples:

(1) The White House isn't saying anything.

(2) An earlier ferry had got me a front seat in one of the waiting buses.

She argues that the first of these examples constitutes a 'typical' case of metonymy in that the vehicle recedes fully into the background as soon as the target has been identified. However, the second example is more complex. In this example, both the buses and the drivers of those buses (who are doing the

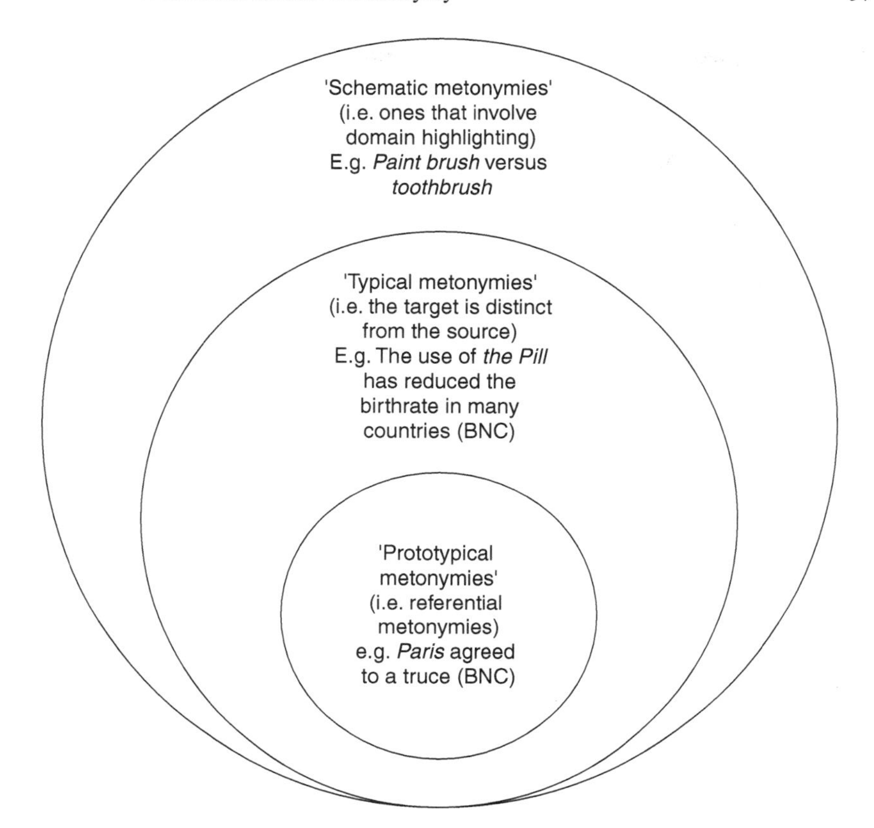

Figure 3.1 Barcelona's progressive membership constraint model

waiting) are part of the intended meaning; the buses do not simply provide 'mental access' to the drivers. Both the buses and their drivers are being referred to at the same time. The sentence therefore lacks the kind of directionality that is inherent in some of the earlier models of (prototypical) metonymy. The metonymic meaning comprises both the target and vehicle and it is 'underspecified' in that it is not entirely clear what is being referred to. It is not clear what direction the metonymic mapping should go in because the weight of its constituent parts is relatively balanced. The same can be said of the following example.

Police stopped *the BMW* from travelling at speed just before midnight with only one headlight on. (BNC)

In this example, the BMW refers to both the car and the driver. It does not simply refer to one or the other, so its exact referent can never be specified.

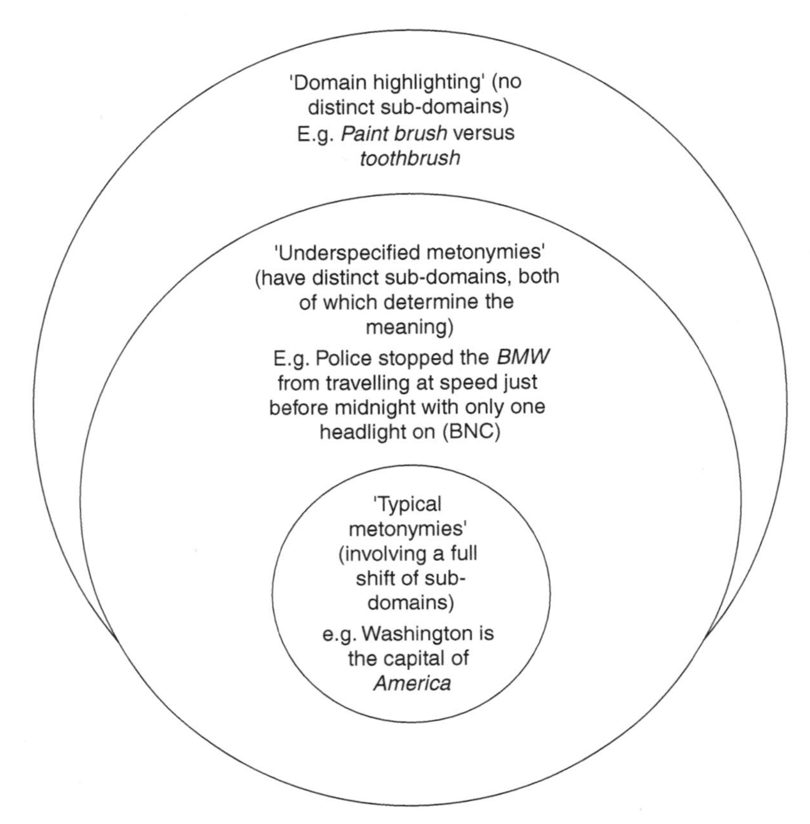

Figure 3.2 Handl's (2012) radial category approach to metonymy

Handl thus proposes the radial category approach to metonymy shown in Figure 3.2, which is a more refined version of Barcelona's earlier model.

In this model, the relatively rare 'typical metonymies' involve completely distinct sub-domains. Washington is not actually the capital of America, it is the capital of the United States of America. 'Underspecified metonymies' involve both the vehicle and the target in their meaning and 'domain highlighting' metonymies have no distinct sub-domains whatsoever, just differences in construal or viewpoint that result from the juxtaposition of the different words.

Handl found that underspecified metonymies tend to involve some sort of containment relation. She argues that this is because people rarely need to differentiate between a container and its contents and that they tend to perceive them in a unified way because they operate as a 'functional unit' (2012: 4). In other words, the metonymic term does not simply 'stand for' the referent in a metonymy, but rather, it stands for both itself and the referent. Her model stresses the fact that linguistic metonymies are not simply another way of expressing an already extant idea, but that they represent an altered conceptualisation of the idea.

As well as corpus data, Handl (2011, 2012) provides experimental evidence indicating that many metonymies are in fact often *understood* in an underspecified manner. She found that the informants in her study usually thought that the metonymy was referring to both the term and its referent. She assigned different weights to the two parts of the metonymy based on frequency of response and was thus able to provide a differentiated description of metonymies in terms of the constituents' weights. In prototypical metonymies, the weight of the vehicle is relatively high. That is to say, the actual words of the metonymy play an important role in its meaning, whereas, when we move out towards the periphery of the radial category, the vehicle recedes into the background. In the more intermediate types of metonymy, both the vehicle and its referent play an equally important role. The fact that Handl's model of metonymy is based on real-world data makes it particularly appropriate for the analysis of the communicative functions of metonymy that will be presented in the next two chapters.

3.3 Other approaches to language that can be used to explain metonymy

In recent years there has been something of a move towards more flexible, context-based approaches to metonymy. Rather than viewing metonymy simply as a 'domain transfer' or 'domain highlighting' process, there has also been much more of a focus on the role of context in metonymy interpretation and production; individual metonymies cannot be seen as independent of what came before them and what will come after them in both the sentence and the text, and even in life more generally. This has led some researchers to view metonymy as a much more fluid and variable and unpredictable phenomenon. There are no specific models of metonymy that incorporate this feature per se, but there are a number of approaches to language, none of which were originally devised with metonymy in mind, that are starting to be applied to the study of metonymy. These are blending theory, relevance theory and complex systems theory.

Metonymy and blending theory

Blending theory is an approach to language and communication which holds that the construction of meaning involves the integration of more than one 'mental space', and that the resultant meaning is more than the sum of its parts (Fauconnier and Turner, 1999). A good account of the role of blending theory in metonymy comprehension is provided by Coulson and Oakley (2003), who illustrate their argument by exploring the expression:

You could end up *digging your own grave.* (BofE).

They argue that this expression involves much more than a straightforward mapping from the source domain of 'grave digging' to the target domain of 'getting oneself into difficulties'. In order to understand this expression, they argue that one needs to form a single conceptual blend in which the person who is getting themselves into difficulties is digging his or her own grave and then presumably climbing into it and dying. The expression cannot be understood by any 'logical' analysis; rather, its meaning is facilitated by the RESULT FOR ACTION metonymy of one's grave standing for one's own death. Once this metonymic relationship is activated the expression makes sense. The digging of one's own grave and the act of dying are compressed into a single utterance. Metonymy is used to unpack meaning from the compressed elements in the blended space. Coulson and Oakley also argue that metonymy holds together the network of mental spaces that need to be activated in order for reasoning to be sustained over an extended length of time. They go on to show how metonymy comprehension involves two key concepts that are involved in the formation of a conceptual blend: 'compression' and 'vital relations'. For example, the metonymy 'a warm coat' involves the compression of the CAUSE of wearing a coat with the EFFECT of being warm. The vital relation between these two is one of property. That is to say, the 'warmth' that the coat endows to the wearer is a property of coat within this blend.

We can see this principle at work in what at first sight appears to be a non-figurative extract from Arthur Miller's play *A View from the Bridge*, which was also referred to above. In this play, an Italian immigrant couple (Beatrice and Eddie) who live with their niece (Catherine) in New York temporarily offer shelter to two cousins who are illegal immigrants and who are thus hiding from the authorities. Before the cousins arrive, Eddie utters the following to his wife and niece:

CATHERINE: No, I just mean . . . people'll see them goin' in and out.
EDDIE: I don't care who sees them goin' in and out *as long as you don't see 'em going in and out.* And this goes for you too, B. *You don't see nothin' and you don't know nothin'.*
BEATRICE: What do you mean? I understand. (Miller, 1995: 13; emphasis added).

In the italicised segments, he means that they must act as if they do not have guests staying with them in order to avoid attracting undue attention from neighbours and potential spies. In order to understand what is meant here one has to create a blend between the actual non-noticing of the guests and the ability to behave as if one has not noticed them. In order to unpack the blend and to make sense of it, one needs to evoke the metonymic EFFECT FOR CAUSE relationship between actually seeing something and behaving as if one has seen it. One issue that has been raised with respect to blending theory is that it is extremely hard to prove or disprove (Gibbs, 2000) as the theory itself is basically infalsifiable and it is difficult to test it out against alternative hypotheses. Having said this, it does present an intuitively appealing explanation for the more difficult-to-explain aspects of metonymy.

Metonymy and relevance theory

Relevance theory is an approach to meaning, proposed by Sperber and Wilson (1987, 2004), which foregrounds the fact that in any communicative encounter the hearer or reader will assume that what is being said is relevant to him or her and will use this as a guiding principle in the interpretation process. Traditionally, relevance theorists have not dealt with metonymy, preferring to focus instead on metaphor and hyperbole. For them, metonymy simply constitutes a 'loose' way of speaking alongside metaphor and hyperbole, and the principle of relevance is sufficient for its interpretation (Carston, 1997). More recently however, relevance theorists have begun to pay more attention to metonymy. Relevance theory approaches to metonymy tend to emphasise the role of world knowledge in metonymy comprehension and attempt to show how such world knowledge explains why some metonymic expressions are deemed much more 'acceptable' than others. For example, Nunberg (1995) takes the sentence: 'I'm parked out back' and argues that two conditions need to be satisfied before 'I' can be taken to mean 'the car'. The first is that there needs to be a 'salient correspondence' between the properties of the person and the properties of the car. In this case, the 'salient correspondence' is that the person is the owner of the car and he or she has just parked the car 'out back'. The second is that it has to be 'either useful or interesting to know that these acquired or inherited properties apply to their carriers' (1995: 192). In the case of the parking example, one would probably be interested to know that the person was 'parked out back' if one was going to be given a lift by their friend, or borrow their friend's car, or if the two people were comparing notes on where they had parked. Papafragou (1996) provides further examples showing how relationships that are salient or relevant *in context* play a key role in determining whether and how a particular metonymic expression will be understood. She argues that there is no need to draw on lists of typical metonymy-producing relationships, as the relationships are generated in an ad hoc manner as the need arises. She describes this process as 'interpretative'.

An advantage of relevance theory is that it emphasises the role of context in the comprehension process and this is useful when studying metonymy in real-world data. On the other hand, it appears to lean slightly too far in this direction, claiming that context is everything. When we analyse metonymy comprehension in more detail we can see that, as well as contextual cues, metonymy types such as those listed by Radden and Kövecses (1999) are also involved in the meaning-making process. For example the 'I'm parked out back' sentence referred to in the preceding paragraph clearly involves a POSSESSOR FOR POSSESSED metonymic relationship. Context plays an important role in activating and exploiting this relationship, but this does not mean that the metonymic relationship itself is absent. Indeed, recent work in cognitive linguistics has thus challenged relevance theory. For example, Ruiz de Mendoza Ibáñez and Pérez Hernández (2003) show how metonymic mappings are repeatedly involved in the interpretation process. Hearers draw on their knowledge of typical metonymy types, *alongside* the principle of relevance, when interpreting metonymic uses of language. In order to illustrate their theory, they provide numerous examples of utterances whose illocutionary force has to be derived through pragmatic inferencing, and show how, in every case, the inferencing draws on a limited number of fundamental metonymic relationships.

Metonymy as an emergent phenomenon: the role of complex systems theory

Complex systems theory is an attempt to explain human behaviour by taking account of all the factors that are likely to have led to a particular event taking place (Larsen-Freeman and Cameron, 2008). Complex systems theory has been shown to provide a useful framework for discussing the interaction between linguistic and conceptual metaphor. Gibbs and Santa Cruz (2012) make a convincing case for the dynamic emergence of conceptual metaphor in discourse. They discuss how conceptual metaphors 'unfold' over time in conversation according to specific types of dynamics. They see conceptual metaphors as temporary instances of stability in the system, which are described in complex systems theory as 'attractor states'. Other conceptual metaphors also act on the conversation at the same time, and tend to 'pull' it in other directions. Thus no single conceptual metaphor has complete control over the way in which an utterance is interpreted. In their words:

> This possibility offers a very different view of the traditional question regarding whether a single conceptual metaphor is activated or not during verbal metaphor processing as many conceptual metaphors, along with many other constraining forces, may have partial, probabilistic influence on one's understanding of verbal metaphor. (Gibbs and Santa Cruz, 2012: 305)

Gibbs and Santa Cruz go on to argue that conceptual metaphors will facilitate metaphor understanding to differing degrees, depending on the interaction of different variables, along multiple timescales, at any given moment in the conversation. This argument is taken even further by Gibbs (2013: 60), who shows how any metaphoric utterance, at any time, may be influenced by any or all of the following: evolutionary forces that lead to group cooperation to ensure basic survival, historical forces that have shaped the development of the language that they are speaking, previous topics of conversation that these particular interlocutors have engaged in, social forces determining what it is and is not appropriate to say in certain contexts, and physical sensations that are being experienced by the interlocutors at the time of speaking.

Complex systems theory has recently been applied to the study of metonymy by Biernacka (2013) in her study of focus group conversations about terrorism. She found that, in the same way as metaphors, metonymies partially shaped the participants' understanding of the topic under discussion, and that more than one type of metonymy was exerting a force at any one time, pulling a particular conversation in different directions. Different types of metonymy were called upon to differing degrees depending on the context of the utterance and the timeframe within which it took place. A particular metonymy would be employed by a speaker or writer at a particular point in time for a myriad of reasons and it was impossible to separate the purely cognitive from the purely social. This complex systems approach to metonymy does not usurp the theories that have been outlined above. It simply enriches them by providing further information about when and why particular metonymies are employed. This idea is discussed in depth in Chapter 4, where among other things I explore the role played by metonymy in anaphoric reference and textual cohesion.

3.4 Conclusion

In this chapter, we have looked at a number of theoretical models of metonymy and we have seen that each model provides valuable new information about metonymy, and reflects a different way of viewing it. The different models will all be used in subsequent chapters when we explore the role played by metonymy in performing various functions in real-world data. Particular use will be made of Panther and Thornburg's notion of illocutionary metonymy, Ruiz de Mendoza Ibáñez and Diez Velasco's notions of SOURCE IN TARGET and TARGET IN SOURCE metonymy, and Handl's radial category approach to metonymy, in which prototypical, salient metonymies shade into more peripheral examples that reflect the status of metonymy as a reference point phenomenon. The advantage of this last approach for the study of metonymy in real-world data is that it allows researchers to move between the centre and the periphery of the category depending on the context and the particular metonymy under discussion. It therefore allows the analyst to delimit the definition of metonymy in different ways, according to the needs of the study. In subsequent chapters, we will also see further evidence of the ways in which some of the distinctions proposed by some of these theorists become blurred when confronted with authentic data in language and other modes of communication. Throughout subsequent chapters, I will also refer, in places, to blending theory, relevance theory, and complex systems theory as these approaches allow for greater focus on the flexible, dynamic and context-specific nature of metonymy.

4 '"BBC", her mother would have said'

What do people use metonymy for?

4.1 Introduction

The previous chapters have looked at a number of theoretical models of metonymy, and have touched briefly on some of the communicative functions that metonymy performs. Here in Chapters 4 and 5, these functions are explored in more depth, in order to provide an answer to the question 'What do people use metonymy for?' This is a relatively under-explored area in the literature, which has tended to focus more on theoretical models of metonymy. As well as focusing on the functions that it performs in language, I also consider the roles that it plays in different modes of expression. I then go on to consider interactions between these different modes of expression and look at multimodal instantiations of metonymy. Where previous studies have looked at the functions performed by metonymy, they have tended to focus mostly on its referential function and, to some extent, its illocutionary function. However, when we look at metonymy in real-world data, we can see that it does much more than this, and therefore needs to be given far more consideration in usage-based models of language. In this chapter, I show how, in addition to referential functions, metonymy serves as a basis for highlighting and construal, anaphoric reference, cohesion and coherence, exophoric reference, illocutionary acts, relationship-building and the establishment of discourse communities. I show how a cognitive linguistic approach to metonymy can help to explain the way it functions in real-world data, and, in turn, I show how a focus on real-world data can help to refine models of metonymy that have been proposed by cognitive linguists.

4.2 Referential functions of metonymy

We have seen so far that one of the main functions of metonymy is to provide a kind of shorthand in which a relatively simple or concrete entity is used to provide easy access to an entity that is much more complex or abstract. Many of the canonical examples used to illustrate the term 'metonymy' (e.g. 'Wall Street' to refer to the American financial industry or 'the Kremlin' to refer to the Russian government) are primarily referential. The relatively widespread use of metonymy to serve referential functions has been attested in studies of the language used in real-world settings, such as the workplace, spoken academic discourse, football reporting and commentary, and descriptions of pain (Deignan *et al.*, 2013; Harrison, forthcoming, 2015; Tang, 2007).

A good, detailed example showing how referential metonymy works is provided by Panther and Thornburg (2002), who carried out an in-depth study of its role in the comprehension of –er nominals, such as 'teacher', 'hatter', 'Londoner', 'stewer' and 'goner'. They show how each of these –er nominals is motivated in a different way by metonymy. They argue that 'teacher' is the most prototypical of these types of –er nominals, which is reflected in the fact that it is most often chosen as the exemplifier in English-language teaching textbooks. Here, the metonymic relationship is one of the activity being metonymically extended to refer to the person who does the activity. The other examples involve different types of metonymic relationship: 'hatter' involves a metonymic relationship between the person and what the person makes; 'Londoner' involves a metonymic relationship between a person and the place where they live; 'goner' involves a metonymic relationship between the person and the process that they are about to undergo (in this case dying); similarly, 'stewer' involves a metonymic relationship between a chicken and a process that it will eventually undergo, but here the emphasis is on the characteristics of the chicken that mean it will eventually be stewed (because it is too bony or stringy for cooking in any other way). Each of these –er nominals is motivated, but they are all motivated in different ways, and they all involve different types of metonymic relationship. Metonymic thinking is required to work out the meaning of each word although, as with much metonymy, the words become conventionalised within the language, and 'active' metonymic thinking is unlikely to be involved unless one encounters a 'new' –er nominal of this type.

Metonymy is also involved in what Panther and Thornburg (2002) refer to as 'event level' –er nominals, such as 'thriller', 'eye-opener', 'groaner' and 'sundowner'. In these –er nominals, events are reified as objects. 'Thriller' involves a metonymic relationship between the event (the watching of a film) and the effect that it has on the participant in that it 'thrills' the participant; 'eye-opener' is similar, though it contains the additional metonymy of opening one's eyes standing for surprise; 'groaner' involves a metonymic relationship between a joke and the activity that it may provoke in the person who hears the joke; and 'sundowner' involves a metonymic extension from a particular time of day to what a certain group of people might do at that time of day (i.e. have an alcoholic drink), as in:

As I was sitting drinking my *sundowner*. (BofE)

In British English, the term 'sundowner' is more likely to be used by middle-class, rather than working-class people, and for some it conjures up an image of people standing on a terrace sipping cocktails. In the Bank of English, the term 'sundowner' occurs fifty-two times, and of these, ten citations appear in *The Times*, which is a middle-class newspaper, and sixteen appear in literature. Here and elsewhere, it tends to be used in rather arch, formal-sounding contexts, such as:

Lucy Victora d'Abreu yesterday sipped her customary *sundowner* brandy and dry ginger ale. (BofE)

Sundowner time found me at the Clachaig Inn. (BNC)

We can see from these examples that referential metonymy combines universal cognitive principles with collocational restrictions and genre-specific preferences.

More recently, Panther and Thornburg (2012) have shown how referential metonymy plays a role in understanding different forms of antonymy. More specifically, they are interested in describing how metonymy is evoked when we try to make sense of the construction:

both xx and xx alike [. . .]

This is a fairly productive construction in English, producing expressions such as:

[The attraction will appeal to both] *young and old alike*. (Panther and Thornburg 2012: 171)

The traditional definition of this construction is that it neutralises the conceptual contrast between the two terms and that there is a quality which applies equally to X and Y. In other words, the traditional interpretation of the construction is that, in the above example, it simply means that both young and old people will enjoy the attraction. Panther and Thornburg point out that although superficially the expression involves the polar antonymy 'young and old', its actual meaning is 'young and old and everyone in between'. They argue that the understanding of this construction involves a SUBCATEGORY FOR CATEGORY metonymy. This type of metonymy follows the pragmatic principle of informativeness: 'say no more than you must' (Levinson, 2000).

They also show how this process applies to antonyms that involve 'multiple incompatibilities', such as the string 'summer and winter visitors', which we saw in Chapter 2. 'Multiple incompatibilities' are antonymic relationships that involve more than two co-hyponyms. Here, all four seasons are involved: namely, spring, summer, autumn and winter. As is typical of metonymy, it is the two most salient hyponyms (summer and winter) which stand for the whole set here. They go on to show that this pattern also applies to contrasts in prototypicality. They illustrate this by analysing the string 'both sparrows and shoebills alike'. Here there is a metonymic inference to the whole list, ranging from the most prototypical member (sparrow) to more peripheral members (such as the shoebill). The same principle also applies to strings such as 'it will appeal to both academics and laypeople alike'. They conclude that if the terms X and Y are 'maximally contrasted' in this way, an inference is triggered from the string X and Y to a list of all members of the class to which the quality applies. If X and Y are not maximally contrastive, this 'open list' inference is blocked. This is why, for example, it sounds fine to say that a book will appeal to 'both young and old people alike' but it sounds odd to say that it will appeal to 'both middle-aged and old people alike'. They go on to point out that if X and Y are genuine binary antonyms, such as 'dead and alive', where there is no real intermediate stage, the 'X and Y alike' construction does not license an open list interpretation. However, when we look at corpus data, we do see examples of binary antonyms being used in this construction:

An inspiration to *both men and women alike.* (BofE)

Both players and fans alike. (BofE)

The effect here is to imply that everyone involved in the situation being discussed has the trait being described. Although 'both dead and alive' sounds odd (probably because of its apparent internal contradiction) 'both the living and the dead' does not sound unusual, and indeed four instantiations of this phrase can be found in the Bank of English. As with the two examples listed above, the meaning here is quite literal and does not involve metonymy in the way that it does with maximally contrasted pairs.

The 'maximal contrast' between the X and Y terms does not necessarily have to be an intrinsic, objective feature of these terms. The key thing is that they should be *construed* as being maximally contrastive in the context of the sentence or utterance. For example, let us look at the following citation from the Bank of English:

A breathy old-school style Chicago vocal hook [. . .] capable of napalming *both dance and trance floors alike.* (BofE)

One would not necessarily see 'dance floors' and 'trance floors' as intrinsically sitting at opposite ends of a continuum, but when they are presented in this context, a maximal contrast is set up between 'old fashioned' and 'modern' forms of dance. This contrast is then exploited using metonymy to refer to 'people who like all kinds of dancing, old and new'. This example illustrates the key role that is often played by context in determining the meaning of metonymy, and the ad hoc nature of the meaning-making process in some types of metonymy (see Section 3.3).

Referential metonymy can also be found in a variety of other modes of communication besides written and spoken language. It is particularly abundant in gesture. In many ways it is somewhat artificial to separate gesture from language, and most gesture theorists would view gesture as part of language (see, for example, Langacker, 2008; Müller and Cienki, 2009). However, gesture is somewhat different from spoken and written language as there is often a more transparent form-meaning connection in gesture. Mittelberg and Waugh (2009) have shown how in iconic gestures (that is to say, gestures that represent concrete entities), this connection relies almost exclusively on metonymy. For example, in order to gesture a 'house', one might make a triangle with one's hands to refer to one of the most salient parts of a house: the roof. This would involve a PART FOR WHOLE metonymy whereby the shape of the roof represents the whole house. We can see the same phenomenon if we think of the gestures one might use to indicate other concrete items, such as a tree (where we might gesture the branches, or the trunk), a table (where we might gesture the flat top), a bed (where we might gesture the act of sleeping), or someone absent-mindedly gesturing the opening and closing of a pair of scissors, while looking for scissors. The same principle also applies to verbs, such as 'write', 'sing', 'eat', 'grow' and so on. In each case, an accompanying gesture would highlight a salient part of the action. In fact it is difficult to imagine an iconic gesture that does not involve metonymy, a fact which leads Mittelberg and Waugh (2009) to argue that all iconic gestures involve metonymy and that gestures that are used to indicate abstract concepts involve both metonymy and metaphor.

Like gesture, a great deal of sign language is motivated by metonymy (Wilcox, 2004; Wilcox *et al.*, 2003). Sign language is inherently iconic (Taub, 2004) and, as with gesture, iconicity nearly always involves metonymy, as signs tend either to represent only one aspect of their intended referent, or they refer to something to which it is closely related. The role of metonymy in iconic sign language has been noted to some extent in the literature. For example, both Taub (2004) and Wilcox (2007) point to the use of PART FOR WHOLE metonymies to refer to animals, such as the use of 'whiskers' in the sign for a cat and the use of 'beak' in the sign for a bird. Wilcox goes on to report an interesting combination of metonymies in people's names whereby the first letter of their name is combined with a gesture representing a characteristic of that person, so for example, Oscar Peterson's sign name might involve the combination of an 'o' shape with a piano-playing gesture, both performed by the same hand. Wilcox also reports a series of signs that involve an EFFECT FOR CAUSE metonymy. For example, she notes that in Catalan sign language, 'crazy' eyes can be used to mean 'really good' and an open mouth can represent 'astonishment', and in Italian sign language a straining jaw can be used to mean 'make an effort'. We can see a clear role for ICMs in the generation of these metonymies, as they rely heavily on encyclopaedic knowledge.

However, the role played by metonymy in sign language has not been explored systematically or in depth, and such a study would probably reveal an extensive role for metonymy. Taub (2004) shows how iconicity in sign language never represents objective universal images of the phenomenon being described, and always reflects different ways of construing it. In other words, signs are neither fully arbitrary nor fully predictable, but they are motivated. To illustrate her point, she discusses the ways in which the sign for a tree varies across languages. In American Sign Language (ASL), the hands and forearms are positioned to resemble a tree growing out of the ground. In Danish, the hands are used to trace the outline of the tree's branches, and in Chinese the two hands trace the outline of the tree's trunk moving upwards from the ground (Yu, 2000). Each of these constitutes a PART FOR WHOLE relationship and provides a different *perspective* on the tree. Taub argues that iconicity is therefore much more than just 'form-meaning resemblance' and that an accurate account of the phenomenon needs to take account of this kind of perspectivisation or conceptualisation. She points out that resemblance is not an objective feature of two entities and that there is always a degree of cognitive processing which inevitably involves a subjective viewpoint. She goes on to argue that iconicity is constrained by the conventions of sign language and that it needs to fit into a 'language-internal system'. What Taub does not do is to describe this 'language-internal system' in detail or say how it is motivated.

A full consideration of the ways in which metonymy operates in sign language may help to explain many of its form-meaning relationships. Mandel (1977) proposed three types of iconicity in sign language. In the first type, the articulators (i.e. the hands and forearms) sketch the outline of the entity. In the second type, the articulators somehow resemble a salient part of the referent, and in the third type, they point to a referent (such as a part of the body) that is present in the signing situation. All three of these types involve PART FOR WHOLE metonymies in which some aspects of the phenomenon are highlighted and others are downplayed. Consideration of work in the sign language literature, and indeed a brief look at the uses of sign language in the British Sign Language dictionary, reveals the presence of a number of metonymy types that are listed in Radden and Kövecses' (1999) taxonomy. Here are some examples:

ACTION FOR OBJECT
The sign for 'gloves' involves putting on a glove.
PART FOR WHOLE
The sign for 'cat' involves miming whiskers.
DEFINING PROPERTY FOR CATEGORY

The sign for 'Ireland' involves the playing of a harp.
OBJECT FOR ACTION
The sign for hairdresser involves miming a pair of scissors.
EFFECT FOR CAUSE
The sign for 'nervous' involves tapping one's heart with one's index finger.
The sign for 'late' differs from the sign for 'not yet' in that the signer has an exasperated look on his or her face. Apart from this, the hand signalling is the same.

A focus on sign language also reveals the presence of metonymy types that are not listed in Radden and Kövecses' taxonomy. For example, there are many instances of what Mandel (1977) describes as 'shape for shape' iconicity where one signs the shape of a particular object (as in the 'tree' examples mentioned above) and of 'path for shape' iconicity as illustrated by the signs for necklace, road and river, where the signer traces the 'path' that these items create. From a metonymic perspective these could easily be described as SHAPE FOR OBJECT and PATH FOR OBJECT metonymies, thus adding two new metonymy types to Radden and Kövecses' taxonomy. 'New' metonymy types can also be found in sign-language classifiers, which are used to categorise certain types of shape, movement, object and so on. Classifiers are less specific than frozen signs as they identify larger classes or referents (for example, long thin objects). The features of some of these classifiers have traditionally been thought of as being unmotivated, but when we take a metonymic perspective, we can see that they are in fact partially motivated. For example, 'F-shaped' hands, with the little fingers pointing in the air (like one might do when drinking a cup of tea in a 'posh' way) are used to outline a long thin cylinder, when signing 'delicate' scrolls, such as degree certificates. This sign reflects the fact that one needs to handle such objects with care. Here we have evidence of a MANNER OF HANDLING AN OBJECT FOR AN OBJECT metonymy, which is not included in Radden and Kövecses' taxonomy. We also have evidence of embodied cognition, as discussed in Chapter 2.

We can see evidence in sign language for many of Radden and Kövecses' guiding principles for selection, such as STEREOTYPICAL OVER NON-STEREOTYPICAL, HUMAN OVER NON-HUMAN, SUBJECTIVE OVER OBJECTIVE, CONCRETE OVER ABSTRACT. These principles may help explain features of sign language that have up until now been considered 'arbitrary' by some researchers. For instance, both the 'tree' sign and the 'Ireland' signs mentioned above reflect the stereotypical over non-stereotypical principle. The 'tree' sign also adheres to the symmetrical over non-symmetrical principle and, of course, the simple over complex principle. The fact that one signs a 'scroll' to indicate a degree certificate, and by extension a degree itself, is a clear manifestation of the CONCRETE OVER ABSTRACT principle. The fact that the sign for 'home' is a combination of the signs for 'eat' and 'sleep' reflects the principle of BASIC OVER NON-BASIC, as these activities are much more basic than other activities that one might engage in at home. The HUMAN OVER NON-HUMAN principle is at work in a group of signs referred to as 'instrument classifiers'. Here, the signer describes or names objects by showing their interactions with them. For example, in many of the world's sign languages, the sign for 'cricket' involves a batting motion, whereas in Icelandic it involves bowling. In all of these, it is the human involvement in the sport that is salient. The sign for 'car' also foregrounds the human interaction with the car in that it involves a person turning a steering wheel. This foregrounding of human experience is important as it shows that we categorise objects in both sign language and spoken language according to the way in which we interact with them. Related to this, the SUBJECTIVE OVER OBJECTIVE principle is also manifested in sign language. For instance, the BSL sign for 'child' involves patting an imaginary child on the head, which reflects the subjective perspective of an adult. Adjectives such as 'near' and 'far' and verbs such as 'give' and 'take' are also signed from the speaker's perspective, and this involves both articulators and eye gaze. Sign language linguists have observed that as signs become conventionalised over time, they become more symmetrical, more simple and more stereotypical (Frischberg, 1979). All of these processes adhere to vehicle-determining principles outlined by Radden and Kövecses.

We have seen that by employing a cognitive linguistic approach to metonymy in the analysis of sign language, we are better able to understand the precise nature of the relationships between the signs and their intended meanings, and to explain these in terms of over-arching metonymy types. Using metonymy to analyse sign language can also help to extend our knowledge of metonymy itself by identifying new metonymy types. Moreover, viewing sign language in this way helps narrow the gap between sign language and spoken language. Historically, and largely for political reasons, the two have been seen as very different entities. The fact that sign language is largely iconic has made some people view it as a form of mime. The reason for this is that in language the link between form and meaning is supposed to be predominantly arbitrary (Saussure, 1915) and not iconic. Sign language researchers keen to assert the status of sign language as an actual language have emphasised the role of iconicity in spoken language, thus drawing parallels between the two. By identifying metonymy types that are shared by both spoken language and sign language and by showing that the over-arching principles that guide metonymic vehicle selection are identical in both spoken language and sign language, I have provided further evidence for the proposition that both types of language share key features and that sign language should indeed be considered a true 'language'. The status of sign languages in comparison with that of spoken languages is the subject of much passionate, ongoing debate within the deaf community (Sutton-Spence *et al.*, 2012).

4.3 Highlighting and construal

As we saw in Chapter 2, Langacker's notion of 'active zones' demonstrates how metonymy highlights some features of a particular phenomenon, while downplaying others. This phenomenon of 'construal' or 'perspectivisation' is well documented, not only in the cognitive linguistics literature (e.g. Croft and Cuse, 2004), but also in other approaches to language, such as systemic functional linguistics (Halliday, 1994, 2004). One of the most common uses of metonymy in the highlighting/construal process is to foreground the information that is most important to the *speaker*. We can see a good example of this in the following extract from Charles Dickens' (1836–7) novel *The Pickwick Papers*. In this extract, a visitor to a London coaching inn asks Sam Weller, a servant, who is responsible for cleaning the boots of the guests staying at the inn, about who is present at the inn:

> 'We want to know,' said the little man, solemnly; 'and we ask the question of you, in order that we may not awaken apprehension inside – we want to know who you've got in this house at present.' 'Who is there in the house!' said Sam, in whose mind the inmates were always represented by the particular article of their costume, which came under his immediate superintendence. 'There is a vooden [sic] leg in number six, there's a pair of Hessians in thirteen, there's two pairs of halves in the commercial, there's these here painted tops in the snuggery inside the bar, and five more tops in the coffee room.'
>
> 'Nothing more?' said the little man.
>
> 'Stop a bit' replied Sam, suddenly recollecting himself. 'Yes, there's a pair of Vellingtons a good deal vorn, and a pair o' lady's shoes, in number five.' (Dickens, 2004: 137)

In this passage, Sam's primary interest is with the footwear that the various guests wear and he uses this to categorise the guests themselves. We can almost 'see' these guests through his eyes; we know nothing about them except for what footwear they own. As we will see in Chapter 7, metonymy is often processed as if it were 'literal' language, and in this passage we get the impression that the knowledge of people's footwear is so engrained in Sam's consciousness that for him the utterances are almost literal. It doesn't matter to Sam who is actually staying in the various rooms; all that matters to him is the footwear, a fact which emphasises the usage-based nature of metonymy. The fact that this knowledge is so detailed and idiosyncratic, combined with the almost complete lack of shared referents between Sam and his interlocutors, contributes to the humour of the passage. The rhetorical effect of the passage is further enhanced by the fact that Sam's use of metonymy interacts with a conceptual metaphor whereby low social status is 'down' and high social status is 'up' (Lakoff and Johnson, 1980/2003). The fact that his job leads him to constantly look down and focus almost entirely on people's feet emphasises his low social status. Sam's low social status is further emphasised by the fact that he himself is often referred to metonymically, simply as 'The Boots'.

The highlighting function of metonymy is particularly prevalent in oxymora, where two apparently contradictory words have to be reconciled into a single meaning. To illustrate this, consider the following two examples:

The venue only serves drinks in *plastic glasses*. (BNC)

She stared down at the *living dead* face. (BNC)

These expressions both involve domain-highlighting metonymy of the sort discussed by Langacker. In 'plastic glasses', the function of the glasses is highlighted, while the idea that glasses are usually made of glass is downplayed. In 'the living dead' example (which refers here to the face of someone in a coma), the focus is on the fact that the person is alive but that their quality of life is so reduced that it is as if they were dead. The fact that it is impossible to be both dead and alive at once is downplayed. Herrero Ruiz (2011) explains this phenomenon in terms of blending theory (see Chapter 3), arguing that two mental spaces are generated linguistically: one by the first part of the expression and one by the second part of the expression. The metonymy then involves domain reduction and highlighting operations whereby the most relevant part for the interpretation is brought into focus. In these examples, the most relevant parts of the domain are the function of the glasses and the fact that being alive normally involves consciousness and movement. Thus the apparent 'clash' between the input domains is resolved by focusing on the most relevant parts of those domains. As we will see in Chapter 5, oxymora, such as these, are also very common in art, particularly modern art, where this type of incongruity is designed to surprise the viewer and challenge existing beliefs.

The highlighting function served by metonymy is also used in non-linguistic forms of expression. For example, Forceville (2012) points out how film music is used metonymically to draw a viewer's attention to different aspects of a particular scene in a film, thus contributing to the meaning-making process for that particular scene. He argues that it can be used to reinforce meaningful information in the scene, but that it can also function 'contrapuntally' in that it can 'unexpectedly evoke elements of meaning that are not, or only latently, present in the visual and/or verbal track' (2012: 2). For example, he discusses a scene in Resnais's documentary film *Nuits de brouillard* (1955), which features views of Auschwitz and descriptions of the lives of prisoners. The scene begins by showing the deserted camp, and this is accompanied by a full orchestra. This is immediately followed by a scene depicting a large number of soldiers, which is accompanied by solo instrumentation. The solo instrumentation contrasts with the mass of soldiers and has the effect of focusing one's attention on the soldiers as individuals. Forceville argues that there are two contrasting metonymies at play here. The full music represents the thousands of people who experienced Auschwitz (which creates a sharp contrast with the empty scene). This contrasts with the solo instrumentation, which metonymically focuses the viewer's attention on the individuality of the soldiers. The relationship of opposition has been described as metonymy by Vosshagen (1999), who claims that opposites belong to 'a single conceptual domain' and that the relation of opposites is one of 'close mental contiguity' (1999: 291). He argues that opposition is a basic associative relation, pointing to word association studies that show how words with an opposite meaning to the prompt are often produced.

The use of metonymy to single out individual features of a scene and to emphasise their poignancy is also found in the musical *Les Miserables*. In one scene, the only survivor of a group of revolutionaries returns to the bar where he and his compatriots had prepared their campaigns. He looks around at the empty chairs, each of which triggers the memory of one of his compatriots via a process of metonymy. He then begins to sing a song entitled 'Empty Chairs at Empty Tables', in order to reinforce the message. The pathos is further emphasised by the metonymic use of accordion playing to represent an older, more 'innocent' France. We hear the accordion but it isn't actually there, in the same way as the people who used to frequent the cafe are no longer there. Both of these metonymies draw on a single ICM of a 'France in the olden days', typified by traditional, lively cafes and accordion playing. This ICM helps the metonymies to work together to make the viewer construe the scene in a particular way, reinforcing the image of what has been lost.

4.4 Anaphoric reference, cohesion and coherence

Metonymy has been shown to play a key role in creating and maintaining cohesion and coherence in discourse through anaphoric reference (Al-Sharafi, 2004; Ruiz de Mendoza Ibáñez and Diez Velasco, 2004). In his discussion of grammatical cohesion, Al-Sharafi points to the contiguous metonymic relationships between nouns and their corresponding pronouns, and shows how conceptual metonymy sanctions ellipsis. In his discussion of lexical cohesion, he shows how synonymy, hyponymy and meronymy all involve metonymic PART FOR PART or PART FOR WHOLE relationships within a single ICM. In order to explain the role of metonymy in coherence, he highlights the importance of CAUSE FOR EFFECT metonymic relationships and shows how they link together different parts of a schema or scenario. In order to do this, he cites Gibbs' (1994: 330) example:

He wanted to be king.
He was tired of waiting.
He thought arsenic would work well.

In order to understand the relationship between these three sentences one needs to evoke a scenario involving a specific set of plans, which are linked to one another by the metonymic relation of CAUSALITY.

Work on the role of metonymy in text cohesion and coherence has also been conducted by Brdar-Szabó and Brdar (2011). They analysed the CAPITAL FOR GOVERNMENT metonymy in media discourse, and were able to show how repeated yet varied uses of the same types of metonymy contributed to the overall cohesion and coherence of the text. They found that different vehicles could be used to refer to the same target:

> '*Moscow* is playing on the contradictions between Europe and the US, aiming to show that Sarkozy's pragmatic and respectful approach, rather than Washington's hard-line rhetoric, is the way to achieve concrete political results with *Russia*,' says Sergei Strokan, a foreign-policy expert with the liberal Moscow daily Kommersant. 'You can't help but notice that the harsher *the Kremlin's* tone toward the US becomes, the gentler and more subtle becomes its approach to Europe.'

The International Herald Tribune, 16 June 2009 (Brdar-Szabó and Brdar, 2011: 233).

In this extract, the italicised uses of Moscow, Russia and the Kremlin all refer to the same thing but they subtly highlight certain aspects of it and downplay others. Brdar-Szabó and Brdar point out that one of the advantages of metonymy is that although one concept is thought to stand for another, both are actually activated in the mind (a fact which is confirmed in psycholinguistic studies of metonymy, as we will see in Chapter 7), which means that metonymy is therefore 'an efficient way of saying two things for the price of one' (2011: 236). Previous usages of the same source domain or ICM shape the meaning of subsequent uses and these repeated uses build up to form a coherent whole. They also found that the same metonymic vehicle could be used in the same text to represent different, yet related phenomena, as in the following example:

> After months of detention amid widespread condemnation from Capitol Hill and UD academics, Li's swift court proceedings and promised release just hours after the Olympics vote leave an appearance of tit for tat justice, raising questions about whether Li and other detainees with US ties are being used as bargaining chips by *Beijing*, observers said.
>
> Li was 'a hostage in the Olympics bid', said Frank Lu, director of the Hong Kong-based Information Center for Human Rights and Democratic Movement in China, which tracks arrests and harassment of dissidents and activists. 'We know that just two weeks ago the Chinese government told the US government that if the US voted against *Beijing*, they wouldn't release him.'
>
> *Boston Globe*, 15 July 2001. (Brdar-Szabó and Brdar, 2011: 239)

Brdar-Szabó and Brdar point out that the first use of Beijing in this extract is a clear case of the CAPITAL FOR GOVERNMENT metonymy, whereas the second occurrence is much vaguer and is more likely to refer to the upcoming

Olympics. They thus show how metonymic targets can shift, arguing that the context is crucial for identifying the target of a metonymy and that there is not necessarily a clear one-to-one mapping between source and target, as has been argued in some of the more traditional accounts of metonymy. This again has been found to be the case in psycholinguistic studies of metonymy, where the actual meaning has been found to be underspecified until the very last moment (see Chapter 7). In order to explain their findings, they make use of Ruiz de Mendoza Ibáñez and Pérez Hernández's (2003) work on the Domain Availability Principle. According to this principle, either the source domain or the target domain can be the point of co-reference, and both remain 'available' for access by the reader long after their first mention. Because the source domain is so large and flexible, it allows for forms of anaphoric reference which, at first sight, may not seem to be syntactically 'logical'. So, for example, when talking to a colleague about a customer, a waiter or waitress might refer to a 'ham sandwich' as 'he or she' long after the actual 'ham sandwich' has been consumed and paid for. Brdar-Szabó and Brdar reject the notion of 'mapping' in metonymy resolution, arguing instead that it is more appropriate to talk in terms of inference-based elaborations (involving either expansion or reduction) of the metonymic source. Their reasoning is thus very much in line with that of Ruiz de Mendoza Ibáñez and Diez Velasco (2002) who, as we saw in Chapter 3, talk about SOURCE IN TARGET metonymies (which involve domain expansion) and TARGET IN SOURCE metonymies (which involve domain reduction). Brdar-Szabó and Brdar also identify a key cohesive role for 'metonymic chaining', which was discussed briefly in Chapter 1.

Examples of the cohesive role played by metonymy can also be found in literature, where it can provide cohesion across an entire novel (Lodge, 1977). A good example of this can be found in Pat Barker's novel *The Eye in the Door* (1993). This novel, which is set in the First World War, features a number of deserters and people who have helped them, who are imprisoned for their crimes. In each of their prison cells there is a 'peephole' in the door that is designed for prison warders to watch them. Around this peephole, again in each prison cell, someone has painted an actual eye so that the prisoners never forget that they are being watched, or that they could be being watched at any moment. The description of the eye is as follows:

> He found himself looking at an elaborately painted eye. The peephole formed the pupil, but around this someone had taken the time and trouble to paint a veined iris, an eyewhite, eyelashes and a lid. (Barker, 1993: 36)

Individual eyes are referred to repeatedly throughout this novel and in most cases they refer metonymically to the idea of being watched. However, at one point there is a graphic description of a scene in the First World War trenches where a shell explodes and the main protagonist, Prior, finds himself holding the eye of his best friend, Tower, who has just been blown up. He finds it difficult to get the image of his friend's eye sitting in the palm of his hand out of his mind. The fact that Prior has this very literal image of an eye permanently in his mind, and that this is frequently referred to throughout the novel, strengthens and complicates the 'eye in the door' metonymy. Here is the second part of the extract that was just cited:

> This eye, where no eye should have been, was deeply disturbing to Prior. For a moment he was back in France, looking at Tower's eyeball in the palm of his hand. He blinked the image away. 'That's horrible', he said, turning back to Beattie.
>
> ''S not so bad long as it stays in the door.' She tapped the side of her head. 'You start worrying when it gets in here'. (Barker, 1993: 36)

Here we can see a cohesive link between the metonymic 'eye in the door', the literal eye that Prior held in his hand, and the metaphorical reference to the eye 'getting into his head'.

The interweaving metonymic use of 'eyes' and 'doors' develops into a theme throughout the novel. Doors are used metonymically to refer to the separation of public and private space, which relates back to the theme of always being watched, and to 'things that happen behind closed doors', which also adds strength to the 'eye in the door' metonymy. For example, in a discussion with his psychologist, Rivers, Prior turns the tables and starts to talk to Rivers about *his* (i.e. Rivers') troubled childhood, and asks him about the abuse that he suffered as a child, which he has subsequently suppressed to the extent that he has impaired visual memory:

> 'This terrible-in-big-black-inverted commas thing that happened to you, what do you think it was?
>
> 'I don't know. Dressing gown on the back of a door?'
>
> 'As bad as *that*? Oh my God.'
>
> [. . .]
>
> 'For God's sake you *blinded* yourself so you wouldn't have to go on seeing it.'
>
> 'I wouldn't put it as dramatically as that.'
>
> 'You destroyed your visual memory. You put your mind's eye *out*. Is that what happened or isn't it?'
>
> Rivers struggled with himself. Then said simply; 'yes.' (Barker, 1993: 38–9)

The repeated uses of 'eye' and 'door' metonymies work together in this exchange (and indeed throughout the book) in a very powerful way to create and develop both tension and cohesion in the novel. The strong rhetorical effect of the repeated 'eye' metonymies can be accounted for in cognitive linguistic terms. As we saw in Chapter 2, one of the key tenets in cognitive linguistics is that our understanding of the world around us is *embodied*. Here, our embodied cognition allows us to experience the protagonists' view of the eye and to make the connection between the eye and the acts of seeing and being seen. As we saw in Chapter 2, there is even a cluster of neurons that has been identified as being particularly strongly associated with this process. Thus when we see an eye, we automatically think of our own eyes, and of what we use our eyes for. Related to this is the fact that when we see someone performing a particular action (such as running, walking or drinking) neural motor circuits are activated in our brains that are identical to those that would be involved if we were performing those actions ourselves (Gallese, 2009). Thus when other people's actions or feelings are being described, we, in some ways, experience those actions or feelings ourselves. Thus, on some level, we too 'feel' the eye looking at us, we 'feel' it entering our heads, and we 'feel' the pain involved in putting out our own eyes and subsequently going blind. This is then extended via metaphor to refer to psychological blindness. This is why the text is so powerful.

Simple repetition of a linguistic metonymy also contributes to textual cohesion, as we can see in this extract from a text-messaging corpus that was analysed for metonymy use by Littlemore and Tagg (in preparation):

A: Just in case you need rescuing from work or dissertation or both, we are meeting again tomo at 6 in staff house. Hope week 3 ok.
B: It's a toss up between that and going for a balti with cherry blossoms. Not sure what would be more fun.
A: Ooh i wouldn't like to have to make that decision . . . [time passes]
B: Sorry cherry blossoms and balti win out. Maybe we could meet up tomorrow if you fancy. Joe's busy tonight and haven't asked about tomorrow yet.
A: Damn, passed over for a cherry blossom. Yeah give me a shout if you're doing anything tomo. Happy balti – and happy end of course.

In this extract, 'baltis' and 'cherry blossoms' are alluded to several times, in order to refer back to the previous message and create a sense of cohesion. 'Balti' is a MEMBER FOR CATEGORY metonymy, referring to the act of going out to eat curry, and 'cherry blossoms' is a PLACE FOR INHABITANTS metonymy, referring to a group of students who are from a Japanese college which is called the 'Cherry Blossom' college. Access to this shared knowledge is essential if we are to understand the metonymy here. The fact that metonymy comprehension relies so heavily on shared referents contributes strongly to its relationship-building function. This is discussed in more depth in Section 4.7 below.

Littlemore and Tagg also observe how the repetition of the same metonymy type can contribute to text coherence. We can see this in the following example from the same text-messaging corpus, which contains three sub-event for whole event metonymies, one after the other:

Happy daddy day to you. happy daddy day to you. happy daddy day to daddy. happy daddy day to you. hope you've had a nice day. i bet you've been *screwing something down or building something*. anyway *make yourself a cup of tea on me, kick back and enjoy*

The cohesive function of metonymy can also be found in other modes of expression, such as gesture. Cienki and Mittelberg (in preparation) note that, in conversation, gestures can occur in full in the first instance and then become progressively shorter. They observe that:

> [the] progressive reduction of gestural forms through repeated use seems to rely on principles of economy and metonymy: less effort is needed to produce anaphoric gestures, but they still may evoke the original more fully articulated gestures and the referent object they depict through pragmatic inferencing. (Cienki and Mittelberg, in preparation: 3)

As with language, this repetition of the same gesture, though in a somewhat reduced form, is likely to contribute to the cohesion of the overall text. Studies of gesture in interaction show that the reduction of a single gestural metonymy can be shared by different speakers in a conversation. For instance, several studies have found that speakers pick up each other's gestures and modify them slightly while retaining an overall gestalt (Kimbara, 2006; McNeill *et al.* 2001; Müller, 2008). In their study of the gestures employed in oral exchanges, Ladewig and Tessendorf (2008) found that the slight differences in the gestures employed by the interlocutors indicated that they were seeing the object or event under discussion from different angles, thus construing it in different ways that were not made explicit in the linguistic code. In this way, their gestures were metonymically highlighting different aspects of the same phenomenon. They concluded that the use of these metonymic gestures created and sustained cohesion across the different turns as they provided repeated access to the same object, albeit from differing perspectives. Taub (2004) points out that this phenomenon is also common in sign language. Once an item has been described via a specific sign, subsequent signed references to it tend to be much less detailed and may highlight different aspects of it.

The role of metonymy in anaphoric reference is particularly prevalent when we look at music, where repeated extracts or 'motifs' occur with slight variations and in different instrumentations. There are metonymic relationships between these different occurrences which are similar to those observed for gesture. In his study of metonymy in video game music, Whalen (2004) points out that, at the syntagmatic level, music often serves as a metonymy for progress in the game. He finds that music is most often used as positive reinforcement for good or bad performance in the game, and argues that it 'encourage[es] the player to maintain the syntagmatic continuity of the game experience by successfully progressing through the game's content' (2004: 13). In other words, variation in the music is designed to keep people playing. For example, the music speeds up when time is running out, it provides clues about approaching enemies, therefore giving the player an edge over the enemy, and 'reward' music is played after successful completion of a level, thus providing positive reinforcement and an incentive to keep playing. The fact that these motifs are repeated throughout the game, with changes in changing pitch, key and tempo depending on the context, also contributes to the cohesion of the game.

Cohesive metonymy also occurs in various art forms. A well-known manifestation of metonymy in cartoons is the 'Mickey Mouse protocol'. Drawings of Mickey Mouse have become so distinctive that it is now possible to represent him with just three simple curved lines, and this has become shorthand for him. In films, the same vehicle is often used metonymically to represent different things. For example, Forceville (2009) shows how in Robert Bresson's film *Un Condamné à mort s'est échappé* (A Man Escaped) close-ups of hands are used repeatedly throughout the film to metonymically represent phenomena that either aid or impede the protagonist's escape from a Nazi prisoner of war camp.

The use of 'hands' as a cohesive metonymic device is no new phenomenon. Chenard (2005) shows how, in his *Ecclesiastical History of the English People*, Bede (731) made repeated use of references to King Oswald's hands, paying them very close attention and thus providing the narrative equivalent of visual 'close-ups', throughout his account of Oswald's reign, in order to emphasise his saintliness. She argues:

> Bede's images of Oswald's hands metonymically represent the relationship between ecclesia and regnum in its ideally intimate and pristine form, especially in the limbs' perpetual incorruption after the king's death in battle. Bede brings Oswald's hands into narrative relief in various episodes depicting the king as a prayerful monarch, even when he is at war. The full metonymic import of these episodes is made particularly clear when other references to hands in the Ecclesiastical History are examined for what they reveal about the ideals of sanctity that Bede attributes to this warrior-king. (Chenard, 2005: 34)

King Oswald's hands are brought into sharp focus in extracts such as:

> [he] seized the cross himself in the ardour of his faith, placed it in the hole, and held it upright with both hands until the soldiers had heaped up the earth and fixed it in position. (Chenard, 2005: 36)

Chenard points out how, in this extract, Oswald's hands are '(quite literally) in touch with God, ardently seizing the wooden representation of the cross onto which the body of Christ was nailed' (2005: 37). She argues that this contrasts with the way in which the Saxon warlord Caedwalla (who was killed by Oswald) is represented. Caedwalla's deeds are carried out with 'impia manu' (*Ecclesiastical History of the English People*, cited in Chenard, 2005: 37), and Chenard points out that although this phrase means 'with unrighteous violence', its literal translation is 'with unrighteous hand'. Bede makes use of the double meaning of 'manus' here to create a link between 'hands' and their potential for perpetrating good or evil. Thus the cohesion created by the metonymy in this text emphasises relations involving both synonymy and antonymy that contribute to the overall cohesiveness of the text.

4.5 Exophoric reference

Metonymy can also be used in *exophoric* reference, where it invokes complex information outside of the text. In literature, it is often used to illustrate the things that a particular character represents either in the eyes of the author or of a protagonist in the book, or both. We can see this in the following sentence from Sebastian Faulks' novel *A Week in December*:

Jenni sat back in the modern chair and folderd her hands in her lap. Gabriel Northwood had a low, cultured voice – 'BBC', her mother would have said – suggesting layers of knowledge and unvoiced jokes at her expense. (Faulks, 2010: 73)

In this extract, Gabriel Northwood's 'BBC' voice immediately evokes, in Jenni's eyes a world populated by confident, middle-class, possibly privately educated individuals, which she finds highly intimidating and alienating. 'BBC' is thus metonymic shorthand for a whole set of associations and class prejudices that are peculiar to British culture. Somewhat ironically, we find out later in the novel that Gabriel Northwood is in fact extremely unconfident and not all that successful in his chosen profession.

The fact that metonymy is closely entwined with exophoric reference makes it particularly suitable for use in ancillary discourse. In their comparison of metonymy use on the touchline at a children's football match with online match reports written by the manager of one of the teams, Deignan *et al.* (2013) found small but noticeable differences in the amount of metonymy used, with 2.5 per cent of the words in the reports and 4.9 per cent in the supporters' discourse being used metonymically. They pointed out that this increased use of metonymy in the supporters' discourse is likely to reflect the fact that it was spoken and ancillary, and that there was a need for rapid communication. We can see these features in the following examples.

Matthew, you're *centre midfield*. (Deignan *et al.*, 2013: 211)

Go on, *Reds*. Go for it, *Reds*. Well done, *Reds*. (Deignan *et al.*, 2013: 211)

In the first example, the player is being metonymically defined by his position, and a particular area of the pitch stands for the player who primarily occupies that area. In the second example, the players are being addressed as a group with single group identity, referred to metonymically by the colour of their shirts.

In their data, they found that the 'ball' was often used metonymically to refer to a particularly good piece of play or to an opportunity for good play:

Good ball. (Deignan *et al.*, 2013: 214)

Boys that was a *great ball*, and we're not attacking it. (Deignan *et al.*, 2013: 214)

Other metonymic uses of the word 'ball' in their study included: 'drop it' (three occurrences) and 'run it' (one occurrence). In each of these cases there is contiguity between the basic meaning and the meaning in context, so the relationship is one of metonymy (Warren, 1999). For example, 'run it' means 'guide it with you as you run'. There were also some metonymic uses of 'on', in the structure 'V + on it', such as:

Patrick, Patrick, Patrick, *stand on it*. (Deignan *et al.*, 2013: 214)

Get on it Tom. (Deignan *et al.*, 2013: 214)

According to the manager of the team, 'stand on it', in this example, meant 'stay near the site of an opposition free kick to stop them from taking it quickly' and 'get on it' meant 'get near it'; the word 'on' in both of these examples stands metonymically for 'in the region of'.

Deignan *et al.* (2013) also discuss findings by Tang (2007), who found frequent instances where metonymy was used to refer to objects and actions taking place that are outside the text, in her description of the language used by staff working in a children's nursery. For instance, children who ate meat and children who didn't would be referred to respectively as 'meat bowls' and 'veg bowls', and the nursery office and its management team were usually referred to as 'upstairs'. The need for speed appears to have been the main motivating force behind these metonymies.

The impact of the speaker's physical environment can also have an impact on the use of metonymy for exophoric reference, as Harrison (forthcoming, 2015) showed in his study of gestural metonymy in communication between workers working in a salmon packing factory. In this particular workplace, there was so much background noise that the workers had to gesture to one another. Harrison found gestural metonymy to be far more common than gestural metaphor in this setting. He explains that this is because the participants were always referring to concrete artefacts and not abstract concepts. He also points out that the gestural exchanges were very short and did not form part of lengthy or elaborate utterances. Both Deignan *et al.* and Harrison attributed the use of metonymy to the discourse communities that they were describing characteristics of, and the registers that were being used, factors which are discussed in relation to both studies in Section 4.7 below.

Metonymic exophoric reference also plays a role in the recognition of lectal variation (i.e. the recognition of different styles of speech, including standard varieties, regional dialects, sociolects, registers and styles). According to Kristiansen (2008), the linguistic features of particular language varieties and dialects can serve as metonymic shorthand for the characteristics of the social groups that use them. She argues that metonymic reasoning underlies 'the step from a linguistic trigger to a social schema, activating stored encyclopaedic knowledge in the broad sense, including ideological aspects and psychological attributes associated with the group in question' (2008: 50). These linguistic triggers can be as small as individual allophones. When this is the case, the two main metonymic relationships involved in the meaning-making process are the PART FOR WHOLE relationship and the PRODUCT FOR PRODUCER relationship.

Kristiansen goes on to argue that lectal varieties operate within radial categories in which some realisations are more or less 'prototypical'. The most prototypical instantiations (i.e. those exhibiting all or most of the features typically associated with that particular variety) tend to form the stereotypes that we use to index certain groups of people. The knowledge that we draw on in order to recognise a stretch of speech as being from a particular lectal variety is acquired experientially (Kristiansen and Geeraerts, 2013), and we can of course choose how to project our own identity by selecting a variety that is nearer to, or further away from, the prototype. This form of metonymic shorthand can also be used to categorise other people. Soukup (2013) reports how, when 'quoting' words used by a presidential candidate from the opposing party, an Austrian activist uttered them in a 'low status' Bavarian-Austrian dialect, even though the presidential candidate did not actually speak with this dialect. The Bavarian-Austrian dialect is sometimes associated with lower education and levels of intelligence as well as sounding coarse, rough and aggressive. By giving the presidential candidate this dialect, the activist was able to imply that he too exhibited these characteristics. Again, we can see that metonymic inferencing involving PART FOR WHOLE relationships is implicated in this process.

Finally, metonymic exophoric reference is also common in music, particularly sampling, where short extracts from other songs are adapted and incorporated into one's song. This provides metonymic, often ironic, shorthand references to other pieces of music or even whole styles of music. The same phenomenon can be found in art, where coded references to phenomena outside the work of art itself abound.

4.6 Illocutionary functions of metonymy

In Chapter 2, we looked at the illocutionary function of metonymy and at the role played by metonymy in indirect speech acts. We saw how indirect speech acts do not simply involve random relationships between the words and their meaning, and observed that many of the relationships are motivated by metonymic principles. A focus on metonymy thus allows one to propose a more robust explanation for the way in which indirect speech acts work. Other studies have shown how illocutionary metonymy is involved in polite requests. For example, Stefanowitsch (2003) uses collocational criteria to demonstrate that requests such as 'can you close the door?' are not predictable from their form and meaning components and can thus be classified as constructions. He argues that despite their unpredictable nature, they are partially motivated by metonymy and posits metonymic 'inheritance links' between direct questions and indirect requests. In other words, he suggests that there is a relationship between these two functions, both of which share the same form. In an indirect request, the questioning element operates in the background, softening the request. In a similar vein, Panther and Thornburg (2003) make a convincing case for the role of illocutionary metonymy in the pragmatic interpretation of truncated '*if*-clauses', such as 'if you wouldn't mind ... ' or 'if you could just ... '. Illocutionary speech acts do not involve random form–function relationships, but involve clear metonymic links between what is said and what is intended.

4.7 Relationship-building and the establishment of discourse communities

The various functions of metonymy that have been described so far all rely to varying degrees on the existence of shared knowledge between the speakers, and it is this property of metonymy which explains the role that it performs in the development and maintenance of discourse communities. Discourse communities and communities of practice make use of community-specific overlapping genres that are defined by their overall communicative purposes. Overlapping with these genres there will often be a range of different registers, each of which has distinct field, tenor and mode. Metonymic meanings become attached to particular words, partly as a result of the genre and register of the language employed by particular discourse communities, and this can sometimes be misunderstood by people who are not members of those communities. For example, doctors and nurses will often use the term 'bed' to refer metonymically to all of the necessary equipment and staff that allow a hospital bed to be occupied by a patient. When they say that there are 'not enough beds', they usually mean that there are insufficient supplies of equipment and staff. This metonymy has occasionally been misinterpreted (perhaps wilfully) by journalists, who will ask 'why can't they simply buy more beds?' This question shows a fundamental misunderstanding of the metonymic meaning of 'beds' in this context. Misunderstandings such as these can occur even between people who know each other well and who have sufficient shared knowledge to facilitate extensive use of metonymy.

Deignan *et al.* (2013), whose work was mentioned above, report on a series of investigations into the ways in which genre and register features can affect the types of quantities of metonymy that are likely to occur. They show how the use of metonymy is largely governed by the communicative needs of the genre as well as register features such as the topic under discussion, the relationship between the speakers and whether the language is written or spoken. Of these different features, they found that those most likely to lead to metonymy are shared background knowledge and a need for speed in spoken workplace settings. They observed that metonymy has a particularly prominent role in spoken discourse, and found that metonymy is particularly prevalent in situations where the communication is primarily concerned with people and entities located within a shared physical space, and where sequences of actions are constrained by time pressures. Examples include busy 'hands-on' workplaces and sporting events, where the use of metonymy often reflects the tenor of the discourse.

Three of the studies that they discuss are particularly useful in highlighting the relationship between genre and register and metonymy use, and show how metonymy plays a role in the formation of discourse communities. These studies focused on the language of football, the language employed by workers in a children's day nursery and the language used by a lecturer when explaining abstract academic content to two interlocutors with different amounts of shared background knowledge.

The first of these studies (which was referred to above) focused on the language used by a discourse community that had grown up around a children's football club. The study looked at how a group of parents and carers standing on the touchline at one of the matches made frequent use of the term 'kick it' to refer metonymically to the action of 'kick the ball very hard, with conviction'. As Deignan *et al.* point out, this reflects a more widespread tendency within football-related discourse communities to make use of metonymy in order to develop their own specialist lexis. In a study of fixed phrases in football commentaries, Levin (2008) found that most of them carry very specific meanings that are motivated by metonymy. Many of these meanings are unlikely to be transparent to people outside the discourse community. For example, the expression 'he had the ball in the net' usually means that a goal was apparently scored but then disallowed, and an empty net refers to the fact that the net is unguarded. Levin argues that there are three reasons why certain metonymic phrases appear to be so common in football commentary. Firstly, there are some concepts that need to be expressed that simply do not occur outside football, and thus a new term has to be coined. 'He had the ball in the net' is an example of this. The second reason why a metonymic lexicon has developed in this field is the speed at which commentators need to produce language. When football commentators are describing a live match they are under considerable time pressure. Brief expressions with precise meanings shared by the discourse community are essential in this context; metonymy is helpful here as it allows a whole scenario to be represented by a single aspect of it. For instance, Deignan *et al.*'s data include the widely used term 'through ball'. This is a metonymy for a team-mate kicking the ball through the defenders' line into a space for another player to run into; the metonymy sums up the whole scenario in just two words. The third reason that Levin gives for the use of these metonymies is that they serve as register markers: their use serves to include those familiar with the register and to exclude others. Deignan *et al.* identify a further reason for the use of metonymy in their data, which relates to tenor. They discuss the following example, which is a common shout from the parents and carers on the touchline:

That's it, stay in front *son*. (Deignan *et al.*, 2013: 211)

This example involves a metonymic extension from one's own son to all the players in the team. In their corpus, their term was only rarely used to address one's own child. This reflects the tenor of the discourse where the parents and carers have a close but asymmetrical relationship to the children on the football pitch. The parents and carers aim to be both protective and encouraging.

Deignan *et al.* also discuss the findings from a study by Tang (2007) who (as we saw above) observed a large number of metonymies in the language used by staff working in a children's nursery. As well as the terms 'veg bowl', 'meat bowl' and 'upstairs' that were mentioned above, she also found that the term 'agencies' was used metonymically to refer to staff who were hired from an agency, and 'do your numbers' was used to refer to the act of counting the children in one's charge. 'Going on visits' was used to refer to a practice whereby children who were about to move up to the next age group spent some time with that age group in order to get used to the room and the new carer. Deignan *et al.* found that these metonymies were highly specific to the discourse community. None of them was in more general use in language corpora, although in many cases the underlying metonymy types were. These uses of metonymy can be attributed to genre and register, their use being largely a reflection of the high degree of knowledge shared by staff, to which the speakers can refer implicitly. It is also a reflection of the highly interactive setting and the need to exchange information quickly in order to achieve concrete, and sometimes urgent, goals.

In the third study, Deignan *et al.* compared the use of metonymy in two exchanges: one between a university lecturer and a colleague and one between the lecturer and a departmental outsider. Both conversations were about the same two management models. They found that in both exchanges the lecturer used a metonymy in which particular people (all previous heads of her department) stood for particular styles of management. In the colleague exchange, the metonymy was picked up by the interlocutor, who used it when giving his own view of the management style of the university. In contrast, in the outsider exchange, the departmental outsider did not pick up on and use the lecturer's metonymy in this way. In the colleague exchange, there was also a tendency on the part of both speakers to make their use of the metonymy more personal by asking questions about each other. Deignan *et al.* report three possible reasons for these findings: firstly, the outsider was not a member of the discourse community of the staff of the university and as such would have far less insight into its management style. Secondly, he was a newcomer to the field of the discourse, and therefore probably less confident at manipulating the models and using the sections of the diagram metonymically in order to compare different management styles. Thirdly, in terms of tenor, he was in a subordinate position to the lecturer within the university and therefore likely to be more inhibited about contributing.

In addition to linguistic metonymy, *gestural* metonymy has also been found to relate to discourse community membership. In the aforementioned study of a French salmon-packing factory where it was too noisy to communicate orally, Harrison (forthcoming, 2015) found that metonymic gestures served key transactional functions and that the use of metonymic gesture was crucial when workers needed to exchange urgent information about the state and quantity of the salmon fillets that were coming down the production line. Some of these gestures combined metonymy with hyperbole. For example, the gesture used to indicate the need for thicker salmon fillets showed the fillets being half a metre thick, which is much thicker than a salmon fillet would ever be in real life. His study also showed how certain metonymic gestures become conventionalised within that particular discourse community, thus contributing to a strong sense of community.

There is also evidence that the use of metonymy reflects shared background knowledge in sign languages. For example, the sign for 'cricket' in most languages involves some sort of 'batting' action. Exceptions to this are the United States, where the word is spelled out, and Iceland, where a bowling action is used, as we saw in Section 4.2. The fact that the signs are so different in these languages may reflect the fact that cricket is not a popular sport in either of these countries and therefore very few discourse communities containing cricket fans and players who use sign language have emerged. In contrast, in countries where cricket is popular, such as the United Kingdom, the sign for cricket takes a highly contracted form and is very minimal compared with that of other countries where cricket is not so popular. This phenomenon is similar in many ways to the examples of linguistic shorthand, such as 'meat bowl', which were mentioned above, that are favoured by more tightly knit discourse communities whose members can draw on a great deal of shared knowledge.

Metonymy is also used to allude to membership of different discourse communities across different registers. For example, the term 'hashtag' is sometimes used by young people in spoken language to preface an evaluation of, or reflection on, what they've just said, or to link what they're saying to an ongoing topic. Both of these uses are to reflect its original 'written' use on Twitter. It might thus be used in the following way:

Just bumped into my mum on campus – hashtag embarrassing![1]
God, that was an awful lecture – hashtag another wasted morning!

[1] Caroline Tagg, personal communication.

An example of this use of the term 'hashtag' was also found in an extract of transcribed conversation between students from Birmingham University who were chatting over dinner.[2] One of them had just mentioned a 'Kim' in the conversation, and then said (about Kim's boyfriend, who was one of the students present):

Kim's his ex, hashtag just saying.

Here the term 'hashtag' invites the interlocutor to critically evaluate the implications of the fact that Kim is his ex-girlfriend, without necessarily saying anything. The hashtag is also used in gesture where one forms the shape of the hashtag with one's two forefingers on each hand. This 'hashtag' gesture is used partly to show that the speaker is part of a community that uses Twitter and other online forums, and thus shares these conventions.

In her study of public health discourse, Stvan (2012) notes that separate polysemous senses can become conflated via a process of metonymy and that this can cause problems when communicating ideas about health to the general public. This type of miscommunication can reinforce people's sometimes mistaken perceptions of the causes of health risks. She investigated eight pairs of polysemous terms in contemporary American English (cold, sweet, sugar, cholesterol, fat, hot, oil and stress). She identified four types of relations between senses that involve metonymy and which can become conflated in the minds of non-experts. Her evidence for conflation comes from corpus data which shows people using these senses interchangeably. The first type of relation involves similar bodily experiences, so here someone might think that being 'cold' leads directly to them having a 'cold'. Both lead to the same bodily experiences (such as shivering) but for different reasons. The second type of relation she describes as being one of 'shared but reinterpreted value or attribute'. Here, for example, someone might think that by eating 'fat' one will become 'fat' and that if one eats food that for example contains carbohydrates rather than 'fat' itself, one will not get fat. Her corpus data show that people often conflate the two meanings of 'fat' in this way. They also conflate the different meanings of cholesterol, thinking that eating food containing cholesterol leads to high levels of cholesterol in the body, although this is not the case (Stvan, 2007). The third type of relation involves a process which she terms 'visually iconic transferral' between distinct entities that have a similar appearance. Here a person might think, for example, that eating oily foods will lead directly to their having an oily skin. The fourth type of relation is 'unrecognized terminology creation'. Here a term acquires a particular clinical definition, and in conversation one interlocutor assumes a 'lay' sense of the word while the

[2] This example appeared in a piece of assessed work submitted for an undergraduate module on discourse analysis.

other assumes a clinical sense, although this clinical sense may not be officially recognised. Stvan concludes from her study that words can exhibit meaning extension via different types of metonymic extensions and that these are influenced by everyday human experience, patterns of perception and cultural preferences.

Metonymy has also been shown to play a role in developing entrenched religious belief systems in faith communities, helping members of the communities to form opinions about themselves and others in terms of their behaviour and their belief systems. These metonymies are often based on strongly entrenched ICMs which are specific to particular faith communities. Richardson (2013) has observed that when evangelical Christians talk about the importance of saving *souls*, they are using one perceived aspect of a human being, this notion of a soul, to represent the human being as a whole. This involves a PART FOR WHOLE metonymy. Conservative religious discourse is filled with vocabulary that represents individuals and communities by referring to one perceived aspect of their behaviour or status, such as, for example: *sinners*, *adulterers*, *non-believers*, *true believers*, *disciples of Satan*, *followers of Christ*, *souls*, *the lost* and so on. Thus we have a number of TRAIT FOR PERSON metonymies. The inevitable result of such metonymies is that highly heterogeneous groups of people can be construed and treated as very simple, often binary, stereotyped groups. This can contribute to tension between different faiths.

One of the repercussions of the use of metonymy by different discourse communities is that when these communities come into contact with one another, there may be misunderstandings, such as those described in Stvan's study. Additional misunderstandings may relate to the role of metonymy in pragmatic inferencing, where the pragmatic information is missed or extra pragmatic information is inferred by the perceiver. Metonymic vague language is another area where there is scope for confusion as it may be mistakenly taken literally. Different academic discourse communities attach different meanings to words, many of which are metonymically motivated, and these differences may cause problems when they are working together on a single project. The potential problems caused by metonymy when people from different discourse communities come into contact are discussed in more depth in Chapter 8. Finally, as we saw above, the use of particular linguistic features that are associated with certain lectal varieties serves as an efficient way of metonymically projecting one's identity as a member (or otherwise) of a particular discourse or speech community.

4.8 Conclusion

We have seen in this chapter that metonymy is used to serve a wide variety of functions across a range of discourse types. In addition to serving a straightforward referential function, metonymy is involved in highlighting and construal, anaphoric reference and cohesion, exophoric reference, illocutionary acts, relationship-building and the establishment of discourse communities. The chapter began by showing how metonymy can at times serve straightforward referential functions, though this is much more prominent in gesture and sign language than in spoken language. It then went on to show how in language and in other forms of communication metonymy usually involves some sort of construal operation presenting information from a particular angle, highlighting some aspects of it while downplaying others. We saw that at times metonymy can be highly conventionalised and adhere to the general cognitive principles that determine salience within and beyond language, whereas at other times it can be deliberately manipulated and conventions can be broken to create particular rhetorical effects. Under the heading of 'discourse communities', we saw how metonymy motivates discourse-community-specific expressions that can only really be understood by people who have in-depth knowledge of the genres and registers employed by those communities and of the types of activities typically conducted by members of the communities. We saw how the use of metonymy is particularly useful in ancillary discourse where rapid communication is necessary, and discussed how metonymy motivates discourse community-specific expressions, particularly in registers that have a more constitutive mode, as well as licensing more creative uses of language that may not be readily understood by outsiders. The functions discussed thus far have been relatively well documented. Chapter 5 explores some of the less well-attested functions of metonymy which could be described as more 'attitudinal'.

5 'But what can we expect, after all, of a man who wears silk underpants?'

Playful, evaluative and creative functions of metonymy

5.1 Introduction

Chapter 4 outlined some of the 'traditional' functions of metonymy that have been discussed in the literature. This chapter looks at how metonymy is used to serve a range of slightly 'edgier' communicative functions, such as euphemism, vague language, hedging, evaluating and positioning, humour and irony. Despite the clear role that metonymy plays in performing these functions, there has been very little acknowledgement of this in the literature. For example, there is an extensive body of literature on the role of hedging, evaluation and positioning in academic writing and other forms of communication (e.g. Hyland, 1998) and metonymy is inevitably involved due to its subtle indirectness, but its role has never been explicitly discussed. Similarly, much humour and irony is achieved through the use of metonymy, for example by contrasting the literal and metonymic senses of the same word, and using them in the same sentence. Although there have been extensive treatments of the role of linguistic devices in humour (e.g. Alexander, 1997), metonymy is rarely mentioned. Finally, the discussions of vague language that have been initiated by Channell (1994) and Cutting (2007) have skirted around the topic of metonymy but have not discussed it explicitly, despite the fact that the indirect nature of metonymy makes it a useful device for vague communication. In this chapter, I use data from written and spoken language, as well as other modes of communication, to demonstrate the role of metonymy in supporting these important communicative strategies and functions. I show how the fact that metonymy involves indirectness means that it underlies a great deal of euphemism, hedging and vague language. I consider the evaluative functions of metonymy and the role it plays in positioning, and explore the potential that metonymy offers for 'language play', showing how it is used creatively to convey humour and irony (Brône and Feyaerts, 2003). Finally, I show how metonymy is used creatively in other forms of expression besides language and discuss how a more explicit, conceptual focus on the role of metonymy in different forms of expression can contribute to existing work in semiotics.

5.2 Metonymy and euphemism

There has been some work indicating the role that metaphor can play in the understanding of euphemism (Pfaff *et al.*, 1997) but there has not yet been any discussion of the part played by metonymy. This is somewhat surprising, given that the basic reason for employing euphemism is to find an indirect way of talking about topics that may be embarrassing or face-threatening, and metonymy is the perfect trope for expressing indirectness (Allan and Burridge, 1991). For example, the following are both euphemisms for going to the toilet:

He needs to use the *restroom*. (Webcorp)

'Us girls,' she said, 'are going to *spend a penny*'. (Webcorp)

Each of these refers to an aspect of 'going to the toilet' that is tangential to the actual process of what one does when one gets there. They rely respectively on a PLACE FOR EVENT metonymy and a SUB-EVENT FOR WHOLE EVENT metonymy. Indeed, even the expression 'go to the toilet' is itself a PLACE FOR EVENT metonymy and the word 'toilet' is itself a historical euphemism involving a metonymic relationship between two parts of the same event (it is derived from the French expression: 'faire sa toilette', which means to get washed and possibly put on make-up).

Not all metonymic euphemisms are as conventional as those we have just discussed. As we saw in Chapter 4, Tang (2007) and Deignan *et al.* (2013) report the use by staff working at children's nursery of the expression 'loose nappy' as a euphemism for a child having diarrhoea. Within this expression, Deignan *et al.* (2013: 19) argue that the word 'nappy' serves as a metonymic reference to the 'stool' via a CONTAINER FOR CONTAINED metonymy, with 'loose' providing a metaphorical description of liquid stool, or of the gut that produces it, as in the more widely used expression 'loose bowel'. As we can see in all of these examples, metonymy is particularly well suited to euphemism as it allows us to avoid making direct reference to the potentially embarrassing topic.

The use of euphemism in business and politics is well documented, but again very few studies have explored the role of metonymy in this context. One exception to this is Gradečak-Erdeljić's (2004) account of the role played by a type of metonymy in which PART OF THE SCENARIO stands for THE WHOLE SCENARIO in the sorts of euphemisms that governments use to describe events in war. She documents for example, the use of the term 'body count' to refer to dead people, or 'air support' to refer to bombing and killing people. Interestingly, these examples also employ nominalisation to reify the concepts being discussed, which renders them one step further removed from the actual events being described. Here we have a superficially 'referential' metonymy performing a highly specific communicative function.

Metonymy is also used in dysphemism, where again there is usually some sort of contiguous or PART FOR WHOLE relationship between the utterance and its referent. This is particularly prevalent in gestural dysphemism, when symbols are used, such as the raising of one's middle finger to serve as an insult. Metonymic dysphemism can also contribute to a feeling of discourse community membership. People who work in professions that involve daily encounters with death often use dysphemism to talk about dead people, which most people outside the discourse community might perceive as offensive (Allan and Burridge, 1991). For example, people working in morgues have been known to refer to the dead bodies as 'stiffs', thus using a PROPERTY FOR OBJECT (or even a TRAIT FOR PERSON) metonymy in which a characteristic of the human corpse (its 'stiffness') stands for the corpse itself. This jocular approach arguably helps these workers to deal with death on a daily basis and it would not be at all appropriate in other circumstances. It would be entirely inappropriate for a doctor to inform close family that their loved one had 'pegged it' during the night and was now a 'stiff'. This use of language would be regarded as insensitive and unprofessional in a different context.

5.3 Metonymy and hyperbole

Many hyperbolic expressions, such as those we saw in Chapter 1 (e.g. 'The *whole town* is livid') rely on WHOLE FOR PART metonymies, or what Ruiz de Mendoza Ibáñez and Diez Velasco (2002) refer to as 'domain reduction' (see Chapter 3). Here 'the whole town' stands metonymically for 'a very large number of people who live in that town'. This is part of a broader phenomenon whereby hyperbole involves 'domain reduction' in order to be properly understood. The rhetorical strength of these hyperboles relies on the fact that, in metonymy, both the vehicle and its referent remain available, allowing the speaker to say two things at once. In other words, while the term 'the whole town' would never be understood as literally referring to the whole town, the fact that these words have been used contributes to the power of the overall message. Another example of a hyperbolic expression that relies on a WHOLE FOR PART metonymy is Barnden's (2013) example 'music was his life' (Webcorp) in which 'his life' actually refers to 'the most important thing in his life', which is just one element of his life.

Metonymic hyperbole can be achieved through the use of particular constructions, as we can see in the following sentence:

They booed him off the stage. (BofE)

As we saw in Chapter 2, this is an example of what Goldberg (2006) refers to as a 'caused motion' construction. The implication in this construction is that the man left the stage as a direct result of the booing. The use of the word 'booed' in this construction is not prototypical and it is made transitive by the construction. As is often the case in this sort of example, metonymy is involved in the interpretation of the sentence. The word 'booed' stands metonymically for the effect that the booing has both on the feelings and behaviour of the actor or comedian (i.e. he feels unwanted and therefore leaves the stage). This CAUSE FOR EFFECT metonymy could be interpreted either as domain expansion (the idea of booing is expanded to include the effect of the booing on the behaviour of the actor) or contiguity (the word 'booing' is used to represent the effect of the booing).

5.4 Metonymy and irony

During the European financial crisis, when the collapse of the Greek economy was thought to be threatening the future of the European Union, the French President, Nicolas Sarkozy was overheard referring to 'our friends the Greeks'. 'Our friends', in this extract has a useful double meaning. On the surface, it is a friendly reference to the Greeks and hints at an inclusive stance. However, when we look at the pragmatic meaning of 'our friends', it is much more nuanced than this. A Bank of English search for 'our+friends+the' reveals that it is nearly always used to talk about people who are in fact, our enemies, or at least people to whom we do not feel particularly well disposed, as we can see in the following extracts:

The millions of victims of *our friends the* Chinese Government. (BofE)

I'm getting regular calls from *our friends the* barley barons. (BofE)

I had to give a seminar on *our friends the* earwigs, or some damn fool thing. (BofE)

We can't even demonstrate about it, thanks to *our friends the* Americans. (BofE)

We can see a similar pattern in the French equivalent of this expression: 'nos amis les', which is of course the original language in which the words were uttered by Sarkozy. Apart from references to films and exhibitions, whose titles begin with those words, the main collocations in French are cockroaches, germs and animals:

Arrh, j'avais oublié *nos amis les* cafards qui ici sont énormes !!! (Webcorp)

[Arrh, I had forgotten our friends the cockroaches, which are enormous here!!!]

Nos amis les microbes (Webcorp)

[Our friends the germs (heading of an article on the omnipresence of germs)]

Nos amis les bêtes (Webcorp)

[Our friends the animals (heading of an article about the dangerous animals that live in Australia)]

The films and exhibitions that use this expression appear to be using it ironically, as they refer to 'our friends the humans' and 'our friends the terrestrials'.

In all of these examples, the underlying metonymy FRIENDS FOR ENEMIES is invoked, so when Sarkozy uses the string 'our friends the Greeks', he actually means 'our enemies the Greeks'. He thus manages to convey his position without overtly offending the Greeks. The utterance contains a strong element of irony, which is based on a relationship of opposition, and, as we saw in Chapter 4, this form of opposition constitutes a form of metonymy.

Metonymic irony does not always involve opposition, as we can see from the example below, which appeared in a heading of an article in the *London Review of Books* (February 2013) that endeavoured to explain the recent attempts by the French army to fight Islamic extremists in France's former colony:

What are they doing in Mali? (London Review of Books, February 2013)

This heading plays on the construction 'what is X doing in Y?', which is typified by the well-known joke opening: 'what's that fly doing in my soup?' meaning 'what on earth is that fly in my soup?' The strong implication here is that the fly should *not* be in the soup, and by extension the French army should *not* be in Mali. This is an example of illocutionary metonymy as there is a conceptual link between the question of what the fly (or the French army) is doing, why on earth it is doing it, and the idea that it should *not*, in fact, be doing it. These meanings are linked by an EFFECT FOR CAUSE metonymic relationship. The irony derives from the fact that both the literal and the metonymic readings are possible in this context.

Herrero Ruiz (2011) uses Ruiz de Mendoza Ibáñez and Diez Velasco's (2002) the notions of 'domain expansion' and 'domain reduction' to account for the role of metonymy in irony. For example, if someone sarcastically declares that 'it's not rocket science', this carries far more rhetorical force than the expression 'it's not difficult'. Here 'rocket science' stands for the class of 'things that are difficult to understand' and thus involves an expansion of the scale of 'things that that particular person might be expected to understand'. It could also be interpreted as a scalar metonymy where the extreme end of a scale stands for a more central part of the scale. It follows one of Radden and Kövecses' key principles for vehicle selection as it is an *extreme* example of the scale of 'things that are difficult to understand'.

5.5 Metonymy and vagueness

As we saw in Chapter 2, the referent(s) in metonymy can often be vague and unclear, and, as we will see in Chapter 7, psycholinguistic studies have shown that the meaning often remains unspecified until the very last minute. This vagueness, or lack of specificity, can be manipulated for communicative purposes. For example, both Channell (1994) and Cutting (2007) have shown that people use vague language in order to avoid sounding too pedantic and knowledgeable as this is potentially very face-threatening. Sounding imprecise opens up space for one's interlocutor to contribute to the conversation, and people sometimes therefore make themselves sound deliberately vague in order to do this. Consider for example, this extract from a conversation on the BBC's 'Listening Project' website which contains short, intimate conversations between individuals. In this particular conversation, Elizabeth and her son Kevin are discussing Kevin's childhood and the fact that Kevin had known about some of the events that took place in the family home, which his mother had thought he was unaware of:

ELIZABETH He had a habit of flirting, and every time he did it, I saw it as a threat. Now remember I'd had a lot of bad stuff in my early life and I knew about things like that.
KEVIN Hmm
[...]
KEVIN Did you know that I knew about all of this?
ELIZABETH No.
[...]
KEVIN I don't think you should think of it as being burdened. I feel as though I got a comprehensive grip on life very, very early. And some of it stems back to *Longfield Terrace* actually.
ELIZABETH Yes.
KEVIN 'Cos I also was aware of all of that [...] even though you didn't ever tell me about it there was my grandmother [...] and my grandfather.
ELIZABETH Yes, I know.
KEVIN although you never told me anything about it, there was my grandmother and my grandfather [...] [laughs] and this other bloke sleeping with my grandmother in the same house. (BBC, n.d.) (emphasis added)

In this extract, Kevin uses the expression 'Longfield Terrace' to refer indirectly to an awkward situation that occurred while he and his family were living in a house in Longfield Terrace. In a nutshell, his grandmother was having an affair, and her lover was living under the same roof as the rest of the family (including her husband, Kevin's grandfather). This had never been spoken about openly by the family. He presumably uses a PLACE FOR EVENT metonymy here because the events that he wants to talk about are extremely sensitive. By using this metonymy he does not need to talk about the events themselves or about the people involved. By talking simply about 'Longfield Terrace', he manages to remain on fairly safe ground, allowing Elizabeth time to prepare herself for what is coming next. Up until the final extract, where he talks explicitly about what happened, both interlocutors have the opportunity to pull back and talk more generally about other aspects of their life in that house. It is only when he receives the cues 'yes' and 'yes I know' from Elizabeth that he launches into his more graphic description of what went on in that house. He thus uses metonymy to keep things vague until he is sure that he can go ahead and say exactly what he wants to say.

Metonymic vague language is often used by journalists who do not want to specify exactly what it is that they are talking about. This could be because the information is sensitive or libellous, because they do not know all of the facts, or because they simply want to whet the listener's appetite. We can see this in the following sentence, which was used on a BBC radio news programme to introduce a news item about the European Union:

Angela Merkel clearly wants *more* Europe, whereas David Cameron clearly wants *less* Europe. (BBC Radio 4 breakfast discussion, 12 April 2013)

We have a good idea of what the journalist means here: presumably that Angela Merkel, the German Chancellor, wants the European Union to have increased amounts of power and influence while David Cameron, the British Prime Minister, wants it to have less power and influence over its member countries. The connotative meaning of this sentence is clear, but its denotative meaning is imprecise. It could be that Angela Merkel wants the European Union to have more political power, more economic power or more constitutional power. What exactly it is that she and David Cameron disagree on is unclear. This indeterminacy allows for flexibility in determining over which areas of influence the two politicians disagree most strongly. The journalist's use of this sentence means that the listener has to carry on listening to the programme in order to find out.

Halverson and Engene (2010) found examples of indeterminacy in their corpus of metonymic uses of the European city Schengen in Norwegian newspapers. The 'Schengen Agreement', which was made in 1995, led to the creation of a borderless area consisting of five European countries. This area has since been extended to included most of the European Union. They found far more cases of metonymic than literal uses of the word Schengen in their data. The four main types of metonymy were as follows (2010: 7):

PLACE FOR EVENT (TREATY)
fatt i signaler om energi, fisk og Schengen, for å ta tre eksempler, . . .
[Received signals regarding energy, fish, and Schengen, to mention three examples . . .]

PLACE FOR TREATY CONTENTS (PROVISIONS, CLAUSES, ARTICLES, PRINCIPLES)
Myndigheter ville imidlertid søke via Schengen på nytt, . . .
[Thus the authorities wanted to reapply via Schengen . . .]

PLACE FOR MEMBERSHIP, (GROUP OF) MEMBERSHIP COUNTRIES
er de automatisk nektet visum i Schengen, et samarbeid Norge er med i.
[They are automatically denied a visa in Schengen, a collaboration that Norway is part of.]

PLACE FOR GEOGRAPHICAL AREA (CREATED BY TREATY)
at ingen uroelementer kommer inn i Schengen.
[That no troublemakers enter Schengen.]

The first of these four types of metonymy is a kind of super-ordinate of the remaining three. They found considerable amounts of indeterminacy in their examples, particularly between PLACE FOR EVENT (TREATY) and PLACE FOR TREATY CONTENTS, as well as between PLACE FOR MEMBERSHIP and PLACE FOR GEOGRAPHICAL AREA. They attributed these ambiguities to the kinds of part/whole ambiguity that are common in metonymy. For example, in the following example, reference could be being made to the treaty itself or to parts of the treaty (Halverson and Engene, 2010: 8):

Det betyr hull i Schengen, . . .
[That means a hole in Schengen, . . .]

This level of indeterminacy is convenient for the journalist, who may not need or want to commit to an exact knowledge of the part of the treaty that has the 'hole' in it. In their diachronic study of the word 'Schengen' they identified differing levels of indeterminacy. They found evidence of a gradual increase over time in the metonymic uses of the word 'Schengen' that followed a steady loosening of strength of contact between vehicle and its referent, which is in line with Peirsman and Geeraerts' (2006a) model of metonymy (discussed in Chapter 3), which emphasises the varying strengths of contiguity in different types of metonymy.

Vagueness can also be conveyed through the use of metonymic gesture. In their corpus of videoed tutorials involving English-speaking lecturers and Spanish-speaking Erasmus students, MacArthur *et al.* (2013a) found cases where a lecturer would wave vaguely in the direction of another building on campus to refer to the activity that took place in that building. The aim, in these cases, was not to specify precisely what activity was being referred to, but to refer to the sort of thing that is being done 'over there'.

5.6 Metonymy and evaluation, ideology and positioning

The fact that metonymy is able to highlight some aspects of a given phenomenon while downplaying others means that it is a very useful device when one seeks, either consciously or subconsciously, to present one's own perspective or to influence the views of others. We can see evidence of the evaluative function of metonymy when we take some of the invented examples of metonymy that are used in the metonymy literature and look them up in language corpora. For instance, an oft-cited example of a purely referential metonymy is 'she's just a *pretty face*' (Lakoff and Johnson, 1980/2003: 37), which is meant to illustrate a PART FOR WHOLE relationship whereby the face stands for the whole body. A search for this string in the Bank of English corpus reveals sixty-four instances, of which sixty are preceded by the word 'not', 'more than' or 'far from'. The remaining four examples are all critical of the idea that someone might be 'just a pretty face', as in 'just a pretty face isn't enough'. Thus it is not really appropriate to analyse the expression 'she's just a pretty face' without taking account of the fact that it nearly always involves negation, as this is how it is most often used in English. It would be more appropriate to analyse the expression '*not* just a pretty face', which means to be savvy and intelligent. The expression also contains elements of irony and humour as well as a subtle criticism of the implicit sexism behind the idea that it is unproblematic to talk about someone as behind 'just a pretty face'. Thus when we look at the ways in which the expression is used in authentic data, a much richer picture of its meaning is revealed and it no longer works simply as an example of a pure referential metonymy.

The role of metonymy in ideology and positioning can be seen when we look closely at traditional accounts of rhetoric, an academic discipline that is designed to help writers and speakers to inform, persuade or motivate their audience (Corbett, 1990). In his second book on rhetoric, Aristotle identifies three means of persuasion that an orator can rely on. These are 'ethos', which is grounded in the credibility of the orator, 'pathos', which involves appeals to the emotions and the use of psychology, and 'logos', which involves patterns of reasoning. In his third book he introduces the notions of 'style', which involves word choice, metaphor, sentence structure, and textual organisation (Cockroft and Cockroft, 2005).

Metonymy can be involved in all three types of rhetoric, as well as style. For example, it plays a role in ethos when a person is used to stand for a particular quality that that person has. As Hamilton (2012) points out, David Beckham has often been used to advertise football boots and trainers. These advertisements rely heavily on our knowledge of Beckham as a famous, good-looking footballer, and he would be less likely to be found in (say) an advertisement for a plumbing business. In this capacity, Beckham is serving as a metonymic 'paragon' (Barcelona, 2004: 363) for the category of 'great professional footballers'. The success of the advertisement rests on our ability to see Beckham as standing metonymically for the activity for which he is most famous.

As far as 'pathos' is concerned, metonymy can be used to create a new category, which the author then evaluates by means of appeals to negative emotions. For example, Meadows (2006) notes the use of metonymy in the following extract from a speech by George Bush:

> And like fascism and communism before, the hateful ideologies that use terror will be defeated by the unstoppable power of freedom [applause]. (President G. W. Bush, 30 November 2005)

Meadows points out how the Bush administration refers to past enemies in metonymic terms. The term 'fascism' is used metonymically to refer to the entire German Nazi political and military establishments. Likewise, the term 'communism' is used metonymically to refer to the political establishment of the Soviet Union and its army. By grouping these together with the 'hateful ideologies that use terror', Bush implies a connection between the current enemy (terrorists) with past enemies (fascism and communism). The three concepts are all contextualised as enemies of the Bush administration and the USA, and are objects of hate. 'Hateful ideologies' is itself a metonymy for the people who hold those particular ideologies and the actions that they take. Meadows goes on to point out that when Bush does speak of the enemy in concrete terms, he does so with heavy metonymic overtones. In the same speech, Bush stated:

The enemy in Iraq is a combination of rejectionists, Saddamists and terrorists. (President G. W. Bush, 30 November 2005)

The word 'enemy' here is clearly a loaded term. In this statement, Bush provides a new, additional framework for the 'enemy' category. He uses a TARGET IN SOURCE metonymy to reduce one segment of the larger domain (Iraqi people) according to a set of deliberately chosen characteristics. As Meadows points out, the three metonymies are difficult to miss:

(1) *rejectionists* are those who reject the pending constitution in Iraq, (2) *Saddamists* are those who the Bush administration deems as supporting Saddam Hussein and, by mutually-exclusive implication, in opposition to American interests, (3) *terrorists* are those who incite terror. (2006: 7)

As Meadows shows, these metonymies resemble racial stereotypes in that they take away human individuality and replace it with broad, impersonal group generalisations that rely on metonymic shorthand.

Of the three forms of rhetoric, 'logos' is the one where metonymy arguably features most prominently. Metonymy plays a key role in the development of patterns of reasoning which are created by the speaker or writer with the express purpose of shaping the thinking patterns of the listener or reader. This function of metonymy is exploited extensively in political rhetoric. For example, in her discussion of the widespread fear that was promulgated by the press in the United States after the 9/11 bombings, Ferrari (2007) draws attention to PART FOR WHOLE metonymy in this Address to the Nation given by George Bush in 2006, in which the 'eyes' and 'ears' are used to look out and listen out for potential bombers:

Add your *eyes* and *ears* to the protection of our homeland. (Address to the Nation given by President G. W. Bush, 2006) (emphasis added)

This metonymy focuses attention on the protective role of the citizen, emphasising their role as part of a single entity, and gives the impression that every citizen could help to guard their own country, the 'homeland', if they wanted to. As one might expect, George Bush is clearly appealing to the 'in-group' in this address.

Politicians often use metonymy to emphasise positive characteristics of the 'in-group' while highlighting the negative characteristics of the 'out-group' (Van Dijk, 1998). However, politicians are not the only people to use this strategy. Unsurprisingly, journalists have been found to use it too. For example, Pinelli (2012) found metonymy to be heavily implicated in the framing of identities in media reporting of terrorist incidents. She analysed newspaper coverage of the Beslan school hostage crisis, which took place in 2004, when a group of armed Chechens attacked a school in one of the main cities in the North Caucasus region of the Russian Federation taking 1,123 hostages, of whom 777 were children. She looked at two newspapers which addressed different audiences, with different attitudes towards Russian politics. One was pro-government and the other was anti-government. She conducted a qualitative investigation of her two corpora, followed by a collocational analysis of keywords, such as 'terrorism', 'terrorists', 'children' and 'Russian government', to show how identities of the different groups were framed, allowing an 'us and them' culture to emerge in both newspapers. Unsurprisingly, she found that in the pro-government newspaper, the term 'Russia' was used metonymically to refer jointly to the Russian people and members of the Russian government. In the anti-government newspaper the Russian identity was framed in such a way as to exclude the government. In this second newspaper, the Russian government was frequently compared to the terrorists, and thus identified as part of 'the enemy' group. Pinelli also found that the conceptual framing of 'terrorism' involved metonymies in which different elements were highlighted or downplayed depending on the political viewpoint of the newspaper involved. Both newspapers employed PLACE FOR INHABITANTS metonymies, but they each did so in different ways, which favoured their own political viewpoint.

This 'in group' and 'out group' mode of thinking is discussed from a theoretical perspective by Moscovici (2001), who refers to two main processes by which social representations are formed: 'anchoring' and 'abstracting'. 'Anchoring' refers to the process whereby we endeavour to fit an event, person or idea into a preformed category that we have for a particular social group. For example, when we meet a person who holds the Islamic faith, we may attempt to fit our view of them into preconceptions that we have of their faith, and look for evidence of traits that correspond to this stereotype and thus fit into the 'category' that we have created for them, while ignoring evidence indicating that they do not. 'Abstracting' refers to the process of selecting a feature at random and using it as a category. For instance, we might think of the wearing of the veil as representing Islam in general, when of course Islam involves much more than this. Koller (2013) points out that this latter conceptualisation process is metonymic, as an instance of a category comes to stand for the category itself.

This strategy is by no means limited to English. Zhang *et al.* (2011) explored the use of metonymy to refer to 'outsiders' in the headlines of a Chinese newspaper and a Taiwanese newspaper. Their aim was to test Brdar and Brdar-Szabó's (2009) finding that emotionally charged capital-city names are more likely to be referred to metonymically than those that are less emotionally charged. They found that metonymic uses of the capital names Beijing and Taipei were ideologically motivated. They found that capital names were more likely to be used metonymically if they appeared in subject position, if they appeared in a political context and (most importantly) if the country being referred to was being negatively evaluated. They found that the Chinese newspaper never used the word 'Taipei' metonymically to refer to the municipal Government of Taiwan (although the Taiwanese newspaper did); in contrast, the Taiwanese newspaper never used the word 'Beijing' metonymically to refer to the government of China, but it did use it to refer to the municipal government of Beijing. Thus we have a subtle manipulation of metonymic meaning by both parties, which reflects their ideological positioning.

Finally, of the three elements of style proposed by Aristotle, word choice clearly involves metonymy. For example, at a very basic level, the use of metonymy in one's word choice can betray a conservative word view, as evidenced by sentences such as:

> In the framework of the village community, within the company, and finally in the state, everyone is assigned a place; *his* identity is based on *his* contribution to the welfare of the whole. (BNC)

The use of the masculine pronoun *he* in this extract is clearly intended to refer to people as a whole and involves a PART FOR WHOLE metonymy as one gender is used to represent both genders. This metonymy follows four of the criteria for vehicle selection outlined by Radden and Kövecses (1999): TYPICAL OVER NON-TYPICAL; CENTRAL OVER PERIPHERAL; BASIC OVER NON-BASIC and IMPORTANT OVER LESS IMPORTANT, which is why the use of 'she' to represent humans as a whole would appear marked to many readers. It also reflects the implicit sexism behind the generic use of masculine pronouns. The fact that metonymy, unlike metaphor, appears to be processed in much the same way as literal language (see Chapter 7) suggests that uses of metonymy such as this may have a stronger and more lasting effect on the development of people's world views than metaphor. Indeed, research has shown that the use of the generic masculine pronoun in texts causes readers to produce predominantly male imagery, leads to a male bias in accompanying drawings and results in reduced self-esteem in female readers (Hamilton, 1988). Metonymy thus has the potential to be a more manipulative trope than metaphor, because it is more subtle and less likely to be noticed. For this reason, it is good to see that the use of the generic masculine pronoun is becoming increasingly rare in British and American English (Lee and Collins, 2008).

So far in this discussion of the use of metonymy for evaluative or rhetorical purposes we have focused on rather negative uses; however, it should not be forgotten that metonymy can be used in more positive ways to mitigate the possible face-threatening effects of the presence of opposing perspectives. For example, Liebscher (2006) analyses a televised interview, recorded in 1982 in north west Germany, when Germany was still divided into 'East' and 'West' Germany. In this interview, the host is interviewing an actor who had lived in East Germany before escaping to West Germany, where he had been living for five years at the time of the interview. Liebscher shows how both the interviewer and the interviewee made use of certain rhetorical devices to pre-empt conflict and to emphasise their shared background and build common ground. Although Liebscher does not refer to these devices as metonymy, in many cases that is what they are. For example, the interviewee refers to weekends spent in the 'Datsche'. The word 'Datsche' was borrowed from the Russian word 'Datscha' during the time of the Russian occupation of East Germany, and thus serves as a PART FOR WHOLE metonymy for an 'East German' lifestyle. The interviewer replies in the affirmative but then adds 'only we say bungalow for Datsche here ['here' being West Germany]' (Liebscher 2006: 169). This use of the word 'bungalow' is a metonymic reference to a more 'West German' lifestyle,[1] but both interlocutors are acknowledging that they are talking about essentially the same thing. This example displays a subtle yet effective evocation and exploitation of the relevant ICM.

5.7 Metonymy and creativity

Traditional accounts of metonymy emphasise its referential function and see it as a rather utilitarian trope. However, more recent work has emphasised the creativity that is often inherent in metonymy, and has identified ways in which new meanings can emerge from metonymies (Barcelona, 2012). As we saw in Chapter 3, researchers are starting to pay increasing attention to the role of conceptual blending in metonymy production and interpretation, and they note that new meanings can often emerge from the blend of source and target that are not intrinsic features of either the source or the target. Within the context of metonymy, these blends can provide a 'creative mechanism for meaning construction that can provide novel insights into a discourse situation' (Alač and Coulson, 2004: 23).

[1] The word 'bungalow' is of course of Indian origin and came into the English language as a result of the British occupation of India.

In this section we look at these creative functions of metonymy, starting with language but then broadening out into other forms of expression, such as art, music and film. We see how, as well as creating new meanings in and of themselves, metonymies can be played with and reliteralised for comic effect, which constitutes a common form of language play. Some of the analyses, but not all, draw on blending theory.

The creative use of metonymy in language and the role of metonymy in linguistic humour

One of the most influential monographs on creativity in everyday language is Carter's (2004) book *Language and Creativity: The Art of Common Talk.* Although Carter discusses figurative language, he hardly mentions metonymy. This is surprising given that metonymy is often involved in creative language production and comprehension due to its ability to shift focus of attention from one part of a domain to another, and to form chains of association. By doing this, it has a unique capacity to make people see things from different perspectives. Many jokes derive from differences in reference point phenomena. For example, one might ask: if olive oil is made from olives, and sunflower oil is made from sunflowers, what is baby oil made from? As we can see in this example, because elements of the source domain are often preserved, jokes that are based on metonymy are able to combine novel and familiar elements. As we will see in this section, many but not all creative uses of metonymy in language are used for humorous effect.

Much creative language play involves the re-literalisation of metonymy, and this often results in humorous exchanges. Consider this extract from Julian Barnes' (2009) novel *Staring at the Sun*, in which Jean (the protagonist) goes to visit Olive, the widow of a soldier (Tommy) who had been billeted in Jean's house during the Second World War. Olive, who is now living with her new husband, Derek, suspects Jean of being one of Tommy's former lovers:

'One of his popsies were you?' Olive enquired with a genial laugh.

'No, no, not at all . . .'

'It doesn't bother me if you were love. I like to think of old Tommy having a last cuddle or two. He always were a bit of a charmer.'

Was he? Jean certainly didn't remember him as a charmer. A bit awkward, fierce, even rude sometimes; capable of being nice. No, charm hadn't seemed one of his components.

'No. I mean, I can see why you might have thought . . .'

'First thing I said, didn't I Derek? Fancy that, I said, one of old Tommy's popsies popping out of the woodwork after all these years. I wouldn't have thrown him out if I'd known.'

'Thrown him out?'

'When we moved yes. I threw him out. Well, what was the point?
When was it Derek, nine or ten years ago?'

Derek pondered the question as he slowly inhaled and exhaled, then replied, 'It's always longer than you think nowadays.'

'Well, whenever it was, ten or twelve years ago, I *threw Tommy out*. We were moving and something had to go, and I hadn't looked at the stuff for years, and his old what-jercallit, battledress or something, I don't know why I had it anyway, it got the moth. So I threw it all out. Letters, photos, a few silly things I didn't look at cause it might upset me. Derek were all in favour.'

'No, that's putting it a bit strong, love.'

'Derek wasn't against, anyway. But what I say is, Tommy's got his little place in my heart, what does he want a place in my attic as well for?' Olive, who had seemed to be moving towards tears, suddenly roared with laughter, her motion shaking some ash from Derek's cigarette. 'He was a lovely boy, from what I remember of him, Tommy. But then life must go on, mustn't it?' (Barnes, 2009: 101) (emphasis added)

In this example, Olive's assertion that she has 'thrown Tommy out' confuses Jean. This turns out to be a POSSESSOR FOR POSSESSED metonymy whereby 'Tommy' represents 'Tommy's possessions'. The humour in this passage plays on the relationship between the literal and metonymic interpretations of 'threw him out'. The idea that Tommy himself would still be in the attic after all these years makes Olive laugh. The humour here relies on the ambiguity and the underspecified nature of metonymy.

Sometimes the humorous nature of the relationship is made even more explicit in the text, as we can see from this short extract from Pat Barker's novel *Liza's England*, where the main character, Liza, is thinking about the iron dust that her father brings home from the factory on his clothes, which annoys her mother:

She just wanted to nestle up close to him and feel his prickly black beard and breathe in the heavy smell of *iron dust* on his clothes. Iron dust was what made the work, but once, when her mother complained, her Dad said, 'Don't argue with our *bread and butter*,' and Liza had wanted to laugh, it was so funny, her Mam arguing with a piece of bread and butter. (Barker, 1996: 22) (emphasis added)

In this passage, *iron dust* refers metonymically to the hard manual labour that Liza's father does and *bread and butter* refers metonymically to the money that he earns. Both examples involve RESULT FOR ACTION metonymies and this contributes to the cohesion of the passage. The *bread and butter* metonymy is literalised at the end of the passage for comic effect.

One of the reasons why metonymy is so often used for creative purposes in literature is that it has the ability to evoke several scenes at once. Pankhurst (1999) shows how, in Toni Morrison's novel *The Song of Solomon*, a single trigger (an earring) evokes metonymy at a variety of different levels. Starting with the premise that metonymy is 'a poetic thought process that is fundamental to our way of thinking' (1999: 385) she goes on to show how the earring that is worn by the main protagonist in the novel (Pilate) provides the reader with access to information about Pilate's identity, her family history and the folk memories of the society in which she grew up.

Creative uses of metonymy can also be found in much more mundane forms of communication, outside the field of literature. For instance, the relationship between metonymy and personification is often exploited for humorous effect in everyday communication. The extract is taken from an email exchange about a proposed 'blue plaque' that was going to be placed on a building where the well-known author David Lodge had previously taught. In the UK, a 'blue plaque' is a permanent sign attached to a building or place to commemorate a link between that location and a famous person or event. Presumably, prior to this exchange, it had been assumed that David Lodge was dead and that he could not be consulted:

Dear Karen,

Not at all. My fault entirely for forgetting that he was an 'alive' blue plaque who I could have run it past! (Quote from an email exchange regarding a blue plaque)

The reference to David Lodge as an 'alive blue plaque' could be interpreted here as an instance of personification (the blue plaque is personified as 'David Lodge') or as a metonymy in which the blue plaque metonymically represents David Lodge and the work that he did. Referring to an actual person or their work as a 'blue plaque' is not really conventional and it does not map easily onto any of the metonymy types identified by Radden and Kövecses. However, the relationship appears to involve metonymy rather than metaphor as there is a relationship between the two. In schematic terms there is an EFFECT FOR CAUSE relationship involved, though obviously the exact relationship is more fine-grained than this.

In their study of the use of metonymy in text messaging, Littlemore and Tagg (in preparation) found multiple instances of playful, creative and sometimes humorous uses of metonymy. Once example is:

Oh no *never in blue jeans* might be coming back to Eastenders – what are we going to do? (CorTxt)

Here, 'never in blue jeans' refers, via a TRAIT FOR PERSON metonymy, to a person who is always over-dressed, possibly alluding to the song 'Forever in Blue Jeans', by Neil Diamond, which evokes a metonymy of opposition.

Barcelona (2003d) argues that in many cases the inferential work that is necessary in order to understand jokes is facilitated by pre-existing metonymic connections within cognitive frames or ICMs. These metonymic connections help the hearer to achieve the 'frame adjustments' that are necessary in order to grasp the humour. He illustrates this by referring to the following exchange, which took place in 1930s Spain in a parliamentary debate between the Prime Minister and a Member of Parliament:

Opposition MP (referring to the Prime Minister):

But what can we expect, after all, of a man who wears silk underpants?

Prime Minister:

Oh. I would never have thought that the Right Honourable's wife would be so indiscreet! (Barcelona, 2003d: 93)

In the first part of the exchange, the opposition MP attempts to compromise the Prime Minister by using the term 'wears silk underpants' metonymically to imply that he is effete and possibly homosexual. In the social climate of 1930s Spain, this might have been taken as a reference to the Prime Minister's inability to govern the country as he was not a 'real man'. In his response however, the Prime Minister uses metonymy to change the viewing frame into one of implied adultery on the part of the opposition MP's wife: only a lover could possibly know what sort of underwear he wore. By doing this he re-establishes himself as an 'alpha male' who is therefore fit to run the country, and establishes the opposition MP as a cuckold who is thus 'less of a man'. Veale *et al.* (2006) use Barcelona's example to illustrate how metonymy, along with metaphor and salience, is one of the key mechanisms underlying 'adversarial humour'. This is a particular (often aggressive) type of humour where a speaker will somehow twist his or her opponent's own words and use them differently to win a verbal sparring match. Veale *et al.* argue that the key feature of adversarial humour is that it has to involve some sort of parallelism across turns. In the above example, the parallelism involves the fact that both utterances refer to the same context, and the fact that they both incite a contiguous relationship between the Prime Minister's underwear and the hearer. The Prime Minister in the above example uses this parallelism to give his interjection an extra edge.

In sign language, too, there is a great deal of language play which exploits metonymy, often to creative and/or humorous effect. For example, Sutton-Spence *et al.* (2012) show how the modality of sign language is particularly suited to some forms of metonymic language play. For example, in 'Macbeth of the Lost Ark' by Paul Scott (www.bristol.ac.uk/bslpoetryanthology), the poet becomes the three witches cackling over the three communication methods of 'manually coded English' ('oralism', 'sign supported English' and 'Paget Gorman signing'), which are widely despised within the deaf community as they have been artificially created for them by the hearing community. For each method, he blends a witch-like hand movement with the particular hand shape that represents that particular method. Each hand shape involves a different metonymy and the three metonymies are incorporated into an over-arching 'witch-like' hand movement that involves a TRAIT FOR PERSON metonymy.

Attardo (2006) points out that work in cognitive linguistics that attempts to explain aspects of humour by appealing to notions such as metaphor, metonymy and construal could usefully be conducted within the context of the two main existing models of humour, namely the Semantic Script Theory of Humour (SSTH) (Raskin, 1985) and the General Theory of Verbal Humour (GTVH) (Attardo and Raskin, 1991). Both of these models emphasise the role played by 'focal adjustments' – that is, sudden shifts from, or within, an expected script or schema which cause the hearer or viewer to see things in a different way. People use scenes and scripts in order to infer entire sets of information or sequences actions from having seen or heard a very small subcomponent of those scenes or scripts. When people are half way through doing this and the scene or script is suddenly subverted, this is often viewed as being creative and/or humorous. We can see a good example of the role of metonymy in script subversion in the following extract from Monty Python's 'Undertakers' sketch:

UNDERTAKER: Morning!
MAN: Ah, good morning.
UNDERTAKER: What can I do for you, squire?
MAN: Um, well, I wonder if you can help me. Um, you see, my mother has just died.
UNDERTAKER: Ah, well, we can 'elp you. We deal with stiffs.
MAN: *(aghast)* What?
UNDERTAKER: Well there are three things we can do with your mother. We can burn her, bury her, or dump her.
[...]
UNDERTAKER: Where is she?
MAN: She's in this sack.
UNDERTAKER: Let's 'ave a look.
(sound of bag opening)
UNDERTAKER: She looks quite young.
MAN: Yes, she was.
UNDERTAKER: Fred!
FRED: Yea?
UNDERTAKER: I THINK WE'VE GOT AN EATER!

Extract from Monty Python's 'Undertakers' sketch

In this extract, we have two metonymic uses of language that are highly marked in this particular script. Normally one would expect a conversation with an undertaker to be conducted in relatively formal register, with respectful language being used about the deceased. In this scene, the undertaker usurps our expectations by using a TRAIT FOR PERSON metonymy and referring to the deceased as a 'stiff'. We saw above, in Section 5.2, that these sorts of metonymies are sometimes employed between employees working in the profession, but they are never used in conversations with clients. In the last line, he refers to the deceased as an 'eater'. This is similar to the use of the word 'stewer' that we saw in Section 4.2, where the word is used to describe a chicken that needs to be stewed because it is too bony or stringy to be cooked in any other way. What he is suggesting here is that they eat the body, rather than burying or cremating it. Again, he has gone completely 'off-script' and the humour is reinforced by his use of a metonymic expression that is normally only used to talk about animals.

At times creative metonymy use involves 'figure-ground reversals', where the reader or hearer is suddenly invited to focus on a part of a scene or event that would normally be seen as background to the scene or event. These involve a metonymic relationship of opposition, of the type seen in Chapter 4. We can see a good example of this in the final part of Catherine O'Flynn's (2010) novel *The News Where You Are*. In this passage, one of the characters, Michael, reflects on the way he feels about his dead wife, Elsie:

> He's never once felt Elsie's presence since she died. He watched the last breath leave her body and then the world changed. She was gone.
> He feels her absence, though, all the time.
> It's there in specific things:
> *The dip in the bed* where she used to lie,
> *The shape of the crack* in the vase that she dropped,
> And it's everywhere:
> The air around him,
> The colour of night in their bedroom,
> The shapes he sees on the insides of his eyelids.
> He understands now. Our absence is what remains of us. (O'Flynn, 2010:308–9)

The main focus in this passage is on the traces that she has left behind both emotionally (as in 'he feels her absence') and physically ('the dip in the bed' and 'the shape of the crack in the vase'). These last two expressions involve EFFECT FOR CAUSE metonymies that evoke an image of his wife engaged in habitual activity (lying in the bed) and an image of a one-off event (dropping the vase). This powerful figure–ground reversal thus evokes images which represent his deceased wife. These images cause painful memories. The passage resonates with the rest of the novel, which is about the destruction of the legacy of a Birmingham architect who designed many of the Modernist buildings that were built in the city in the 1960s, and about the effect that his obsession with his work had on his wife and child.

We have seen how metonymy is used creatively in language. The creative use of metonymy is also ubiquitous in other forms of expression, such as art, music, film and advertising, although it is only really beginning to be noticed and studied seriously in these contexts. In the following sections, we look at some of the work that has begun to investigate metonymy in different modes of expression. We will see that, in many ways, the functions that metonymy performs in these modes of expression are similar to those that it performs in language, but there are some important differences which have the potential to inform and enrich existing theories of metonymy.

The creative use of metonymy in art

A brief survey of the literature on art history suggests a changing role of metonymy in the various art movements. For example, the 'metonymical' nature of Cubism has been contrasted with the more 'metaphorical' nature of Surrealism (Jakobson, 1971b). By this, Jakobson means that Cubist paintings often focus on what 'isn't' there, or the spaces left by objects (very much like the extract from the Catherine O'Flynn novel that we have just seen). The Cubist artists' approach was to show the opposite of what was there. In this way, their paintings are somewhat like negative photos. Surrealist paintings, on the other hand, invite the viewer to make metaphorical comparisons between everyday objects. Each thus involves a different form of creativity.

The view that metaphor is the primary mechanism for creativity in art is beginning to be challenged, and researchers are beginning to suggest that art theorists pay more attention to metonymy. Particular attention is starting to be paid to the role played by metonymy in Impressionism. For instance, it has been argued that Cézanne's frequent use of water and bathing is a metonymy for 'simple pleasures', and harmony between humans and nature (Friedman, 2012). This relationship is clearly one of contiguity rather than comparison so it is more appropriate to see it as metonymy rather than as metaphor. Although it is difficult to see how the relationship fits into Radden and Kövecses' (1999) taxonomy, it could be described as a case of 'domain expansion' (Ruiz de Mendoza Ibáñez and Diez Velasco, 2002), in which the simple act of bathing represents all the feelings that one might have about that experience, the nostalgic associations that some viewers of the painting may have, and the feelings that other viewers may have of having 'missed out' on these simple pleasures. Ironically, at the heart of the complex network of meanings and emotions that can be associated with or provoked by Cézanne's paintings is a straightforward desire for simplicity. Metonymy is at the heart of this creative meaning-making process.

Attention is also beginning to be paid to the role of metonymy in contemporary art (Green, 2005). For example, Ryland (2011) uses a number of case studies of contemporary artworks to show how metonymic meaning is both 'held within' and 'created by' processes, materials, objects, language and context in these art works. One of the artworks that she discusses is Cornelia Parker's (1996) 'The Negative of Words'. This artwork consists of a pile of residue accumulated from the engraving of words on a piece of silver. The residue has a metonymic relationship with the words themselves as it is both the messy 'leftovers' of the neatly engraved words, as well as being the actual material that was contained in the words themselves. Ryland points out that, by doing this, Parker is emphasising the material quality of the words and downplaying their objective authority. She is making use of metonymic

PART–WHOLE relations to allude to absence and loss, to show how some of the parts are undervalued or marginalised. This use of 'negatives' also involves a metonymy of opposition, like those we discussed in Chapter 4.

Another artwork that she discusses is Susan Hiller's (2007/8) 'Auras: Homage to Marcel Duchamp'. In this artwork, fifty photographs of people's 'auras' are presented together in a rectangular display. Even though many viewers of the artwork may be of the opinion that visible auras probably do not exist, and that they would certainly not be photographable, the fact that they are presented in the same way as x-rays are presented in hospitals gives the impression that they constitute scientific 'evidence'. Thus the viewer fluctuates between two possible interpretations of same artwork. Here, metonymy is operating as a reference point phenomenon, creating a relationship between two conceptual domains that one would not normally consider related (rational science and the belief in 'auras') and highlighting different aspects of them. The fact that the auras are displayed in the same way as x-rays are displayed in a hospital involves a STYLE OF PRESENTATION FOR PRODUCT metonymy. This kind of relationship is not listed in Radden and Kövecses' (1999) taxonomy.

A third artwork that she looks at is Ceal Floyer's (1995) 'Door'. In this exhibit, a slide projector shines a band of light along the base of a closed door. This creates a strip of light in the gap between the bottom of the door and the floor. This creates the illusion that there is a brightly lit room the other side of the door (in which interesting events may be occurring), whereas in reality the light is coming from the projector itself. It apparently takes viewers between 30 and 90 seconds to work out that the light is coming from the projector, rather than from the room the other side of the door. This exhibit highlights the fact that our minds are automatically tuned to use metonymy in order to interpret stimuli (the light shining under the door is a PART FOR WHOLE metonymy for the non-existent brightly lit room the other side). When we are faced with unexpected 'literality' (such as the fact that the light is coming from the projector), we suddenly become aware of the metonymic nature of our thinking. In Ryland's words: 'human brains are simply not set up to read the world literally, so this literality occurs as a novel experience' (2011: 166).

In her analysis, Ryland finds support for Nerlich and Clarke's (2001) view of metonymy as 'a force of *conceptual spreading* inside and across adjacent conceptual domains', which contrasts with the idea of metaphor as 'a force of *conceptual binding* between domains' (2011: 245–72). This conceptual spreading is what, in Ryland's eyes, gives rise to the creative potential of metonymy. Her argument is:

> The cognitive linguistic view is that metonymy 'gives access to' and 'highlights' meaning within a cognitive domain or domain matrix. This, however, implies a return to something already known. But metonymy has the capacity to offer new connections within a domain, and expansions into related domains not previously regarded as

contiguous. When we draw on our personal experiences, we generate *ad hoc* categories that group in a domain elements that may not previously or conventionally have formed groups. The act of forming an unconventional cognitive domain and identifying things that might be contained within, and related to it is an act of creativity. (Ryland, 2011: 45)

She concludes that a focus on metonymy could usefully be integrated into the teaching of art theory. It is useful because it can reveal other meanings that are hidden by a focus on only metaphor; it exposes ambiguity between literal, metonymic and metaphoric readings of the same artwork; it allows for the inclusion of metonymic chaining in the analysis of art; and it explains how viewers shift between alternative frames of reference that highlight and downplay different meanings of the artwork. Such a focus could also be extended to the study of more everyday art forms, such as Japanese 'manga' cartoons, where, as we saw in the Introduction, the absence of hands (and sometimes feet) in the pictures can metonymically represent loss of control (Abbott and Forceville, 2011).

It is interesting to note that Susan Hiller's aforementioned (2007/8) work has the words 'Homage to Marcel Duchamp' in its title. The reason for this is that Marcel Duchamp was particularly interested in painting people's imaginary 'auras', and he was producing his work at a time when x-rays had just been invented and many artists were working with the concept of x-rays in their work. Marcel Duchamp was a member of an art movement whose members made extensive use of metonymy in their work. This is the 'Orphism' movement, which was an extension of Cubism. The difference between Orphism and Cubism is that Orphism has no recognisable subject matter and relies solely on form and colour to express its meaning. An example of an Orphist artwork is František Kupka's 'Katedrála' (The Cathedral), 1912–13, which depicts a series of vertically aligned parallelograms in different shades of blue slotted together to resemble a modern stained-glass window. In this work he manages to convey the atmosphere of a cathedral simply by picking out elements of one part of a cathedral. He thus makes successful use of a chained PART FOR WHOLE metonymy in which elements of a stained glass window stand for the window as a whole, and the window stands for the cathedral. The metonymy works well as the work is extremely atmospheric and one feels as if one is actually in a cathedral when looking at it.

The creative use of metonymy in music

A great deal of metonymy can be found in music. It appears in the lyrics, the melody and in human interactions with the music (such as conducting, dancing and the memories evoked). We have already seen how repeated extracts – or, more recently, sampling – can provide metonymic (often ironic) references to other pieces of music or even whole styles of music. Like Proust's madeleine, just the opening bars of a song can take the listener back to a particular time in their life, and reawaken memories of the feelings that they had at that particular time or even of people long since forgotten. Wagner's leitmotifs are a good example of the way metonymy can work in opera. These are short, constantly recurring musical phrases that are associated with particular characters in his operas. In Wagner's *Ring Cycle*, when the listener hears Siegfried's leitmotif, he or she knows that Siegfried is about to appear on the scene. As Siegfried becomes more heroic, his leitmotif acquires more orchestration and becomes louder, evoking a strong TRAIT FOR PERSON metonymy. As we saw in Chapter 4, in his study of metonymy in video game music, Whalen (2004) points out that, at the syntagmatic level, music often serves as a metonymy for progress in the game. He also shows how this combines with other features of the game to create an overall feeling of progression.

Another way in which metonymy can appear in the music itself is via the musical motion. In their analysis of the Beatles song 'Something', Johnson and Larson (2009) point to the role of embodied cognition in the conceptual metaphor MUSICAL MOTION IS PHYSICAL MOTION. This conceptual metaphor is metonymically motivated, as people often experience a desire to physically move when they hear music, and the type of movements that they make in response to the music usually reflect the character of the music itself. Johnson and Larson also draw attention to the way in which the song ends,

I don't wanna leave her now
You know I believe and how
[Short guitar solo]

The words end before the musical phrase, and the final 'sentence' is provided by a short, six-note guitar solo. Johnson and Larson comment that 'where the text leaves off, embodied musical meaning answers' (2009: 82). They argue that the use of a short guitar solo here is the Beatles' way of saying that 'in the end, only music can say what needs to be said'. They also point out that the rising pitches in the final four notes of this solo (A–B♭–B–C) are the exact reverse of falling pitches used in the opening lines of the song (C–B–B♭–A). Thus an upward movement is used metonymically to refer to a previously heard downward movement via a relationship of opposition.

The first researcher to propose a model of the ways in which metonymic thinking operates in musical understanding is Pérez-Sobrino (2013b). She identifies four levels of 'metonymic reasoning', some of which resemble those already discussed. The first level is 'metonymic echoing', where a piece of music echoes aspects of sounds from nature, such as bird sounds, the sounds of the wind, and so on. The second level, 'metonymic cueing', involves the selection of relevant material for metonymic thinking to take place. Here, she cites Smetana's 'Vltava' (which is the name of the longest river in the Czech Republic), which starts as two small streams, coming together to form a flowing river. In the third level, which she labels 'musical SOURCE-IN-TARGET metonymy' a musical theme illustrates the mood of the character. This theme can be a rhythmic motif, a musical scale, or a certain musical key. Finally, at the fourth level which she labels 'musical *multiple* SOURCE IN TARGET metonymy', a whole piece of music or an extract might come to stand for a brand. Naturally these different levels of metonymic reasoning interact with each other in different ways.

Given the extensive role played by metonymic reasoning in musical comprehension, it is unsurprising to discover that orchestral conducting also involves metonymy, as do the gestures employed by music teachers when teaching musical concepts (Chuang, 2010). It has been claimed that most conducting and music teaching gestures are based on metaphoric or metonymic connections between aspects of the music and physical interactions that people have with objects in their everyday lives (Bräm and Bräm, 2004). Litman (2010) shows how conductors of choirs make extensive use of gesture to make metonymic reference to concrete objects that reflect emotions and other aspects of human experience that are difficult to express in words, and argues that this encourages the singers to reproduce these experiences through their singing.

Metonymy also features in the verbal instructions that conductors and music teachers give to performers. Johnson and Larson (2009) show how the metonymy THE PERFORMER IS THE MUSIC PERFORMED is extensively exploited and demonstrate how the way in which the performer is metonymically identified with the music licenses instructions such as: 'You speed up and go higher, just when she slows down and goes lower' and 'This is where you take over'. They also show how the INSTRUMENT FOR PERFORMER metonymy further facilitates instructions, such as 'the violins were sluggish' and 'the drums got lost' (2009: 76). Finally, metonymy is sometimes used to refer to different types of music, as we can see in this quote from Sebastian Faulks' novel, *A Possible Life: Part V 'You Next Time'*, which is set in the USA in the 1970s:

I didn't like the production. It was too *West Coast*. (Faulkes, 2012: 204)

It does not take too much imagination on the part of the reader to understand that what is being referred to here is the fact that the music sounds like it might be from California. What exactly this might mean to an individual depends on what they know of 1970s music from California. The particular ICMs that are triggered here may vary considerably according to the readers' age, and their exposure to different types of California music.

The creative use of metonymy in film and advertising

So far we have looked at metonymy in different modes of expression. We now turn to two types of media that involve 'multimodal metonymy': film and advertising. In these types of media, metonymy is particularly likely to appear in more than one mode at once, and these modes work together to form a coherent message. Although we are not always aware of the fact, we are usually on the receiving end of information from a variety of sources, even when we think we may 'just' be reading or 'just' be listening; there are usually other sources of information which contribute to the overall message in varying subtle ways, serving several different functions at once. What we are interested in here is the extent to which these multimodal forms of metonymy contribute to creative expression in the media concerned.

The role of metonymy in film is well attested, reflecting the enormous potential for metonymy afforded by changes in angle and camera focus. In both film and advertising, complementary metonymic messages can be conveyed in a single scene through the language, camera angle, actor movement and music. In Chapter 3, we looked at Forceville's (2012) work on the importance of metonymic sound in film. He argues that this is often a highly creative force as the sound track can be used to enhance the salience of visual elements in the film that one may not normally notice. Other uses of metonymy in film are more mundane: a red front door may imply that the person who lives there leads an exciting lifestyle, a single empty whisky glass on a kitchen table may indicate that someone has a drinking problem, a broken child's toy on the floor may be a reference to the presence of uncared-for children, and so on. Camera angles are often used to make metonymic reference to the viewpoint of a particular character or to the sorts of things he or she might focus on in a particular scene. Ortiz (2011) points out that in countless horror films we see just the shadow of the evil character, suggesting that they are lurking in a dark area, beyond the reach of the camera, about to commit their evil deed. At other times, we simply see the shadow approaching the victim, perhaps with a knife in its hand. As with the works of art discussed above, the shadow is the reverse representation of the person, and here this is combined with the primary metaphor EVIL IS DARKNESS to create tension and fear. This is a somewhat conventional use of metonymy, but creative extensions of this idea and of other metonymies abound in cinema. This particular metonymy is taken to an extra level in vampire films, where the vampire casts no shadow, indicating that he or she is not actually human.

Two good examples of the use of metonymy in film are provided by Rudicell (1992). In the first, he refers to the 1961 film *101 Dalmatians*, in which the evil Cruella De Vil wants the Dalmatian puppies for their skins. She is regularly seen smoking a cigarette that spreads yellow smoke throughout the room. About half way through the film, a newspaper is shown with a voice-over reporting the theft of the puppies. Suddenly, trails of yellow smoke start to appear in front of the newspaper, which make one think of Cruella. In the second, he refers to the film *Gal Young 'Un* in which the male character, Trax, starts to abuse the female character, Mattie. In an early scene, he gets hold of Mattie's well-loved cat and throws it violently off the bed, which is a metonymic reference to the way in which he is going to treat Mattie herself. Rudicell makes the point that these examples both involve metonymy, but does not go any further than that in his analysis. The models of metonymy outlined in Chapters 2 and 3 provide useful tools for the analysis of these metonymies. On one level, the two metonymic relationships could be defined in Radden and Kövecses' (1999) terms as ACTION FOR AGENT and POSSESSED FOR POSSESSOR respectively, but there is far more involved in the actual meaning interpretation than this. The smoke does not just evoke Cruella De Vil herself; it evokes her evil presence. And the cat does not just evoke Mattie, but her relative weakness in relation to Trax. In order to offer a fuller explanation of the meanings of these metonymies, it is useful to bring in Peirsman and Geeraerts' (2006a) 'varying strengths of contiguity' model that was discussed in Chapter 3. In this model, metonymies radiate out from prototypical instantiations in three different ways: they gradually become less contiguous, less bounded and less concrete. This is what is happening here. Although the basic metonymic relationships are fairly prototypical, their actual meanings in context are more distinct, less easy to define and more abstract, and therefore lie more towards the periphery of the category.

Metonymy can frequently be found in advertising, where it is used to hint at sought-after lifestyles and other aspirations and to serve as a persuasive device. Many of these uses are creative, involving a subtle combination of the verbal and the pictorial elements to convey a strong and coherent overall message (Forceville, 2008). Urios-Aparisi (2009) demonstrates the role played by metonymy in four television commercials, showing how it performs important rhetorical functions in its own right, as well as motivating some of the metaphor in the commercials. There is insufficient space to discuss all four commercials here, so we will limit our focus to just two. In the first commercial, a tea tag for 'Hornimans' tea is shown swinging slowly in the same way as a hypnotist would swing a watch, and as the tea tag swings, the picture goes slightly out of focus. This commercial thus invokes the metaphor A TEA TAG IS A HYPNOTISER'S WATCH, and the drinking of the tea makes the tea drinker relax. Underlying this metaphor, however, are two important metonymies: an EMBLEM FOR PRODUCT metonymy (the tea tag represents the tea bag) and an EFFECT FOR CAUSE metonymy (the relaxed state results from drinking the tea). The whole commercial is filmed in soft gold and brown colours, which metaphorically represent the warm feelings that will allegedly be experienced by the tea drinker. They might also be said to stand metonymically for the colour of the tea and its smooth taste. The voice-over is spoken in the sorts of soft tones that might be employed by a hypnotist. Thus, in this advertisement, metaphor and metonymy interact in a range of different modalities to create an overall blend designed to make the viewer associate this particular tea with relaxation. In a second commercial, from Spain, the front of a Volvo car is shown driving through a series of adverse weather conditions, and the voice-over provides advice on the importance of driving safely and prudently in order to protect one's 'cargo' (i.e. one's family). Here there is a clear PART FOR WHOLE metonymy in that the front of the car stands for the whole car. In addition to this, we hear the sounds of children getting into a car, the door closing, the noise of the engine, and the sounds of rain and thunder. These metonymically evoke a scene in which the driver is responsible for his or her (though probably his) family and must look after them by driving a safe car. Urios-Aparisi points out that throughout this advertisement there is no actual driver so that it appears at times as if the car itself is being addressed. This creates a personification metaphor in which the car itself becomes the safe and responsible driver. The fact that the camera focuses so much on the front of the car and its headlights adds to this effect as the headlights begin to look like eyes. This personification metaphor sets up a chain of metonymies in the viewer's mind in which Volvo cars, which are already known for their safety record, become responsible for the safety of the whole family.

Yu (2009) notes the use of metonymy in a slightly different type of 'commercial' and focuses on an 'advertisement for public good', which was shown on China Central Television (CCTV) and was designed to influence and improve people's thinking. This advertisement features the words 'In everyone's heart there is a big stage; however big one's heart is, that is how big the stage is' (2009: 120). This is accompanied by a short film featuring a Chinese woman in traditional dress dancing past a village, then past a wall (which resembles the wall of the Forbidden City in Beijing), then past a statue, and then on a skyscraper, in a city that looks like Shanghai. She then acquires a partner and together they dance past the sculpture and the wall, they briefly acquire and then lose a whole troupe of dancers, then she is shown alone again dancing on the roof of a skyscraper and finally standing on the skyscraper gazing into the distance. The advertisement begins with traditional Chinese music, then Western music is played but at the end there is a return to the traditional Chinese music. Metonymies abound in this advertisement. The traditional clothes and music as well as the village and the wall metonymically represent traditional Chinese culture, the move from the village to the big city represents the move that is made by hundreds of thousands of Chinese people every year and by extension shows a move that is being made by China itself from a predominantly agricultural to predominantly industrialised society, and the final scene in which the traditional music is juxtaposed with the sight of the young woman looking out over the modern city involves a metonymic blend of the old and the new, showing that traditional values do not necessarily need to be lost in the course of economic development.

The use of metonymy in advertisements can at times extend over an entire commercial campaign. Villicañas and White (2013) report on the creative role played by pictorial metonymy in a twenty-year advertising campaign for Purificación García, a Spanish clothing company. These advertisements all involve black and white photographs in which a simple object from the metonymic source domain of 'clothing' is combined with another object, representing something that they sell or that is contextually relevant in some other way, For example, one of their advertisements features a watch. On closer inspection, the watch strap is in fact a tape measure. This advertisement appeared just as Purificación García was starting to produce and sell watches. In another advertisement, which appeared just before Christmas, a series of coat hangers is displayed so as to resemble a rudimentary Christmas tree. In these advertisements, the tape measure and coat hangers metonymically represent the clothing industry. Villicañas and White argue that this campaign is distinctive in a number of ways. Firstly, all of the advertisements have a minimalist feel, rely almost exclusively on pictorial images, and contain very little supporting linguistic material. The fact that none of the products of the company ever appear in the advertisements means that metonymic reasoning is vital to the comprehension process. They show how the repeated use of metonymy over the lifespan of the advertising campaign establishes a 'family resemblance' between the campaigns, which allows for anaphoric reference in some of the later advertisements. Finally, they show how creativity derives from the unexpectedness of the metonymic source and from the metonymic blends, and how the consistent use of metonymy enhances cohesion and coherence, contributing to a strong and distinct corporate image.

A similar longitudinal metonymic campaign was used by Saatchi and Saatchi in a single advertising campaign in the Netherlands for a pain-relieving gel named Voltaren, which is produced by Novartis. Serrano Losado (2013) explores the ways in which pictorial metonymy works in these advertisements. Each advertisement features a silhouette of a person, surrounded by pictures of knives, pins, razor blades or shards of glass. Serrano Losado points out how, in these advertisements, physical damage used as a source domain works via a CAUSE FOR EFFECT metonymy; stabbing, pricking and cutting all represent pain. The advertisements also contain INSTRUMENT FOR ACTION metonymies in that the knives represent deliberate cutting, the razor blades and shards of glass represent accidental cutting, and the pins represent pricking. By making repeated use of these metonymy types throughout the campaign, Saatchi and Saatchi gradually build up a picture of different yet related sources of pain which the product can counter.

How do these findings on the creative uses of metonymy in other forms of expression relate to existing work on semiotics?

In this chapter, we have seen that metonymy is used creatively in a wide range of different forms of expression other than language. This provides evidence for the cognitive linguistic claim that metonymy is more than a linguistic phenomenon. Our investigation into the role of metonymy in art, film, music and advertising has led to new insights about the nature of metonymy itself. The relationship also works in the other direction: incorporating a focus on metonymy in the study of these modes of expression can contribute to existing theories and frameworks that are normally used to analyse them. The study of the semantics, syntax and pragmatics of signs such as these is referred to as semiotics, and dates back to Ferdinand de Saussure (1915). Three widely used frameworks within the field of semiotics are Peirce's (1966) three-way semiotic distinction, Barthes' (1972, 1993) second order of signification, and Kress and van Leeuwen's (1996) grammar of visual design. In this section, I look at each of these frameworks, and assess the ways in which an explicit focus on metonymy may contribute to work in this area. We will see that the main contribution that metonymy can make in this area is to challenge the assumption that the relationship between a sign and its meaning is always arbitrary (see Al-Sharafi, 2004), and that a focus on metonymy types provides more structure and systematicity to the analysis of the relationships that are identified.

Peirce (1966) identified three kinds of signs corresponding to three different kinds of relationship between signifier and signified – arbitrariness, resemblance and causation. In *symbolic signs*, the relationship between the signifier and the signified is purely conventional and largely arbitrary. The majority of words are signs of this kind, but so are some non-linguistic symbolic signs, such as those used in Morse code or semaphore. In *iconic signs*, the relationship between the signifier and the signified is one of resemblance. An example of this would be a 'no overtaking sign' or a stylised picture of a woman on a toilet door to indicate that it is the ladies' toilet. In *indexical signs*, the relationship between the signifier and the signified is one of causation. For example, tracks in the snow would indicate that a human or animal has been there; a contrail in the sky indicates that an aeroplane has gone by. Metonymy relates most closely to iconic and indexical signs. Iconic signs never involve a full representation of the thing being signified, and only ever involve a schematic or partial representation. Therefore they nearly always involve some sort of PART FOR WHOLE metonymy. Indexical signs clearly involve an EFFECT FOR CAUSE or a CAUSE FOR EFFECT metonymy. We can see here that a focus on metonymy provides the analyst with a useful framework for analysing the nature of the relationship between both indexical and iconic signs and their referents. Here we have identified two types of metonymic relationship, but, as we saw in Chapter 2, metonymy researchers have at their disposal many other types of metonymic relationship with which to work. For example, relationships such as MANNER FOR ACTION, INSTRUMENT FOR AGENT, PRODUCER FOR PRODUCT and PLACE FOR EVENT are all likely to be involved in the creation of signs, but the nature of their involvement has not been explored to date. It would be worth examining the roles that metonymic relationships, such as these, play in semiotics as this would allow for a more fine-grained analysis of the relationships between signs and their referents. It would also allow for a more systematic analysis of the ways in which these relationships co-occur and work together in the form of metonymic chaining (see Chapter 1). It could even be that we need to add to Peirce's taxonomy of sign types; the aforementioned metonymic relationships are not easily captured by the notion of iconic or indexical signs as they involve neither PART/WHOLE nor EFFECT/CAUSE metonymic relationships. It might therefore be worth looking at ways of systematically extending Peirce's taxonomy to include signs that involve the construal of contiguous relationships other than PART/WHOLE or EFFECT/CAUSE relationships, and using Radden and Kövecses' taxonomy as a starting point in this endeavour.

Attempts have been made to extend Peirce's framework, although they have not involved a focus on metonymy. For instance, the framework was extended by Barthes (1972, 1993), who tried to take connotation into account. For Barthes, the connotative power of signs was particularly important because it could serve a cultural, ideological purpose, which he referred to as 'mythology'. For example, he pointed out that for the French, a bottle of wine connotes a healthy, robust, relaxing experience, which is somewhat removed from the literal meaning of wine as an inebriating beverage. He argued that these 'mythologies' have the power to make our own view of the world appear somehow 'normal' and 'objective', and the only way of being. Mythologies abound in cultures all over the world and they regularly involve metonymy. The French mythology for wine contrasts with the Anglo-Saxon mythology, which places more focus on the inebriating qualities of wine. A more systematic exploration of the role played by the different metonymy types in the development of mythologies would help to explain how they have arisen and may provide a better account of universality and variation. For example, the 'wine' example that we have just seen involves a SUB-EVENT FOR WHOLE EVENT relationship between wine drinking and activities that may take place at the time of the wine drinking (socialising, relaxing, eating fine food and so on). This SUB-EVENT FOR WHOLE EVENT relationship is less well developed in Anglo-Saxon culture, as in Britain it is more common to drink wine without food than it is in other cultures. In Spanish, 'un vino de honor' (lit. 'a wine of honour') means a reception at which food (in the form of tapas) will always be served. This may be confusing for an English speaker of Spanish who, if asked to prepare 'un vino de honor', would need to know that food is expected. SUB-EVENT FOR WHOLE EVENT metonymies also lie behind the fetishisation of products such as Coca-Cola and McDonald's hamburgers, as the consumption of these products may connote particular sought-after lifestyles, which makes them desirable in countries where those lifestyles are less attainable.

Work on the semiotics of multimodal discourse has been further developed by Kress and van Leeuwen (1996), who emphasise the interaction of the visual and the verbal components. In their *Grammar of Visual Design* they emphasise features such as modality, which can be expressed visually through varying shades of colour; hedged messages might be presented in faded, blurred or pastel colours, whereas strong messages tend to be written in bold colours. Black and white pictures denote history and tradition, whereas bright Technicolor can represent 'Modernism' or ideas from the 1960s. The experiential, metonymic basis of these apparently metaphorical relationships is clear: when we cannot see something clearly we are unlikely to say for certain what it is, thus evoking a CAUSE FOR EFFECT relationship, and use of Technicolor to represent the 1960s involves a PROPERTY FOR CATEGORY relationship. The semiotics here is not random as it involves metonymic extensions from real-world experiences.

5.8 Conclusion

In this chapter we have seen that the functions of metonymy extend well beyond those that have been discussed in traditional accounts. We have seen, for example, that metonymic thinking is often highly creative and that it plays a key role in art, music, film and advertising. Multiple connections between the source and target are possible, and metonymy can create hypothetical relationships, especially in the area of art where items are unexpectedly juxtaposed to create new meaning, which allows us see things in radically different ways, and to question our assumptions about the world. It can also be involved in zeugma, and this is often used to create comic effect. We have also seen that metonymy can serve a wide range of rhetorical functions, and it also serves a key device in meaning extension in both spoken and sign language as well as in other modes of communication such as gesture and music. Its role here is perhaps more subtle than that of metaphor, which makes it more difficult to spot. We have also seen that metonymy can operate above the level of the phrase, and that it can serve as an important form of cohesion in literature, music, film and video games, as well as in everyday language. Metonymy can therefore constitute a suggestive, powerful and economical meaning-making device, as it draws heavily on shared cultural knowledge that can be very rich. Metonymy can extend across large stretches of text and other forms of communication as well as providing intertextual references to other texts via sampling and other more covert forms of reference.

6 'The Government of Britain is sort of there'

How can we identify 'metonymy'?

6.1 Introduction

In this chapter I focus on the identification of metonymy, and its interaction with other types of figurative expression. More specifically, I look at how one can decide whether a particular piece of language constitutes a metonymy or not. Admittedly, this is a rather artificial endeavour given that metonymy is best seen as a dynamic cognitive process underlying language and other forms of communication, rather than as a static feature of language itself. However, dynamic cognitive processes do leave traces in language, and it is these traces that tend to be viewed as 'instances of metonymy'. It is therefore useful to have some sort of procedure for identifying such 'instances of metonymy' in language, as this makes studies replicable and allows researchers to compare the use of metonymy across different genres. Having a reliable identification procedure allows researchers to explore the ways in which metonymy behaves in real-world data and to use that data to develop current theoretical models of metonymy. Having such a procedure is a necessary prerequisite to automatic, computer-based metonymy identification which, as we will see later in this chapter, can make a significant positive impact on human–computer interaction.

Up to this point, the issue of metonymy identification has been presented as if it were relatively unproblematic. Many of the earlier studies of metonymy offered no explanation of the procedure used to identify it. In more recent work, researchers have begun to offer an outline of their rationale for metonymy identification. For instance, in their study of metaphor and metonymy in language used to discuss penal reform, Deignan and Armstrong (forthcoming, 2015) considered as metonymies all situations where the lexical unit has a contextual meaning that is different from its basic meaning, and where the two meanings had a relationship based on contiguity rather than comparison. Using this procedure, they found that the word *court*, the place where decisions about justice are made, was regularly used to stand for the people who make those decisions. This, they argued, served to depersonalise the process of justice. However, even Deignan and Armstrong's study did not involve a systematic examination of all the metonymy in the texts they studied. This difficult endeavour has only been attempted in one study (Biernacka, 2013). Biernacka (whose study was briefly mentioned in Chapter 3) adapted an existing procedure for metaphor identification (Pragglejaz Group, 2007) for use in metonymy identification in a series of focus group discussions on the subject of terrorism and found that this presented a number of challenges.

In the next section, I explore Biernacka's adaptation of the Pragglejaz Procedure for the identification of metonymy. In subsequent sections, I look at the challenges that she was forced to overcome in order to do this, and relate them to more widespread difficulties in metonymy identification. The focus in these sections is on linguistic data as well as others of expression. In the second part of the chapter, I move on to explore advances that have been made in the automatic detection of metonymy by computers, and suggest ways in which this work could be developed still further.

6.2 Metonymy identification in text: a possible procedure and initial challenges

Researchers studying metaphor have developed a fairly robust scheme for identifying linguistic metaphor in text, which is known as the Pragglejaz Group (2007) Metaphor Identification Procedure (MIP). This procedure involves identifying as metaphor *any* lexical unit that has the potential to be processed metaphorically. The analyst begins by identifying all the lexical units in the text and then, for each lexical unit, he or she establishes its meaning in context and then decides whether it has a more basic contemporary meaning in other contexts and, if so, whether its meaning in the text can be understood in comparison with this more basic meaning. Basic meanings tend to be more concrete, related to the human body or more precise. If this is the case then the lexical unit is marked as being 'metaphorically used'.

One problem with the MIP is that it operates at the level of the word rather than the phrase or utterance and this is a somewhat artificial way to view metaphor, given that it often occurs in fixed expressions (Deignan, 2005a). An alternative procedure to the MIP, which gets round this problem, is Cameron's (2003) 'Metaphor Identification through the Vehicle' (MIV), which does not take a word-by-word approach. When using the MIV, an analyst would begin by determining whether a stretch of text is 'clearly anomalous or incongruous against the surrounding discourse', and then consider whether the incongruity can be removed by 'some transfer of meaning' from the incongruous stretch to the topic under discussion (Cameron 2003: 60–1). The incongruous stretch is treated as the 'vehicle' through which the metaphor is expressed, hence the procedure's name.

To illustrate, let us consider the following extract from a university lecture, which is taken from the British Academic Spoken English (BASE) corpus:

[...] you can learn directly the *nuts and bolts* of a writer's craft. (BASE corpus)

Under the 'MIP', *nuts* would be labelled as a metaphor and so would *bolts* but *and* would not. Under the 'MIV', the whole phrase, *nuts and bolts* would be marked as a metaphor. While the MIV seems to be more intuitively appropriate, there are problems identifying the beginning and end of the metaphorically used phrase. Corpus data tells us that *nuts and bolts* frequently occurs as part of the string *the nuts and bolts of*, so a case could be made for labelling the whole string as 'metaphor'. This only really becomes a problem when attempts are being made to calculate metaphoric density, but it could be frustrating for the analyst.

In order to identify metonymy in language, Biernacka (2013) manages to combine both of the above approaches. Her procedure for metonymy identification is as follows:

1. Read the entire text to get a general understanding of the overall meaning.
2. Determine lexical units.
3. Decide on the metonymicity of each lexical unit:
   a. For each lexical unit establish its contextual meaning – taking into account how it applies to an entity in the situation evoked by the text, as well as co-text (i.e. the surrounding text; what is said before and after the examined expression). Take co-text into account.
   b. For each lexical unit determine if it has a more basic contemporary meaning in other contexts than the meaning in the given context.
   c. If the lexical unit has a more basic contemporary meaning in other contexts than the given context, and the contextual and basic meanings are different, determine if they are connected by contiguity, defined as a relation of adjacency and closeness comprising not only spatial contact but also temporal proximity, causal relations and part whole relations.
4. If a connection is found in step 3c that is one of contiguity: check backwards and forwards to determine if any other lexical unit(s) belong(s) together semantically, thus determining the extent of the metonymy vehicle; and mark the lexical unit (or lexical units which belong together) as metonymy vehicle. (Biernacka, 2013: 117)

The key stage in this procedure is 3c, where the analyst must decide whether the contextual and basic meanings are closely connected in terms of the situation evoked by the text. This description is sufficiently loosely worded to accommodate the different types of metonymic relation that were discussed in Chapter 2. It also allows for the coding of an item as both metonymy and metaphor, which, as we have seen throughout the preceding chapters, is not an uncommon phenomenon. To illustrate how this process works, let us look at this extract from the *Guardian* newspaper:

West overlooked risk of Libya weapons reaching Mali, says expert

US, Britain and *France* focused on securing anti-aircraft missiles but neglected other weapons [...] (*The Guardian*, 21 January 2013)

Here, the words 'US', 'Britain' and 'France' are good candidates for coding as 'metonymy'. We can see that their contextual meanings (members of the governments of these countries) differ from their more basic meanings (geographical locations) and that these meanings are closely connected, as in each case the country stands for members of the government of that country. The word 'West' would also be coded as metonymy under this procedure as a geographical location (relative to another geographical location) stands for the countries that are there which in turn stand for the governments of those countries. This metonymy is somewhat less precise than the specific country metonymies (perhaps deliberately so) and relies to some extent on a chaining process, but it still works.

The final part of the procedure allows for the inclusion of more than one lexical unit in the metonymy vehicle. We can see how this would work by looking at the following extract, which is from the same lecture as the 'nuts and bolts' example:

I'm also what you might call a cultural werewolf that is *by day* I'm a scientist but I moonlight also as a poet and as an editor. (BASE corpus)

Here the term 'by day' is clearly metonymic as it has a contiguous relationship with the literal sense shown in the following extract from the Bank of English:

They hunt *by day* and feed mainly on mammals. (BofE)

In both cases, it is the string 'by day' which carries the meaning, rather than just 'day', so it is more appropriate to label the whole string as metonymy rather than just the word 'day'.

Let us illustrate this with one more example:

She has again become *her mother's daughter*. (BofE)

In this citation, 'her mother' stands metonymically for 'the personality of her mother' and the whole citation means that she is very much like her mother in terms of her personality. Therefore we should label the whole string 'her mother's daughter' as metonymy, rather than one particular word. The expression 'her mother's daughter' also contains an element of metaphor as there is an implicit comparison between the mother and the daughter. This reflects the fact that metonymy underlies a great deal of metaphor (Goossens, 2003).

If we are to use authentic linguistic data to challenge and explore the models of metonymy that were outlined in Chapter 2 and 3, then we also need to find a way of identifying the metonymy types that were proposed by Radden and Kövecses (1999). Here again, we might consider adapting a method that has been proposed in the field of metaphor studies for use in metonymy identification. Steen (1999) proposed a five-step procedure for getting from linguistic to conceptual metaphor. The procedure is as follows:

1. Identification of metaphor-related words
2. Identification of propositions
3. Identification of open comparison
4. Identification of analogical structure
5. Identification of cross-domain mappings.

He illustrates this procedure by analysing the word 'sleeps' in the poem by Tennyson 'Now Sleeps the Crimson Petal'. Basically, the word 'sleep' is identified as a metaphorically used word (step 1); the analyst then considers that petals are being talked about as if they could sleep (steps 2 and 3); the analogical structure is then identified, in other words that the petals are inactive (step 4); and, finally, other cross-domain mappings are identified, such as the fact that the petal is being compared to a human, and that as such, it needs rest (step 5). The conceptual metaphor here would thus be: A PLANT IS A HUMAN.

In order to show how this procedure could be adapted to the identification of metonymy types, let us reconsider one of the 'university' examples that were introduced in Chapter 2:

[...] they played a friendly against the *university*. (BofE)

In order to get from a specific instance of metonymy to a 'metonymy type' in this example, one might begin by taking the physical campus as the most basic sense (as it is the most concrete and tangible). One could then adapt the procedure in the following way in order to identify the metonymy type underlying this linguistic metonymy:

1. Identification of metonymy-related words
2. Identification of propositions
3. Identification of a domain
4. Identification of the relationship within the domain.

The word 'university' is identified as a metonymically used word (1), and it is being used to refer to a university sports team (2). The domains are the whole university and the sports team (3) and the team is being talked about as if it were somehow a representative of the whole university, therefore the domain is the university and everything associated with it (4). The fact that 'the university' is referred to, and not just the name of the team means that it is a WHOLE FOR PART metonymy.

6.3 Further challenges in metonymy identification

We have just seen that one potential problem in metonymy identification is the fact that metonymy, like metaphor, often operates at the level of the phrase rather than at the level of the word, and that it is sometimes very difficult to see where the metonymic phrase begins and ends. There are at least two other problems inherent in metonymy identification in text. These are the role played by metonymy in language change, and the fact that it is often very difficult to distinguish between metonymy and other figures of speech, such as metaphor. Not only is it sometimes very difficult to work out whether a particular phrase or utterance is metonymic or metaphorical, sometimes metaphor and metonymy work together in the phrase (alongside other tropes) and each contributes to the overall meaning in its own way. Both of these issues make it very difficult to delimit metonymy. In the following sections, I look at the role played by metonymy in language change and at its interaction with metaphor, and discuss the difficulties that both of these present to successful metonymy identification in linguistic data.

The role played by metonymy in language change

It is well established that metonymy plays an important role in language change and that it therefore has a diachronic as well as a synchronic aspect. This presents the analyst with a problem when it comes to identifying it in text. If metonymy has been the motivating force behind the development of meaning then when do we draw the line deciding whether it still is metonymy or not?

There is a significant body of work on the role of metonymy in grammar and language change. For example, Bartsch (2002) shows how the word 'noise' has been metonymically extended to refer to 'interference', and the word 'mother' has been metonymically extended to refer to typical 'mothering-type' behaviour. Essentially, metonymic relationships play an integral role in shaping grammatical meaning even though by and large, through processes of conventionalisation, the metonymies become hidden and do not need to be accessed upon interpretation. Taylor (2002, 2003) explains this phenomenon in terms of 'category extension'. According to this approach, words have prototypical meanings which generally relate to concrete experience. They then acquire more abstract meanings via the processes of metonymy and metaphor. Of the two processes, metonymy is the more pervasive. For example, Taylor (2003: 129) shows how the French word 'chasser' has an original meaning of 'to pursue an animal with the aim of catching/killing it'. The second, more recent, sense of this word ('to chase someone away') throws into perspective the common knowledge that if we pursue an animal, it will run away. According to Taylor, there is a metonymic relationship between these two meanings because we can establish a mental connection between them in the given ICM of the hunt. For the metonymy analyst this presents a problem as metonymy has been involved in the development of this word's meaning, but it is very difficult to say whether or not it is still present as both senses of the word can be considered 'basic', and the fact that one is historically older is neither here nor there when it comes to language use. This reflects the underlying fact that metonymy is best described as a process rather than as a static phenomenon that can be identified with certainty.

A form of grammatical change that has a particularly strong association with metonymy is noun–verb conversion, where for example the noun 'eye' becomes the verb 'eyeing' in the following expression:

Thank you very much, Maggie thought bleakly, *eyeing* him with even greater suspicion. (BNC)

Here, the fact that 'eyeing' means 'looking at' involves an OBJECT FOR ACTION metonymic relationship. Dirven (1999) argues that in English, the metonymic relationships that are involved in noun–verb conversion in English can be explained by three different types of schema: the 'action' schema, the 'location' schema and the 'essive' schema.

'Action' schemas involve OBJECT FOR ACTION metonymies that focus on the object, such as:

A yacht *crewed* by a man and three laughing women careered dangerously close to the shore.
Hong Kong's people wonder why the Vietnamese are *housed* and *clothed*, while illegal immigrants from China are sent packing. (BNC)

They also involve INSTRUMENT/MANNER FOR ACTION metonymies, such as:

about 10,000 Dall's porpoise were *harpooned* each year. (BNC)

I *spooned* a gob of whipped cream over my gooseberry pie. (BNC)

'Location' schemas involve PLACE FOR ACTION metonymies, such as:

It is often *bottled* and sold as mineral water. (BNC)

Finally, 'essive' schemas involve STATUS FOR ACTION metonymies, such as:

Dhani put him in a Buddhist monastery and *nursed* him back to health. (BNC)

Some of these metonymies are so conventional that many analysts might prefer to label them as literal. It is difficult for the analyst to draw the line in these cases. As has been observed for metaphor, metonymy can exist at different levels of analysis, and a metonymy that is 'dead' in the text or in the language as a whole may or may not be dead in the mind of the beholder. Like metaphors, metonymies can be 'dead', 'alive', 'sleeping' or 'waking' for different interlocutors in different contexts of use (Müller, 2008).

INSTRUMENT FOR ACTION metonymic relationships appear to be particularly productive in English, which means that we still find relatively novel uses, such as the following, which were found by Littlemore and Tagg (in preparation) in a corpus of text messages:

R u driving or *training*? (CorTxt)

Hope red dress is *wowing* at wedding. (CorTxt)

Here the words *training* and *wowing* are motivated by INSTRUMENT FOR ACTION and EFFECT FOR CAUSE metonymic relationships.

A further role played by metonymy in language change involves 'grammaticalization'. This is the process whereby 'lexical' or 'content' words acquire a grammatical meaning over time and, in some cases, start to lose their content meaning. It is thought to be one of the principal processes underlying language change (Hopper and Traugott, 1993) and is uni-directional (i.e. 'content' words tend to become 'grammatical' words, but not the other way round). Three different theories have been proposed to explain grammaticalisation (see Evans and Green, 2006). These are 'metaphorical extension', 'invited inferencing theory' and the 'subjectification approach'. Of these three, the latter two invoke metonymy, as they involve changes in perspective and internalisation.

Invited inferencing theory (Traugott and Dasher, 2002) emphasises the usage-based nature of language change. An invited inference is one that is suggested by the context, based on the hearer's world knowledge, their own point of view and their own set of expectations about what they think the speaker is likely to be telling them. Let us look, for example, at three citations form the Bank of English which contain the word *since*:

We haven't touched it *since* we moved to the house. (BofE)

We are a lot better off financially *since* we slimmed. (BofE)

No one should be surprised that children develop bad habits *since* we all have one or two ourselves. (BofE)

The first of these citations has a clear temporal meaning, the third has a causal meaning and the second arguably has both meanings. The temporal meaning of 'since' pre-dates the causal meaning, and Traugott and Dasher (2002) argue that the meaning change came about because the temporal meaning, in certain contexts, 'invites' a causal interpretation. Over time, this interpretation has become part of the meaning of 'since', giving the word a degree of polysemy. Because the two meanings are linked conceptually, one can argue that the meaning change has a metonymic basis.

The *subjectification approach* (Langacker, 1999) sees meaning change as being motivated by changes in perspective. We can see this in the two citations containing the string 'down the road':

There were monkeys holding hands walking *down the road*. (BofE)

Joe Schmoe *down the road* might start drinking too much. (BofE)

In the first of these examples, *down the road* is literal and involves movement as the monkeys are *walking down the road*. The second refers to the place that one would get to if one walked down the road, but no walking is involved, so 'down' becomes more grammatical and simply operates as a marker of location. The focus is on the end point of the journey. Thus the focus changes and begins to incorporate the subjective viewpoint of the listener. This involves a metonymic shift of meaning within the 'perception' ICM.

It is not always easy to distinguish between the two approaches, as we can see in the following two citations containing 'must' from the Bank of English:

The state *must* take steps to save the fish. (BofE)

Some woman *must* be harbouring him. (BofE)

The deontic meaning in the first citation of 'must' involves direct obligation whereas the epistemic meaning in the second citation is more along the lines of 'it must be the case that'. This meaning also contains a degree of obligation and appears to be a case of category extension. However, the meaning is also internal to the hearer and focuses on the end point of the 'must' relationship, so we can see evidence of both the invited inferencing theory and subjectification in this example. Regardless of which theory one uses to explain the process, we can see that there is a metonymic relationship between the two meanings involving the 'perception' ICM, but it would be very difficult for the analyst to identify every instance of this type of metonymy as it is largely a historical phenomenon.

We see the same process at work in other cases where modal verbs have taken on particular meanings that are different from their core deontic or epistemic meanings. In her analysis of written academic feedback that undergraduate students receive on their essays, Lee (2013) notes that the expression 'can be' is used as a hedge as in expressions such as:

It *can be* a little difficult to understand.
Your style of writing *can be* rather colloquial. (Lee, 2013: 268)

These uses of 'can be' highlight one aspect of the epistemic meaning of 'can', namely that it is 'sometimes the case'. This use of 'can' involves a POTENTIAL FOR ACTUAL metonymic relationship.

The role played by metonymy in grammar and language change also becomes apparent when we look at sign language. For example, Sutton-Spence and Coates (2011) point out that the British Sign Language (BSL) sign for Preston North End football club in the UK involves miming the wearing of a pair of glasses. This sign refers (via a SALIENT PROPERTY FOR CATEGORY metonymic relationship) to the fact that in 1922 goalkeeper J. F. Mitchell became the first and last player to wear glasses in an FA Cup Final. This shows how metonymic vehicles can involve historical facts which for most people are long-forgotten, and which are not particularly salient for the individuals using the language. This is an example of metonymic chaining where the glasses metonymically represent the goal keeper and the goal keeper metonymically represents the club as a whole. Again, we encounter the difficult question of where to draw the line between metonymy and 'literal' language.

The interaction and overlap between metonymy and metaphor

A further difficulty inherent in metonymy identification is that it frequently co-occurs with and overlaps with metaphor, and it can be difficult to separate out the metonymy component in these cases (Kövecses, 2013). For example, in the following sentence both Washington and Tehran could be viewed as metonymies for the politicians who work in those places, or they could be seen as personification metaphors, in which Washington and Tehran take on human characteristics:

Noting that *Washington* is willing to improve relations with *Tehran*. (BNC)

A similar problem of overlap can be found in the following sentence, where 'get hot under the collar' means to get stressed and angry:

The crippled businessman is beginning to *get hot under the collar* as his jealousy deepens. (BofE)

This expression can be viewed as an example of an EFFECT FOR CAUSE metonymy, in that a particular symptom (getting hot under the collar) refers back to its cause (getting stressed and angry). However, usually when the expression is used, there is no real suggestion that the person is actually getting hot under the collar, and in this case it is perhaps more accurately described as a 'metaphor from metonymy' (Goossens, 1990), a phenomenon which is discussed in more detail below. Equally, although the 'pencil in' example that we saw in Chapter 1 involves metonymy, in many cases, such as the following, there is not necessarily an actual diary or pencil involved:

They have *pencilled in* talks with Richards on Tuesday. (BofE)

In this example, 'pencilled in' refers to a provisional arrangement in a hypothetical diary, and, as we will see below, might thus be said to be a 'metaphor from metonymy' (Goossens, 1990, 2003). At times it will be unclear whether or not a real diary and pencil were actually involved, and in some such cases it is difficult to tell whether we are dealing with metonymy or metaphor, or both. The same could be said for the term 'handbagging' (which was mentioned in the introduction) as it appears in the following example:

Reagan got a *handbagging* over US action in Grenada. (Webcorp)

It is extremely unlikely that Ronald Reagan, the US President, was, in fact, struck with a handbag in this case, so the expression must be metaphorical, but it does have a metonymic basis so it could be labelled as containing both metaphor and metonymy. These examples underscore the difficulties encountered when metonymy shades into metaphor.

Metaphor and metonymy are intrinsically 'slippery' concepts, as are the criteria that are used to distinguish between them. Various researchers (e.g. Dirven, 2003;

Radden, 2000) have proposed continua ranging from the purely literal, through metonymy, to metaphor. Croft and Cruse (2004: 220) also give examples that suggest intermediate possibilities between metaphor and metonymy, while also warning that what may appear to be intermediacy may be the result of combining distinctly different processes. Thus, in principle, an expression can never be said to be metaphorical or metonymic in any absolute sense, but only for a given user in a given context. The slipperiness of the metaphor/metonymy distinction has been studied in depth by Barnden (2010). He looks at the two main grounds for differentiation: the idea that metaphor involves similarity while metonymy involves contiguity, and the idea that in metonymy links to the source domain are preserved while in metaphor they are not. He then looks at cases of metaphor and metonymy where these 'rules' appear to be broken. He begins by challenging the notion that metaphor relies solely on similarity, pointing out how many 'primary metaphors', such as KNOWING IS SEEING or MORE IS UP (Grady, 1997) are in fact based on real-life experiential correlations which are essentially contiguous in nature. In other words, when we are first learning our language and its metaphors, KNOWING regularly involves SEEING, and MORE regularly involves an 'upward increase'. The relationship between the source and target domain therefore involves contiguity rather than comparison and is perhaps better described as 'metonymy'. Primary metaphors are thought to underlie whole hosts of conceptual metaphors, so if they are essentially metonymic in nature then this also applies to the conceptual metaphors that they underlie. Barnden goes on to point out that when someone is feeling down, they may not actually be bent over or drooping but that we could perhaps imagine them to be in this state and this hypothetical reasoning could form part of our understanding of the metaphor. Thus we have to acknowledge that some metonymic processing is at least potentially involved in the comprehension of metaphors such as these. As he puts it, 'contiguity is in the eye of the beholder' (Barnden 2010: 10).

In addition to demonstrating how some metaphors can involve contiguity, Barnden also shows how some 'metonymies' can involve similarity. An example that he uses here is that of the name of a country, such as the USA to refer metonymically to a sports team that is representing the USA. He points out that the similarity derives from the fact that they only make sense within the context of a sports competition in which different teams play one another. There is therefore a one-to-one correspondence between the country and its team, and a structural analogy is set up within which competitive relationships between the teams correspond to competitive relationships between the countries. He argues that when seen in context, many metonymies in fact involve structural similarities between the source and target domain and can thus be viewed as metaphor.

Another criterion for distinguishing between metaphor and metonymy that Barnden finds problematic is the idea of 'link survival'. It has been suggested that in metonymy the 'literal' meaning of the vehicle term is still very much part of the final meaning of the metonymy whereas in metaphor it is not. So, for example, we might contrast the following metaphor and metonymy, both of which involve the idea of a 'mouth':

Father and I fished at the *mouth* of the river. (BNC)

He held out his arms and *mouthed* a farewell. (BNC)

In the first (metaphorical) expression, there is no actual mouth present, it is simply that the river opens into the sea, like a mouth, whereas in the second (metonymic) expression, the actual mouth is still very much present in the comprehension process as it is involved in the speaking, or in the imitation of speaking. Barnden finds this distinction problematic, citing the example of the metaphor 'army ant'. Here the ants do exhibit the behaviour of real armies although they are not real armies as such. Reference to the behaviour of a real army is an important part of the comprehension process, particularly the first time one comes across the expression. Therefore the link survives in this metaphor, which makes it difficult to distinguish from a metonymy.

One conclusion that Barnden reaches is that it may be possible to distinguish between metaphor and metonymy on the basis of *the use that one makes* of the links between the source and target domain, an approach which de-emphasises any intrinsic links that may exist between them. He concludes that rather than asking whether a particular expression is intrinsically metaphorical or metonymic, it is more useful to ask questions such as: what type of similarity does it involve, if any? What sort of contiguity does it involve, if any? Does it involve link survival? And is hypothetical reasoning involved? This approach to the study of metaphor and metonymy is much more refined than previous approaches, and provides a promising line of investigation. It could be refined even further if two further factors were included. These are the nature of metonymy as a radial category (as discussed in Chapter 3) and the fact that, in language at least, there are clues in the text or intonation that often indicate whether or not a particular expression should be understood as metaphor or metonymy.

At times, the distinction between metaphor and metonymy is left deliberately ambiguous, as we can see from the extract below from the novel *Goodnight Mr Tom*, by Michelle Magorian. At this point in the novel, Mr Tom is remembering the birth of his child, who died of scarlatina soon after being born along with his mother, Rachel, Mr Tom's wife. Rachel had been fond of painting:

> 'Ent he beautiful', she had whispered and he had nodded and watched helplessly as the familiar colour of scarlatina had spread across both their faces.
>
> 'Yous'll have to git blue' she had whispered to him, for during her pregnancy he had bought her a new pot of paint for each month of her being with child. The ninth was to be blue if she had given birth to a boy, primrose yellow if it had been a girl.
>
> After they had died he had bought the pot of blue paint and placed it in the black wooden box that he had made for her one Christmas, when he was eighteen. As he closed

the lid, so he had shut out not only the memory of her but also the company of anyone else that reminded him of her.

He glanced down at Will, who had become suddenly quiet. He gave a start and opened his eyes. His lips had turned blue. (Magorian, 1983: 230)

In this extract, the blue paint metonymically represents both the baby boy (as boys are invariably given blue clothes, blue bedrooms, and so on) and Tom's wife, Rachel (as it reminds him of her love of painting). The fact that the paint is now locked in a box is a metaphor for the fact that Tom's feelings are now 'locked away' and hidden from the outside world. However, if we consider some of the discussion above, we can see that the source domain is still very much present (the pot of blue paint is still in the box), so this metaphor might be said to contain shades of metonymy. The literal references to the colours red and blue at the beginning and end of the passage ('the familiar colour of scarlatina' and 'his lips had turned blue') strengthen the dramatic effect of the metonymic and metaphorical references to red and blue. This felicitous combination of metaphor, metonymy and literal meaning, and the fact that it is easy to slip between them, contributes to the overall effectiveness of the passage.

Goossens (1990, 2003) has identified four main ways in which metaphor and metonymy interact, and refers to the overall process as 'metaphtonymy'. The first way in which they interact involves *metaphor from metonymy* in which the experiential basis of metaphor is in fact metonymy. The 'hot under the collar' and 'pencilled in' examples mentioned above are what would be described as 'metaphor from metonymy' as they begin life as metonymy and then develop into metaphor in certain contexts. The second way in which they interact involves *metonymy within metaphor*. This occurs when a metonymy functioning in the target domain is embedded within a metaphor. For example, in the expression 'she caught his eye and laughed' (BNC), 'his eye' refers metonymically to the fact that they exchanged glances, but the catching implies a conduit metaphor. Deignan (2005a) points out that *metaphor from metonymy* can lead to ambiguous utterances. For example, when we talk of 'pencilling something in', it could be the case that we have literally taken out a pencil and noted something in our diaries, or it simply might be the case that we have made a loose arrangement. With *metonymy within metaphor* there is no such ambiguity. In the above example it could not be the case that the woman literally 'caught' the man's eye.

The third way in which they interact (which Goossens admits is very rare) involves *demetonymisation within metaphor*. The example that he gives of this is 'paying lip service', as in:

Previous governments have *paid lip service* to the idea but achieved little. (BNC)

At first sight, this expression appears to involve a PART FOR WHOLE metonymy, where the lips stand for speaking, but the expression is only ever used in abstract senses and is therefore always a metaphor. In this metaphor, there is no PART FOR WHOLE metonymy as there is no actual speaking. The expression therefore loses its apparent metonymic element.

The fourth way in which metaphor and metonymy interact (also rare) involves *metaphor within metonymy.* The example that he uses to illustrate this relationship is 'get up on one's hind legs', as in:

David Sprott who wasn't afraid to *get up on his hind legs* at a social gathering and talk, seriously and at length, about teeth. (BNC)

This expression, which means to 'get up and say something in public', is essentially a metonymy, but it relies on the metaphorical construal of a human being as an animal.

Researchers working with Goossens' model have since revealed greater complexity. For example, Wojciechowska and Szczepaniak (2013) looked at idiomatic expressions containing the word HAND whose motivation consists of metonymy mixed with metaphor. They identified different types of metaphor–metonymy interaction in the various expressions and found evidence for all four types of 'metaphtonymy' that were distinguished by Goossens (1990, 2003). However, their data demonstrates more intricate patterns where cumulative and integrated metaphtonymies are combined. They found that the nature of the interplay varies according to whether or not the idioms are in their canonical form, which indicates the importance of phraseology in metonymy analysis. Their findings reflect Geeraerts' (2003) claim that 'metaphtonymy' is part of a more inclusive model, which allows for other ways in which metaphor and metonymy interact, including, for example, successions of metonymies followed by metaphors, metaphors followed by metonymies, and metonymies followed by metonymies. Geeraerts' model provides a more comprehensive description of the semantics of composite expressions such as idioms and compounds.

Many of the problems concerning the close relationship between metonymy and metaphor also apply to its identification in other modes of expression. We saw in Chapter 5 that a number of the metonymies identified in advertising, art, film and music shade into metaphor in much the same way as they do in language. Metaphor and metonymy have been found to interact in complex ways in advertising (Pérez-Sobrino, 2011, 2013a) and sign language (Kaneko and Sutton-Spence, 2012; Taub, 2004), and it is often very difficult to extricate one from the other. Moreover, in art, sign language, poetry and dance it is possible for many metonymies to be used simultaneously, and they interact in ways that are somewhat different from language.

In her study of multimodal advertisements, Pérez-Sobrino (2011, 2013a) discusses the term 'Greenwashing', which is a compound word involving the ideas of 'whitewashing' and 'being green'. This is a form of advertising which actively promotes the (often artificial) perception that a company's policies or products are environmentally friendly. She looks at two advertisements in which the metaphor PRODUCT X IS A GREEN PRODUCT interacts with the metonymic complex GREEN FOR NATURE FOR NATURE-FRIENDLY PRODUCT to misleadingly convey a positive image of the product.

The first advertisement is for Saab cars. This advertisement features the following text, accompanied by a picture of a red Saab:

Grrrrreen.
Every Saab is green. Carbon emissions are neutral across the entire Saab range.

Pérez-Sobrino also points out that the fact that the Saab in the picture is actually red combined with the fact that the word Grrrrreen resembles the roaring of a lion lends the advertisement a degree of irony, ensuring that it also appeals to drivers who like high-performance cars and may not have much sympathy with the 'green' movement. She argues that a full understanding of this advertisement involves a conceptual blending process, in which the boundaries of metaphor and metonymy are blurred.

The second advertisement is for Otis, a company that makes lifts, escalators and moving walkways. Here, the text is:

OTIS
THE WAY TO GREEN™

The word 'green' is written in green in this advertisement, and the text is accompanied by the image of several dots building up in number from left to right and changing colour from blue to green as they do so. In this advertisement, the metonymy GREEN FOR NATURE FOR NATURE-FRIENDLY PRODUCT is combined with the metaphors MORE IS UP, GOOD IS UP and CHANGE IS FORWARD MOTION. Again, the advertisement relies on the reader's ability to blend these metaphors and metonymies in order to reach a full understanding of the advertisement. It is very difficult to tease the metaphor and metonymy apart in these advertisements and to do so would diminish their rich meanings.

Also problematic for the identification of metonymy in other forms of expression is the fine line that exists in some cases between metonymy and more 'literal' forms of expression. If we are to see metonymy as a reference point phenomenon as Langacker does, then in a film every camera angle is a metonymy of one kind or another. The problem is that it is impossible to film something without having a camera angle, which makes metonymy synonymous with perspective. Finally, in art, as with language, it is not always easy to see where a particular instance of metonymy begins and ends. We saw this in some of the artworks that were discussed in Chapter 5. A possible way round these problems is to focus on creative or marked forms of metonymy in other forms of expression, insofar as this is possible, in much the same way as with language.

6.4 The automatic identification and interpretation of metonymy in language

It would be very useful if metonymy could be detected automatically in text. Researchers working in artificial intelligence (AI) have shown that the automatic detection and interpretation of metonymy by computers considerably enhances human–computer interaction. For example, when Stallard (1993) incorporated metonymy resolution into an automated question-answering system about airline reservations, he noted a 27% improvement in performance. Equally, Kamei and Wakao (1992) show how an ability to deal with metonymy resolution is essential for the successful functioning of machine translation systems. Traditionally, techniques for the automatic detection of metonymy in language have relied on 'selectional restriction violations' and 'coercion' (see, for example, Fass, 1991, 1997; Harabagiu, 1998). 'Selectional restriction' refers to the fact that certain verbs can only be used 'literally' with certain types of nouns. For example, the verb 'reading' tends to be used with nouns such as 'book', 'magazine', 'newspapers' and places where one would find printed text. When one encounters the sentence 'I stayed there all summer reading Shakespeare' the selectional restriction of the verb 'reading' is violated, as 'Shakespeare' is not strictly speaking a text, so the meaning of 'Shakespeare' is 'coerced' via a process of metonymic reasoning into meaning 'plays written by Shakespeare'. Automatic detection systems use this information in combination with huge datasets, such as 'Wordnet' (Fellbaum, 1998), which contain vast amounts of information about words and the types of concepts they tend to be associated with, in order to identify potential cases of metonymy.

This approach to the automatic detection of metonymy has been criticised by Markert and Hahn (2002), who argue that metonymy need not always involve selectional restriction violations. For example, they show how, in the BNC example 'I don't really like Shakespeare', metonymy can occur without there being a mismatch between the noun and the verb (it is perfectly possible to 'like' a person as well as an object), but in this example the 'liking' refers to plays written by Shakespeare, rather than to the man himself. Moreover, they argue that traditional approaches to automatic metonymy resolution only operate within the sentence and do not take sufficient account of intersentential information. They propose an alternative algorithm for automatic metonymy resolution in text, which draws together information from five different sources. The first of these is world knowledge (i.e. knowledge concerning the 'typical' relationships between entities that are likely to give rise to metonymies). The second is intrasentential semantic constraints of the type discussed above, but only where these are relevant. The third is 'discourse embedding', which includes intersentential information, such as anaphoric reference. The fourth is 'schematization', which refers to the preponderance of certain types of metonymy-producing relationships, such as those discussed in Chapter 2. The fifth is 'aptness', which refers to the principles involved in vehicle selection, which were also discussed in Chapter 2. They do not include morphosyntactic evidence (such as the fact that in English, PRODUCER FOR PRODUCT metonymies tend to be preceded by the definite article) or language-specific lexical idiosyncrasies (for example, the fact that the animal for meat schema does not apply to pigs in English as we have the word 'pork'). The reason for not including these types of information is that they wish their model to be non-language-specific, though of course it could be adapted to include this sort of information if necessary. When they used their algorithm to identify metonymy in a corpus of computer science texts, they found that it was capable of identifying 15 per cent more metonymies than previous techniques. Of the 622 sentences in their corpus, 106 contained metonymy, which means that if metonymy had not been taken into account, 17 per cent would have been incorrectly interpreted. These findings underscore the importance of a robust metonymy detection and interpretation procedure in automatic text comprehension software.

Automatic metonymy identification procedures, such as those described above, have been found to improve the level of accurate comprehension by machines in texts outside the field of computer science. For example, Leveling and Hartrumpf (2008) showed how computers were able to retrieve much more accurate information from geography texts if they used an automatic detection procedure for metonymically used place names. However, current automatic detection procedures are still not perfect, with Markert and Nissim (2009a and 2009b) reporting that the data they produce tends to be skewed towards frequent metonymy types, with rarer metonymy types tending to be overlooked. Systems for the automatic detection and resolution of metonymy have tended to focus on nouns, and as we have seen in previous chapters many metonymies involve other parts of speech besides nouns. It would therefore be worth exploring other parts of speech, as well as drawing on other findings from linguistics.

6.5 Possible avenues to explore in the automatic identification of metonymy

Although substantial progress has already been made in the field of computer science in the automatic detection of metonymy by computers, other more recent insights from linguistics may also be of benefit. It could be useful to look at the way it is signalled (if it is), the changes in spelling and word classes that are typically associated with it, the types of phraseological patterning that tend to accompany it, and the types of genres and registers in which it is normally found. The following sections explore the work that has been done in these areas and assess whether it has the potential to contribute to the automatic identification of metonymy.

Signalling

One possible way of using linguistic information to help with the automatic identification of metonymy might be to pay attention to the ways in which it tends to be signalled in texts. Two influential studies have identified the use of particular signals for metaphor in spoken discourse. Cameron and Deignan (2003) found a number of signalling devices – such as 'just', 'like' and 'sort of' – that are used to indicate metaphor in spoken discourse. They use the term 'tuning devices' to label these devices as this reflects their interactional nature and focuses on their function, which is to alert the hearer to a possible problem in interpretation and to suggest that a metaphorical meaning is intended (2003: 150). Tay (2011) observed a strong co-occurrence of discourse markers such as 'you know', 'and' and 'right' and the use of extended metaphors in his corpus of psychotherapeutic consultations.

At first sight, this appears to offer a promising avenue for metonymy identification. However, on closer inspection, it turns out not to be as productive as one might hope. The following utterance is taken from a recording of an academic working in the International Development Department at a British university when explaining two management models to a student in that department, who is from Kazakhstan:

The government of Britain is *sort of* there but if you were in a kind of economic task force. (author's own data)

As she utters these words, the lecturer points to a diagram containing four quadrants, each of which represents a different style of management. By pointing to a particular part of the model, she is telling the student that the Government of Britain has a particular style of management, represented by that quadrant. This involves metonymic relationships between the place in the diagram and the style of management that it represents, and between the actual government and its 'place' in the diagram. At first sight, we may conclude that 'sort of' may be a good candidate for signalling device indicating metonymy in this conversation. However, when we look at the lecturer's use of 'sort of' in the entire conversation, we realise that it is used to indicate many other things besides metonymy:

1. The government of Britain is *sort of* there but if you were in a kind of economic task force
2. The *sort of* performance management kind of goal oriented type of organisation
3. But em painted in a *sort of* Kazakh way rather than a Chinese way
4. beautiful little dishes, they were *sort of* er almost like Chinese balls Ma but
5. So these are *sort of* opposites, right?
6. Figure out what is happening here, what *sort of* culture it has

7. Think about what *sort of* organisation you might be wanting to work for
8. We can think of open systems, the *sort of* organisation usually small ones where

The first two uses of 'sort of' in this list are indeed used to signal metonymy. However, in citations three to five, it is used to indicate vagueness and in citations seven and eight it is used to indicate a 'type of'. It is not simply used to signal metonymy. However, these findings are interesting nonetheless. We have already discussed the relationship between metonymy and both vagueness and part–whole relationships in previous chapters, so the use of 'sort of' here appears to be indicating some sort of radial category that includes metonymy along with the semantic and pragmatic meanings with which it is often associated. However, it is insufficiently refined to serve as an indicator of 'pure' metonymy. It could be that the search term simply needs to be more specific than this and that the corpus search needs to be more refined. The first instance of metonymy in this list is signalled by the string: 'is sort of'. Could it perhaps be the case that the string 'is sort of' might be more indicative of metonymy? Unfortunately, a British National Corpus (BNC) search for this string reveals that this is not the case. Of the first fifty lines to appear in a search for 'is+sort+of', only three contain metonymy. This example suggests that this particular signalling device is by no means unique to metonymy. On the other hand, we can see in the eight instances above that the cluster of functions served by the string 'sort of' do seem to be related to one another in some sort of radial category, a fact which has the potential to be exploited in future, perhaps in combination with other features, for the automatic detection of metonymy or related linguistic features.

It could be that there are other signalling devices that are better predictors of metonymy. These could be verbal devices or they could involve gesture and intonation. It would be interesting to investigate whether this is indeed the case. Or it could simply be that metonymy does not tend to be signalled as much as metaphor. This could well be the case. As we will see in Chapter 7, from a psycholinguistic processing point of view, metonymy is closer to literal language than metaphor is, and it could well be that speakers are simply not generally aware of the fact that they are using metonymy. This would not be surprising as, unlike metaphor, metonymy is rarely studied in schools and many people do not know what it is.

Formal features of metonymy

A more promising way of identifying metonymy might be to focus on its formal features. An analyst using this approach would need to identify ways in which the grammatical patterns surrounding metonymy differ from those that accompany 'literal' language and other types of language such as metaphor. It has already been observed that when words are used metaphorically or metonymically there is often some sort of change in terms of their formal features, marking their figurative usage as being different from their meaning in literal contexts (Deignan, 2005a, 2005b). These can take the form of changes in spelling, word class, grammatical patterning and phraseology. It would also be useful to invoke findings from construction grammar (Goldberg, 2006). These features could usefully be explored, and possibly exploited, in the search for a robust method of metonymy identification.

Let us start by looking at the role of spelling. Barnbrook *et al.* (2013) found interesting differences in the meaning of 'blonde' and 'blond' in the British tabloid press. They found that when the word 'blonde' was employed it was used to refer metonymically to a woman with blond hair, whereas when the word 'blond' was used it was more likely to be an adjective. Thus in British English (at least in this register), the word 'blonde' with its original spelling (carrying over the feminine ending from French) appears to have metonymically narrowed its meaning via a TRAIT FOR PERSON relationship, to 'a woman with blond hair' and the word 'blond' with the American spelling has been imported to fill the semantic gap that has been left behind. Thus in order to conduct a corpus search for metonymic uses of the word 'blonde' in the British tabloid press, one would need to focus on the older spelling.

We saw some examples of changes in word class that are associated with metonymy in Chapter 1. For instance, 'pencil' is never used as a verb, except when it has a metonymic meaning of 'to pencil [something] in'; 'muscle' is not usually an uncountable phenomenon when talked about in the context of a living human being, outside the field of medical discourse; 'brains' are usually singular, not plural; 'handbags' do not usually appear in the gerund or 'verbal noun' form (and gerunds themselves are rarely countable in the way that 'handbagging' is); and 'suits' are not normally given agency.

As we can see in many of these examples, a grammatical change that has a particularly strong association with metonymy is that of 'conversion' leading to denominal verbs (Dirven, 1999). Denominal verbs can also be extended via a metonymic chaining process to develop 'verbal nouns' (Quirk *et al.*, 1985) or 'ing' nouns (*Collins COBUILD English Grammar*, 2011), such as the expression 'a good handbagging', which we saw in the introduction. Verbal nouns (which often involve metonymy) tend to be used uncountably, although the words in the pattern would in themselves usually be countable or singular. Thus something that is normally construed as being countable (e.g. a handbag) becomes part of an uncountable phenomenon when it is used in this construction.

Denominal verbs are also found in Japanese, where they are particularly closely associated with borrowings from other languages. Tsujimora and Davis (2011) identified a small subset of so-called 'innovative verbs'. These are denominal verbs that have been derived from borrowing of nouns from other languages and used creatively in Japanese to mean something slightly different from what they mean in their original languages. Although Tsujimora and Davis do not focus on metonymy in their study, it is clear that in many cases the derivational processes involve metonymy, as we can see in the following examples, many of which are taken from English:

Tero-ru	'commit an act of terrorism'
kae-ru	'go to a café'
memo-ru	'take notes'
biri-ru	'play billiards'
jazu-ru	'play jazz'
maka-ru	'go to McDonald's' ('Makudonarudo' is the Japanese transliteration of McDonald's)
sutaba-ru	'go to Starbucks'
kaheore-ru	'have a coffee stain on one's clothes' ('kaheore' is the Japanese transliteration of 'café au lait')
rizo-ru	'hunt for a man at a resort hotel by playing marine sports and the like' ('Rizooto hoteru' is the Japanese transliteration of 'resort hotel')
egawa-ru	'display selfish conduct' (Egawa is a former pitcher in the Tokyo Giants baseball team)

From Tsujimora and Davis (2011: 800)

Tsujimora and Davis make a convincing case for the idea that innovative verbs such as these operate as a single linguistic 'construction'. As we saw in Chapter 2, a construction is a grammar pattern whose meaning is not predictable from its component parts (Goldberg, 2006: 5). Tsujimora and Davis contend that innovative verbs meet these criteria as they all share the same set of properties. Firstly, they tend to undergo a 'clipping' or shortening of the base nouns, and when they do, the resulting verbal root must be at least two syllables long, although in Japanese language in general, there are plenty of verbs whose root is only one syllable. Secondly, they all take the same conjugation pattern, in that they all end in 'ru' rather than the other, more formal verb ending in Japanese, 'masu', and in the past tense they all end in 'tta' rather than the more usual 'ta'. Thirdly, they consistently display a particular accentuation pattern where the stress is on the final syllable of the root (for example, in the word 'jazu-ru', the stress is paced on the 'zu'). This marks them out as being different from other Japanese verbs. Fourthly, they have certain semantic and pragmatic features in common. They are particularly flexible semantically and their meaning can vary considerably from speaker to speaker, depending on factors such as discourse community membership and the age of the speaker. Pragmatically, these are all considered to be playful, informal uses of language, used by the young, and they often constitute an in-group code. Tsujimora and Davis argue that the cluster of properties displayed by innovative verbs suggests that they should be viewed as a 'construction' as defined by Goldberg (2006) as they constitute a 'form-meaning-function complex where phonological, morphological, semantic, and pragmatic information is encoded as a collective property' (Tsujimora and Davis, 2011: 801).

Another grammatical feature that accompanies some types of metonymy, and that might also be considered to be a construction, is 'predicate transfer'. Here, a particular property is reassigned to an object that would not normally have that property. We saw an example of this in Chapter 3, in the expression 'I am parked out back' (Nunberg, 1995). A person cannot normally be parked, but via a series of metonymic links, the sentence makes sense as we naturally understand that it is actually the person's car that is parked out back, not the person him/herself. Predicate transfer makes it possible for one to say 'I am parked out back' without implying that one has become a car or something that can be parked. It also allows for a sensible interpretation of the utterance 'we are parked out back', and for this to refer to a single car, for example in cases where the speakers travelled together.

One could look at construction grammar the other way round and identify metonymy in some of the classic examples that have been proposed by Goldberg. As well as the very obvious role played by metonymy in Goldberg's well-known example 'He sneezed the napkin off the table' (Goldberg, 1995: 55), we can also find more subtle uses in some of the other widely cited examples of constructions, such as the genitive construction and the ditransitive construction. Although they were not looking at metonymy per se, Wolk *et al.*'s (2013) findings regarding the development of these two constructions are of interest here. They tracked the relative use of the genitive construction (labelled 'a' in the following pair) in comparison with a near synonymous construction (labelled 'b' in the following pair) over time from the seventeenth century to the present day:

a. John's friend (the genitive construction)
b. A friend of John.

Type (a) constructions have traditionally been more associated with animate objects, while the type (b) constructions have been more likely to occur with inanimate objects. Wolk *et al.* found that, since the seventeenth century, the relative frequency of type (a) constructions has grown over time while the relative frequency of type (b) constructions has decreased. Moreover, they found that type (a) constructions are increasingly being used with what might normally be seen as inanimate objects, such as companies, countries and machinery. So, for example, expressions such as 'Spain's Prime Minister' or 'IBM's marketing strategy' are much more common than they used to be.

Wolk *et al.* also tracked the relative use of the ditransitive construction (labelled 'a' in the following pair) in comparison with a near-synonymous construction (labelled 'b' in the following pair) over the same time period:

a. I sent Mum some flowers [the ditransitive constructive]
b. I sent some flowers to Mum.

Again, type (a) constructions tend to be more associated with animate objects, while the type (b) constructions are more likely to occur with inanimate objects. Wolk *et al.* found that the relative frequency of type (a) constructions has grown over time while the relative frequency of type (b) constructions has decreased, and that type (a) constructions are increasingly being used with what might normally be seen as inanimate objects. For example, expressions such as the following are much more common in English than they used to be:

It gave the house a Medieval feel. (BNC)

She [. . .] gave the table a cursory wipe. (BNC)

Oliver gave the table a puzzled look. (BNC)

In these examples, it could be said that inanimate objects are increasingly being viewed as being somehow 'animate' and that personification metaphors are on the increase in English. Alternatively, given the blurred boundary between metonymy and personification metaphor that was discussed above, it could also be said that there has been an increase in the metonymic use of inanimate objects to represent the behaviour of those objects or, in the case of organisations, the people who work for them. Therefore one way to begin the search for these particular types of metonymy might involve focusing on these constructions in language corpora.

We have seen in this section that different types of metonymy tend to occur in particular types of grammatical structures and/or constructions. This may well help the reader or listener to distinguish figurative senses from more literal ones and may play a role in identification processes. Future work could usefully identify further sets of constructions that are likely to signal particular types of metonymy. This work would have potential applications to automatic metonymy identification.

The role of genre and register

A final possible aid to the detection of metonymy is an awareness of the types of texts and contexts in which it is likely to be found. We saw in Chapter 4 that Deignan *et al.* (2013), after studying the use of figurative language in a range of contexts, found that certain combinations of genre and register features tended to lead to higher levels of metonymy use. They found metonymy to be particularly prevalent in the language that is used by tightly knit discourse communities, arguing that this is primarily because of its reliance on shared knowledge. They also observed that metonymy serves a slightly more prominent role in spoken discourse than in written discourse. Metonymy was more likely to be prevalent in situations where the communication was primarily concerned with people and entities located within a shared physical space, and where sequences of actions were constrained by time pressures. Examples included busy 'hands-on' workplaces and sporting events. This is arguably because metonymy serves the needs of rapid, efficient communication in shared physical settings where interlocutors are under time pressure, and where language plays an ancillary role to extra-linguistic activities. These findings correspond to Harrison's (forthcoming, 2015) identification of gestural metonymy in a fish-packing factory, where similar conditions prevailed (see Chapter 4). These findings indicate that researchers interested in identifying and exploring metonymy would do well to focus on spoken language employed by closely knit discourse communities in busy hands-on workplace settings. If machines are to successfully identify metonymy and the functions that it performs then they need to take genre and register into account.

6.6 Conclusion

In this chapter, we have explored some of the complex issues involved in the identification of metonymy. We have seen that the main barriers to the development of a reliable system of metonymy identification include the fact that metonymy does not really operate at the level of the word, the fact that metonymy is a diachronic as well as a synchronic phenomenon, and the fact that it can be difficult to extricate it from metaphor. The chapter then looked at the promising developments that have been made in the automatic detection of metonymy by computers and artificial intelligence systems and suggested other possible approaches that might facilitate this process. These included a more detailed consideration of formal features, such as spelling, word class, grammatical patterning and phraseology, and an increased consideration of the impact of genre and register. Of all the issues discussed in this book, the identification of metonymy has the greatest potential for development in the coming years due to the rapid advances that are being made in corpus linguistics and artificial intelligence. This is an area where interdisciplinary research could be particularly productive, and its findings could be of considerable benefit to metonymy researchers.

7 'I found Robbie Williams in the lounge'

How is metonymy processed in the mind?

7.1 Introduction

Throughout the preceding chapters, I have emphasised the fact that metonymy is as much a cognitive process as a linguistic one. In this chapter, I develop this theme, and explore work on metonymy that has been carried out in psycholinguistics and neurolinguistics. I begin by examining the cognitive processes that are thought to be involved in the comprehension and production of metonymy, and then consider evidence from eye-tracking studies and brain-scanning procedures that tells us where and how metonymy is processed in the brain. I then go on to investigate how metonymy comprehension and production develop in childhood in both typically developing individuals and individuals with linguistic impairments. In the final section of the chapter, I look at how metonymy is involved in the formation and expression of delusions by people with schizophrenia and related disorders, and explore the potential role that metonymy could play in psychotherapy in helping patients to recognise and come to terms with their delusions.

7.2 Psycholinguistic and neurological studies of metonymy comprehension

Psycholinguistic studies of metonymy comprehension have tended to focus on the question of how similar it is to the comprehension of literal language, the role of context in metonymy comprehension, and the effect of syntactic patterns on metonymy recognition and production. Research methods have included eye tracking, brain scanning, reaction-time studies, and straightforward metonymy comprehension tasks that have been administered to individuals from different age groups and in some cases with different types of linguistic impairments. In this section, I present and evaluate these studies and, in places, I suggest ways in which they might be adapted to take more account of authentic language data.

Research using eye-tracking software suggests that native speakers process conventional metonymy in much the same way as they do literal uses of language (Frisson and Pickering, 1999). That is to say they do not pause any longer when asked to read metonymic sentences than they do when reading literal sentences. As one might expect, when people are presented with a novel metonymy (e.g. 'the minister had an argument with the cottage') as opposed to a conventional metonymy (e.g. 'the minister had an argument with the embassy') they take longer to process the novel metonymy. Frisson and Pickering argue that, in these cases, the reader engages in a *sense creation* process as opposed to a *sense selection* process, and that this difference explains the difference in processing times.

In a later part of the study, where they compared PLACE FOR INSTITUTION metonymies (e.g. 'The traveller spoke to the consulate') with PLACE FOR EVENT metonymies (e.g. 'A lot of Americans protested during Vietnam'), they found that difficulties experienced by participants when interpreting unfamiliar PLACE FOR EVENT metonymies occurred later and lasted much longer. They inferred from this that the resolution of PLACE FOR EVENT metonymies requires the participant to search through a much larger amount of information, which is why it takes them much longer to find an explanation. In the PLACE FOR INSTITUTION metonymies, participants were able to decide more quickly whether or not the metonymy contained any meaning because they could identify the institution straight away.

Frisson and Pickering interpret their findings as a whole to indicate that in the moments before insufficient context is provided to allow the participant to decide whether a literal or a metonymic meaning is intended, the participant does not need to commit to any particular meaning, and the meaning of the item is therefore 'underspecified' at that point. That is to say, neither the metonymic nor the literal meaning of the item is intrinsically more 'accessible' than the other. The participant develops an underspecified, schematic idea of the word's meaning and then homes in on the appropriate (literal or metonymic) sense by activating relevant parts of the meaning as soon as sufficient contextual information has been provided. This account of metonymy processing is very much in line with work in cognitive linguistics which proposes that an ICM is accessed and then exploited in the search for meaning (see Chapter 2). Frisson and Pickering's findings were replicated for older adults by Humphrey *et al.* (2004), indicating that the ability to comprehend metonymy is not something which deteriorates with age. Frisson and Pickering's study and Humphrey's study are important as they appear to provide empirical support for the idea of underspecified meanings and ICMs. However, both studies focus only on metonymy at the word level and all of the examples of metonymy that were used involved nouns rather than other types of speech. As we saw in Chapter 6, metonymy often occurs at the level of the phrase rather than the word and it frequently occurs in parts of speech other than nouns. It would therefore be useful to apply similar analyses to longer stretches of metonymy and to other parts of speech.

Another way in which these studies could be made more relevant to real-world communication is to focus on the role of phraseology in the meaning-making process. Lowder and Gordon (2013) attempted to address this issue to some extent. They noted that the examples in Frisson and Pickering's study contained two different sentence types. In some cases, the metonymy is the direct object, as we can see in the following example:

The journalist offended *the college.*

In other cases, the metonymy appears in an adjunct phrase, which would change the above to the following example:

The journalist offended the honour of *the college.*

Lowder and Gordon argue that metonymies are likely to be more difficult to process when they appear as a direct object than when they appear in an adjunct phrase. The reason for this is that in an adjunct phrase, the person who is trying to comprehend the sentence is more likely to focus their attention on the information preceding the metonymy (i.e. the 'honour' in the above example) which means that they will spend less time trying to work out the meaning of the metonymy itself. When the metonymy appears as a direct object, it is arguably more salient, and the person comprehending the sentence will accord it more attention and thus process it more deeply. They based their hypothesis on previous studies showing that sentence structure guides the depth to which people process certain parts of a sentence, extrapolating their expectations to metonymy.

In order to test this hypothesis, they repeated Frisson and Pickering's experiment, but split the examples into those where the metonymy was a direct object and those where the metonymy appeared within an adjunct phrase. As predicted, they found that when the metonymy operated as a direct object of the verb, there was a clear and significant lasting processing difference between the familiar and unfamiliar PLACE FOR INSTITUTION metonymies. This difference was more significant when the metonymy was a direct object of the verb than when it appeared within an adjunct phrase.

One way to interpret Lowder and Gordon's findings is to use construction grammar. As we saw in Chapter 2, Goldberg (2006) has shown that constructions shape the meanings of the words that appear within them. This account might also explain Lowder and Gordon's findings. When a metonymy appears as an argument of a verb the construction itself may lead the reader to try to interpret it as if it had human characteristics. In other words, constructions such as the following are likely to lead a reader to seek an interpretation that involves some sort of personification of the word 'college':

The journalist offended *the college.*

When this personification is not possible, the reader may be troubled for longer. This is likely to be the case for the nonsensical 'novel' examples employed by Frisson and Pickering and by Lowder and Gordon's study, such as:

The journalist offended *the pyramid*.

According to usage-based approaches to language, readers of this sentence would generalise from their previous exposure to the construction and from their encyclopaedic knowledge of the word 'offended' to expect a human object in the final position. On the other hand, constructions involving an adjunct phrase are less likely to lead the reader to search for personification, as human objects rarely occur in such a position. Therefore the appearance of an anomalous metonymy in such a sentence would trouble them less, and they would spend less time trying to work it out. This constructionist account of Lowder and Gordon's findings is compatible with their own explanation, as constructions carry semantic and pragmatic meaning. It may therefore be useful to incorporate a construction grammar perspective more explicitly into psycholinguistic studies of metonymy.

Other researchers have used brain-imaging techniques to explore the ways in which metonymy is processed in the mind. The findings from these studies indicate that conventional metonymies appear to be processed in very much the same way as literal language, whereas novel metonymies are processed quite differently. For example, Rapp *et al.* (2011) used magnetic resonance imaging (fMRI) to investigate which parts of the brain are involved in metonymy comprehension, and to compare these with the findings for literal language. They scanned the brains of fourteen healthy participants while those participants were reading literal sentences (e.g. 'Africa is arid'), metonymic sentences (e.g. 'Africa is hungry') or nonsense sentences (e.g. 'African is woollen').

They found that the area of the brain that displays the strongest activation for metonymy (in comparison to literal language) is the left middle temporal gyrus. They report that, in previous studies, this part of the brain has been found to be responsible for semantic processing at the level of the sentence. It has also been found to be involved in the processing of novel metaphor. They also found increased activation for metonymy comprehension in the inferior frontal gyrus of both hemispheres. They report that in previous studies, the left frontal gyrus has been found to be involved in the unification of separate ideas into overall representations. Like Frisson and Pickering, their findings appear to support the role of ICMs in metonymy comprehension. They suggest that one reason why the frontal temporal network is particularly active in metonymy comprehension is because metonymy comprehension involves the integration of world knowledge (such as, for example, the fact that Kyoto was the place where an important environment treaty was signed, which allows Kyoto to stand metonymically for that treaty). They point to growing empirical support for the idea that the inferior frontal gyrus is responsible for the unification of discourse information with previously stored knowledge in the long-term memory, which again indicates a possible role for ICMs. A particular strength of their study is that it involved a number of different metonymy types which exhibited different metonymic relations; however, as with other studies in psycholinguistics, the focus was again on nouns.

Although the studies we have just seen make important contributions to metonymy research, they do have some drawbacks in terms of the language that they study. One concern is that the metonymic vehicles are always nouns, which does not reflect the way in which metonymy is distributed across different parts of speech in real-world data. It would be well worth replicating some of the above studies using verbal metonymies. Although the issue of how grammatical category information is represented in the mind/brain remains a contentious issue, the fact that nouns tend to encode entities while verbs express relational processes (Langacker 1987) may well affect the findings of such studies. It is difficult to predict the sorts of differences this may make, but one hypothesis might be that the effect found by Lowder and Gordon would be even greater for verbal metonymies than for nominal ones. This is because verbs have been found to be more difficult to process than nouns (Kauschke and Stenneken 2008; Spenney and Haynes 1989) and they are more difficult to recall, particularly in adult populations (Earles and Kersten 2000). It would be interesting to replicate some of the above studies using verbs rather than nouns as the metonymic vehicle. Participants would perhaps find processing more difficult, and this increased difficulty in general might allow for differences in processing time between metonymy and literal language to be made even more transparent. However, one potential difficulty in conducting psycholinguistic studies with verbal metonymies is that, unlike nouns, there are usually no literal equivalents in the verb form. For example, verbs such as ‘to eye’ and ‘to shoulder’ are always used metonymically (or metaphorically) and never literally. This would pose a serious problem for researchers hoping to compare processing times for matched sentences in a metonymic and a literal condition.

Another feature of the psycholinguistic studies to date is that in all the prompts used the metonymy can be traced to an individual word. We saw in Chapter 6 that metonymy often operates at the level of the phrase rather than at the level of the word and that it is sometimes virtually impossible to pinpoint the exact metonymically used word. The metonymy prompts used in psycholinguistic studies could therefore be brought more into line with authentic metonymy as it appears in discourse if examples were used where the metonymy hovers over the whole phrase. If examples such as this were used, we may see increased activation in the left frontal gyrus, as this has been found to be involved in the unification of separate ideas into overall representations. It has to be acknowledged, however, that such prompts would constitute a methodological challenge to researchers as these prompts would make it difficult for them to isolate the exact moment at which the metonymy is being processed.

Finally, more attention needs to be paid to the difference between novel and conventional metonymies. Rapp *et al.* (2012) conducted a large meta-analysis of all fMRI studies that have been conducted involving figurative language. They concluded from this analysis that figurative language is processed by a predominantly left-lateralised network involving several areas of both the left and right hemispheres including the inferior frontal gyrus mentioned above. Interestingly, they found a difference between conventional and novel figurative language, with increased right-hemisphere involvement in the processing of novel figurative language. In their meta-analysis there is little focus on metonymy, and it would be interesting to find out whether or not the left/right hemisphere preferences are also found for the processing of conventional and novel metonymy. Such studies might usefully focus on the role of metonymy in indirect speech acts, as this had been discussed extensively at a theoretical level (see Chapter 4). A number of studies have been conducted looking at how individuals with right-hemisphere brain damage comprehend indirect speech acts (Zaidel *et al.*, 2002). Although the findings from these studies are somewhat mixed, they do seem to suggest that individuals with right-hemisphere damage who find it difficult to recover non-literal meaning tend to experience no difficulties in interpreting conventionalised indirect requests appropriately. However, when faced with *non*-conventionalised indirect requests, they experience considerable difficulty. These findings indicate that such individuals may find it difficult to retrieve the appropriate metonymic links that would help them to understand such requests. To date, there have been no studies investigating the role of the right hemisphere in metonymy comprehension in the context of indirect speech acts. Such studies would be useful as they would shed more light both on the nature of metonymic thinking itself and on its role in communication.

7.3 Developmental studies of metonymy comprehension and production

A small number of studies have investigated the rate at which metonymy comprehension and production develops in children, and have attempted to assess whether it develops with age or with vocabulary knowledge. There has also been some interest in the extent to which the development of metonymy comprehension parallels that of metaphor comprehension. This is an important avenue of research from a theoretical perspective as findings from studies such as these help to explain the relationship between metonymy and metaphor and provide information on the extent to which they resemble one another.

The most extensive developmental study of metonymy comprehension in typically developing individuals is that of Rundblad and Annaz (2010a), who looked at metonymy and metaphor comprehension in a range of individuals whose ages ranged from 5:3 to 37:1 years old. In order to measure metonymy and metaphor comprehension, they used a story/picture comprehension task consisting of twenty stories. The participants looked at four pictures, each accompanied by a short text, and were asked to answer a comprehension question at the end. One of the stories used was as follows.

1. Kate and Anne are listening to music in Kate's room. Kate has a lot of CDs with songs on.
2. Kate wants to play her favourite song to Anne. Kate looks for the CD with the song on.
3. But Kate cannot find the CD. She says 'maybe my favourite CD is in another room'. Kate goes to look for the CD in the other rooms. Anne stays in Kate's room.
4. After a while, Kate calls: 'come and look Anne! I found Robbie Williams in the lounge'. Anne goes into the lounge to look. What does she see? (Rundblad and Annaz, 2010a: 506–63)

A similar set of stories was used for metaphor comprehension. Rundblad and Annaz found a similar onset of performance for metonymy compared to metaphor. Furthermore, results showed that typical development in metonymy comprehension is significantly greater than metaphor comprehension at all points in time throughout childhood to adulthood, and that metonymy comprehension develops at a faster rate. They also found that metonymy comprehension, unlike metaphor comprehension, reaches a ceiling around the age of 12, although this could be a result of the items used in the test. They report faster times for metonymy comprehension than for metaphor comprehension, a finding which is in line with other studies comparing reaction times for the two tropes (Klepousniotou and Baum, 2007). In particular, they found that metonymy comprehension was more strongly related than metaphor to vocabulary size. As with the findings cited in section 7.2, this indicates a more straightforward role for ICMs in metonymy comprehension. One of the possible reasons that Rundblad and Annaz give for their findings is that metonymy conforms to a limited number of cognitive patterns (i.e. metonymy types) and that most types of referential metonymies are found across all languages, whereas metaphor is more likely to be involved in the open-ended construction of ad hoc concepts. In other words, they appear to be saying that metonymy comprehension tends to be relatively straightforward and predictable, whereas metaphor comprehension has the potential to be a more creative process.

One way in which this study could be extended to take account of what is now known about metonymy in real-world data would be to focus on creative metonymy. We have seen in previous chapters that metonymy comprehension can be highly creative and involve ad hoc concept generation, in much the same way as metaphor. It would therefore be interesting to repeat Rundblad and

Annaz's study, using novel as well as conventional metonymy, and even incorporating metonymies that involve different modalities.

Other studies have focused on the role of metonymy in language acquisition in infants. The most influential study in this area is Nerlich *et al.*'s (1999) study, whose title begins with the rather intriguing quote: 'Mummy, I like being a sandwich', which was used by a child to refer to the fact that they like being one of the children who takes sandwiches to school rather than one who has school dinners. Nerlich *et al.* noted that the children saw the fact that they took sandwiches to school as being part of their group identity, and were keen to be part of this group. In their study, they identified a phenomenon which they labelled 'creative metonymical shrinking', in which young children use metonymic relationships between concepts in order to communicate new ideas with minimum effort. Examples included: 'I'm eating a bone sandwich' (uttered when the child was eating cheese and biscuits, after having been told that cheese contained calcium, which was good for his bones) and 'I have been wearing this curtsey all day' (uttered when the child had been wearing a long jumper which he used as a skirt in order to practise curtseying).

Evidence of metonymic thinking has even been found in the utterances of 2-year-olds. Pramling and Pramling Samuelsson (2009) identified a number of instances of language play in very young children (aged 2) which indicate that they can make metonymic associations, as we can see in the following example:

> [Together they sing about an elephant that makes different sounds. A child starts to talk about the elephant.]
> CHILD: Farting in there.
> [The children laugh, and some children start to wave with their hands as if wanting to get the 'smell' away from the nose.]
> CHILD: It smells skunk.
> TEACHER: How peculiar, an elephant smelling skunk!
> Pramling and Pramling-Samuelsson (2009: 334)

Here, when the child says 'it smells skunk', they are using the word 'skunk' to refer metonymically to the *smell* of a skunk via some kind of TRAIT FOR ENTITY relationship.

Other studies have taken a more usage-based approach to the acquisition of metonymy, working within a theoretical paradigm that is more in line with Langacker's 'active zones' approach to metonymy. For example, Krott (2012) investigated the role of metonymy and reference point phenomena in children's interpretation of novel noun–noun compounds. She found that children use analogy to interpret unknown compound words. Their interpretations are affected by the knowledge of other compound words they know, in particular compounds with the same headword. She also found that children prefer some interpretations over others, namely HAS and LOCATION relations over FOR relations. In other words, when they first encounter a compound that is novel to them, such as lemon+box, they are more likely than adults to think that it is a box that HAS lemon pictures on it than, for instance, a box that could be used FOR lemons. She argues that her findings support usage-based accounts of metonymy comprehension as their interpretations reflect those that are most frequent in the language input that they have received to date, as well as the most common combinations that are associated with a particular headword.

An area that has not yet been explored to the best of my knowledge is the role played by metonymy in child-directed speech. This would be a useful line of investigation given that language acquisition has been found to be largely usage-based (Tomasello, 2003). The amount and type of metonymy used by the carer is likely to relate to the amount and type of metonymy that is understood and used by the child. Because of its close links with construal, metonymy is likely to be heavily involved in the use of shared referents in first language acquisition.

7.4 Metonymy comprehension and production by children with linguistic impairments

A small number of studies have been conducted on children with different types of linguistic impairment. The focus has been on children with Williams syndrome and on children with autism. Annaz *et al.* (2008) investigated whether children with Williams syndrome develop the ability to comprehend metaphors and metonymies and looked at how their performance compared to that of typically developing children. Williams syndrome is a developmental disorder that is characterised by mild to moderate intellectual disability or learning problems. People with Williams syndrome typically have difficulty with visual-spatial tasks such as drawing and assembling puzzles, but they tend to do well on tasks that involve spoken language, music, and rote memorisation. Affected individuals often have outgoing, engaging personalities and tend to take a strong interest in other people. They have traditionally been described as having 'good language abilities'; however, on closer inspection, they have been found to exhibit a number of impairments in their pragmatic language use. For example, their conversation tends to be somewhat stereotyped, they employ inappropriate turn-taking gambits, and tend to lack rapport with their interlocutors. When recounting narratives, they provide insufficient information concerning the goals and motivation of the protagonists.

Annaz *et al.* tested metaphor and metonymy comprehension using the same picture comprehension task that was employed by Rundblad and Annaz and which was described above in Section 7.3. They found that children with Williams syndrome were generally better at comprehending metonymy than they were at metaphor; however, their performance was significantly poorer than the typically developing group. They found the comprehension of metonymies to be in line with receptive vocabulary, but comprehension of metaphors fell well below this level. Their conclusions were that metonymies may work in the same way as 'ordinary' vocabulary items and be treated as synonyms by people with Williams syndrome, while metaphor involves additional cognitive mechanisms outside language that develop atypically in this disorder. One drawback of their study was that they omitted to discuss the extent to which the participants were familiar with the metonymies used in the study. In order to address this problem, Van Herwegen *et al.* (2013) repeated the study, controlling for novelty versus conformity from the point of view of the participants. They found that development of both conventional and novel metonymy comprehension in the Williams syndrome group was delayed in comparison with the typically developing group, and (unlike metaphor comprehension) it developed alongside semantic knowledge.

Studies have also looked at the development of metaphor and metonymy comprehension skills in children with autism. For example, Rundblad and Annaz (2010b) compared the performance of eleven children with autism with seventeen typically developing children in a metaphor–metonymy comprehension task. They explored metaphor and metonymy comprehension using the same child-friendly story picture task that was described above in Section 7.3. Trajectories were constructed linking task performance either to chronological age or to measures of mental age. They found significantly poorer performance in both metaphor and metonymy comprehension in the children with autism compared with the typically developing children, Metaphor comprehension was impaired in relation to both chronological and mental age, whereas metonymy comprehension was more in line with the children's receptive vocabulary knowledge. They concluded that the autistic children's understanding of metaphors and metonymies was severely affected at all ages examined. They went on to suggest that the reason why the development of metonymy comprehension appeared to parallel the development in literal language comprehension could be that metonymy, unlike metaphor, involves a single domain. Alternatively, it could be because there is still a trace of the vehicle in the contextual meaning and that it is therefore closer to literal language.

To sum up, developmental studies of metonymy comprehension appear to indicate that it develops alongside vocabulary size and that it follows a similar trajectory to the development of literal language comprehension, although the trajectory is somewhat slower. Some of the studies outlined in this chapter could usefully be extended to take account of the way in which metonymy behaves in real-world data. For example, future studies could pay more attention to the differences between novel and conventional metonymy and the phraseological patterns that give rise to different metonymic meanings. They could also study metonymies in different modes of expression besides language. It would be particularly interesting to explore the cognitive processing of metonymy in gesture. Joue *et al.* (2012) are starting to look at the ways in which gestural metaphor is processed in the mind, and early findings indicate that the distinction between novel and conventional metaphor that is found for language is also found for gesture. In other words, the same neural substrates are involved in conventional metaphor comprehension, whether it appears in the linguistic or the gestural mode, and the same is true of novel metaphor (i.e. the same neural substrates are involved, regardless of the mode in which it is presented). The key deciding factor appears to be whether or not the apprehender needs to access a conceptual metaphor to aid comprehension. Given the findings discussed in these last two sections, one might expect to find a similar division for conventional and creative metonymy when it occurs in gesture. If such a distinction were found then this would provide further support for the conceptual nature of metonymy. Although such studies would be challenging from a methodological perspective, their findings would be of considerable benefit to the field of metonymy research.

7.5 Metonymy and psychotherapy

An area of psychology where a focus on metonymy has the potential to make a significant contribution to people's well-being is psychotherapy. Figurative thinking has been found to contribute to the sorts of delusions suffered by people with schizophrenia and related disorders, but the focus has tended to be on metaphor more than metonymy. For example, Rhodes and Jakes (2004) interviewed twenty-five patients with schizophrenia, schizo-affective disorder, manic depression, delusional disorder and psychotic depression about their delusions. They found that metonymy-based metaphor featured heavily in the accounts given by eleven of these patients. However, when we look more closely at the accounts described in their study, we can see that metonymy plays a greater role than their analysis would suggest. Although Rhodes and Jakes did not mention ICMs, we can see that in all eleven cases the patients perceived the different elements within their delusions as existing within a single ICM, which indicates that their thinking was predominantly metonymic rather than metaphorical. In addition to this, there is evidence in their data of a number of metonymy types that can be found in Radden and Kövecses' (1999) taxonomy. In this section, I re-analyse some of the accounts of these delusions, emphasising the central role played by metonymy.

One of the participants in Rhodes and Jakes' study reports how, in the pre-delusion period, she attended a strict religious school where she was forced to attend the school's church on a regular basis. The church contained small statues of 'devils', which 'watched' people as they prayed. She remembered the nuns looking at her as if she was evil and in her head conflated these looks with those of the devil statues. In later life, she developed a delusion in which the devil spoke to her and made her 'bad', and this developed into a feeling that she was possessed by the devil. One could interpret this sequence of events as metaphor, whereby the statues metaphorically represent the devil, but it is perhaps more appropriate and more useful to view the sequence as metonymy, for certainly within this patient's mind the devil statues became conflated with her feelings of guilt and intrinsic sinfulness and the whole delusion appears to have involved a PART FOR PART metonymy within the same conceptual domain. From her point of view, the devil was literally communicating with her. It might be useful for this patient's psychotherapist to explore the metonymic links between source and target of the delusion rather than trying to treat them as solely metaphor. As metonymy sits between metaphor and literal thinking this may contribute to a closer alignment between the psychotherapist's view and that of the patient.

In a second case, Rhodes and Jakes cite a patient who believed that he was a powerful world leader who was imbued with special powers and that he had a body that was based on hydrogen. It transpired that this patient had had a traumatic upbringing during which watching cartoons had been his only source of comfort. This patient appears to have conflated the world of cartoons with his own world and then, from this blend, new CAUSE FOR EFFECT metonymies have emerged, such as the imaginary role of hydrogen in the development of his super-powerful body.

In a third case, Rhodes and Jakes report a patient who saw a light in the sky and assumed it to be a spaceship, which presumably involved a visual PART FOR WHOLE metonymy. This PART FOR WHOLE metonymy was then elaborated to make him strongly aware of the fact that he was part of the Milky Way, which then led to a delusional episode in which he became an interplanetary ruler of extraterrestrial life in the Milky Way. Here we have the development of a whole new frame or ICM, triggered by the viewing of a single light in the sky and multiple metonymic links between parts of that ICM. The patient presumably felt safe within this world, which was different from but tangentially related to the real world, via the light in the sky. Again, if a psychotherapist were to see the whole thing as a metonymy rather than a somewhat far-fetched metaphor, this might provide a point of contact with the patient that allows the patient and the therapist to develop a mutual understanding of their different perspectives on the delusion.

A fourth delusion reported by Rhodes and Jakes also appears to have involved metonymy. Here a patient reported feeling that she was constantly being bitten by insects on her lower back, and that these insects were actually going into her body. Some years before the delusion, she had suffered from serious burns to her lower back from an accident involving boiling water. In this case, there appears to be a metonymic CAUSE FOR EFFECT relationship, and the patient has invented a new cause for a long-remembered effect.

In all of these cases, there is a blend of fantasy and reality, but because the patients have created their own idiosyncratic ICMs that link together things that would not normally be related, the relationships between the different components appear to involve metonymy rather than metaphor. In their minds at least, the relationships involve contiguity rather than comparison, and the links to the source domain are preserved. If we view the problem from a 'rational' perspective in which these imaginary ICMs do not really exist then it will be impossible to enter the 'worlds' that these patients inhabit. For these reasons, it may therefore be useful for counsellors to use metonymy in counselling sessions. Significant inroads have been made into the use of metaphor in counselling. Charteris-Black (2012) found that three conceptual metaphors were used by patients suffering from depression. These were DEPRESSION IS DARKNESS, DEPRESSION IS WEIGHT and DEPRESSION IS DESCENT. Tay (2012) shows how conceptual metaphors provide a powerful tool for counsellors, allowing them to both access and represent the emotions that are being experienced by their patients. They can then be used to foster empathy and provide new frames of reference for the patients. Focusing on the metonymic basis of the patients' 'metaphors' could be an equally powerful tool for counselling. Knapton and Rundblad (2012) found that patients with obsessive-compulsive disorder are likely to exhibit lower levels of personal agency (and the concomitant ability to deal with the disorder themselves) if they conceive of the disorder as standing metonymically for themselves. They argue that treatments such as cognitive behavioural therapy could be enhanced if they included elements whereby patients are encouraged to become more aware of their metonymic thought processes. Future work could usefully test claims such as these.

The fact that patients with schizophrenia tend to see their delusions as 'real' and do not understand them as metaphor or metonymy is perhaps related to the fact that they find it difficult to understand metaphor and metonymy in general. Findings from clinical psychology show that they appear to experience difficulties understanding figurative language when it is used by other people. For example, Gavilán and García-Albea (2011) found that patients with schizophrenia were significantly more likely than controls to offer a literal interpretation for a series of metaphors, even when these metaphors were highly conventional. They found that this deficit correlated with deficits in the patient's ability to see things from another person's perspective, which is known in the psychological literature as 'theory of mind' ability. This finding suggests that it may be difficult for therapists to get their patients to see their delusions as 'metaphors'. In these cases, metonymy could serve as a useful way for counsellors and patients to meet each other half way.

7.6 Conclusion

In this chapter we have looked at psycholinguistic and neurolinguistic studies of metonymy. The evidence from these studies suggests that, although metonymy comprehension does not always involve consideration and subsequent rejection of a literal sense, it often involves knowledge of cultural conventions and idealised cognitive models, if only at a subconscious level. We then moved on to explore studies of metonymy comprehension in individuals with neurological impairments, where we found that metonymy comprehension skills tend to be worse than literal language comprehension skills, but better than metaphor comprehension skills. This finding provides some support for Dirven's (2003) idea of a figurative continuum, from literal language, through metonymic language, to metaphorical language (see Chapter 1). In other words, metonymy comprehension appears to fall part way between literal language and metaphor in terms of its cognitive processing requirements. In these studies, although it is delayed, the developmental trajectory for metonymy is similar to the trajectory for literal language, and is strongly related to vocabulary size. While being less demanding than metaphor comprehension, metonymy appears to require deeper and more extensive vocabulary knowledge than 'literal' language.

Despite the significant advances that have been made in the psycholinguistic and neurolinguistic study of metonymy, there are a number of areas where further research is needed. To date, psycholinguistic and neurological studies of metonymy comprehension have tended to focus on referential, linguistic metonymy and we have suggested that it would be useful to focus on other modes of expression, such as gesture. It would also be worth paying more attention to metonymies that appear in different parts of speech, metonymies that perform different functions, and metonymies whose meaning is strongly affected by phraseological patterning. Although such studies would be difficult to conduct, their findings would provide greater insight into the ways in which metonymic thinking interacts with other types of knowledge-processing in the mind.

Perhaps the most socially relevant part of this chapter is the section in which we saw how metonymy is involved in the formation and expression of delusions by people with schizophrenia and related disorders. It was suggested that therapists might make more use of metonymy in their counselling sessions, as the fact that metonymy sits half way between 'metaphor' and 'reality' means that it could help them to find common ground with their patients. This would be worth exploring in future practice-based research studies.

8 'He started as nobody from Austria'

Cross-linguistic and cross-cultural variation in metonymy: implications for language learning and translation

8.1 Introduction

In Chapter 4, we looked at the role played by metonymy in forming and developing discourse communities. We saw how discourse communities sometimes attach a particular metonymic meaning to a given word or phrase and how this can at times be misunderstood (or interpreted in a different way) by people outside that discourse community (Deignan *et al.*, 2013; Stvan, 2012). The focus was on the types of metonymy that are employed by what Holliday (1999) describes as different 'small cultures', and the problems that arise when these small cultures come into contact with one another, despite the fact that, at least on the surface level, they are all speaking the 'same language'. These problems can become even more acute when people from different linguistic or cultural backgrounds need to communicate, or when translating metonymy from one language to another.

In this chapter, I broaden the discussion to focus on both regional and national cultures, describing the ways in which such cultures develop particular metonymies that help define group identities. I discuss the role of metonymy in cross-cultural and cross-linguistic communication, outlining how metonymy both impedes and facilitates understanding between people who have different cultural and/or linguistic backgrounds. I explore ethnographic research showing how people from different cultural backgrounds employ metonymy in different ways, in language and gesture, as well as in other modes of communication.

There have been recent moves in cross-cultural communication research to explain differences and misunderstandings in cognitive linguistic terms, drawing on concepts such as construal and categorisation (e.g. Bührig and ten Thije, 2006). I argue that some of these findings can also be explained in terms of metonymic mappings, especially if we take Langacker's (1993) definition of metonymy as a reference-point construction. I also discuss problems that the use of metonymy in non-verbal communication can present in inter-cultural communication.

After having discussed cross-linguistic variation in metonymy use, I then go on, in the second part of the chapter, to consider the practical implications of cross-linguistic and cross-cultural variation in metonymy by looking at the challenges they present to language learners and to translators. I begin by analysing the problems that metonymy presents to language learners, reporting findings from the small number of studies that have investigated the comprehension and production of metonymy by second language learners. I then consider the challenge that metonymy presents to translators. Examples are provided of the types of strategies that translators might use to deal with the heavily culture-bound and imprecise nature of metonymy. Because it can conceal subtle evaluations and preconceptions, metonymy can be very difficult to translate.

8.2 Cross-linguistic variation in metonymy

There is a wealth of literature exploring cross-linguistic variation in metonymy and its grammatical repercussions across a wide range of languages. Studies that have investigated this phenomenon include Barcelona (2003c, 2004), Brdar (2007), Brdar and Brdar-Szabó (2003), Brdar-Szabó and Brdar (2004), Hilpert (2007), Panther and Thornburg (1999, 2009), Ruiz de Mendoza Ibáñez and Pérez Hernández (2001), Ruiz de Mendoza Ibáñez and Mairal Usón (2007) and ten Thije (2006). These researchers have explored, among other things, variation in the metonymic use of place names to refer to events that took place there, variation in the ways in which metonymy is used in pragmatic inferencing and indirect speech acts, variation in the ways in which body parts can be metonymically chained, and variation in the ways in which metonymy relates to personification across languages. These studies show how metonymy affects meaning construction in different ways in different languages. In this section, I explore these types of variation, focusing first on those that are unlikely to present difficulties in cross-linguistic and cross-cultural communication and then moving on to those that are perhaps more likely to cause problems.

Some types of cross-linguistic variation in metonymy are fairly unlikely to lead to problems in communication. For instance, Barcelona (2003c) looked at the ways in which place names are metonymically derived from common nouns and at how these place names can themselves be used metonymically to refer to things other than the place. He found considerable differences in the way in which this process works in English, French, Spanish, German and Italian. He also found significant differences across languages in the extent to which these types of metonymy are productive in these different languages. In a similar vein, Jäkel (1999) explored the ways in which people's surnames are based on the place that they are from, and found extensive cross-linguistic variation in the productivity of this metonymy type. He showed that, in German, surnames frequently reflect places associated with the person to whom that surname was originally given, resulting in names such as Niendorf (new village) Hofstater (farm town), Ossenbrugge (oxen bridge), Baumgarten (tree garden) and so on. This type of metonymy is also very common in Japanese, but is less productive in other languages. These differences are unlikely to present serious problems in cross-linguistic communication. Indeed, in some contexts, discussions of the origins of one's surname or a place name even may serve as useful opening gambits in conversations between people with different linguistic and/or cultural backgrounds. Problems may arise, however, when the process is extended beyond individual names and place names. Barcelona (2004) found that the metonymic extension of 'paragon' names (for example, 'he's no Shakespeare' or 'he's England's Picasso') varies considerably from language to language, and points out that this process relies heavily on culturally entrenched metonymic models that may not be transparent to people outside that particular linguistic community.

A type of cross-linguistic variation in metonymy use that perhaps has greater potential to cause comprehension difficulties between speakers of different languages was found by Hilpert (2007), who discovered extensive variation in the ways in which body parts are metonymically chained in different languages. He looked at seventy-six languages and found that virtually all of them had a wide range of semantic extensions. Some of these extensions were common across all the languages studied, whereas others were not. For example, he found that most of the languages studied make use of the ORGAN OF PERCEPTION FOR PERCEPTION metonymy and use 'eye' to refer to seeing and 'ear' to refer to hearing. In some languages, the 'ear' metonymy is chained to imply 'paying attention', and in other languages, 'ears' are used to refer to 'obedience' via a CAUSE FOR EFFECT metonymy. In just two languages, 'belly' is extended via a CONTAINER FOR CONTAINED metonymy to refer to 'pregnancy' and via a CAUSE FOR EFFECT metonymy to refer to 'offspring'. The body parts 'arm', 'finger', 'foot' and 'hand' were found to be involved in INSTRUMENT FOR ACTION metonymies in most of the languages, and in a small number of languages, the term mouth is extended to mean 'word'. The body parts 'back', 'belly', 'buttocks', 'face', 'forehead', 'hand' and 'head' are grammaticalised in some languages but not others. For instance, in a small number of languages, 'forehead' is grammaticalised to mean 'in front' and 'buttocks' is grammaticalised to mean 'behind'. In just two languages, 'belly' is grammaticalised via a CONTAINER FOR CONTAINED metonymy to act as a marker of inclusiveness, meaning 'a member of a set'. This study shows that simple metonymic extensions are reasonably common across languages but that chained metonymies are subject to substantial cross-linguistic variation. The resulting expressions may be less than transparent to people who do not speak those languages fluently.

Other studies have found cross-linguistic variation in metonymy in terms of syntax. Although these variations are unlikely to present comprehension problems in cross-linguistic communication, speakers of a second language may not always produce them correctly because of interference from syntactic patterns in their first language. The findings from these studies are interesting in that they cast doubt on some widely accepted views of metonymy. Brdar-Szabó and Brdar (2012) report on two particular contrastive case studies that they have conducted. The first looks at the different degrees to which the CAPITAL FOR GOVERNMENT metonymy is productive in different languages. Using corpus-based analyses of newspapers from the different languages, they report that this metonymy appears at first sight to be significantly more productive in English than it is in German and Hungarian. However, when they looked at how the CAPITAL FOR GOVERNMENT metonymy is translated from English into German and Hungarian, they found that, in English, noun phrases involving this metonymy are often found in subject position, as in:

Washington has insisted it will not be drawn into a bilateral pact. (Brdar-Szabó and Brdar 2012: 730)

In contrast, in German and Hungarian they tend to function as locative adverbs, as in the following examples:

[. . .] *in Washington*, they doubted this. (2012: 731)

[. . .] it is difficult to find it said *in Islamabad.* (2012: 731)

They attributed their previous finding of apparent 'under-representation' in German and Hungarian to the fact that an analyst would have categorised examples such as these as literal, rather than metonymic. However, they went on to argue that these examples are just as metonymic as the Hungarian examples, but the metonymy is expressed differently. This finding casts doubt on the idea, discussed in Chapter 3, that referential metonymy is usually found in the subject position of the sentence.

Two further examples of the sorts of exact transliterations that they use to illustrate their point are as follows:

Nach mehr als zwanzig Jahren Krieg sei es äußerst schwierig, einen Neuanfang zu finden, heißt es *in Islamabad.*
(lit. 'After more than twenty years war is-SUBJ it extremely difficult a new start to find said-is it *in Islamabad*')
(2012: 731) [*Frankfurter Allgemeine Zeitung*, 7 December 2001]
Moszkvában most úgy látják, . . .
(lit. '*Moscow-in* now thus consider') (2012: 731)

These examples would translate into more natural-sounding English, in the following way:

Islamabad says that, after more than twenty years of war, it'll be extremely difficult to make a fresh start.
Moscow is now considering. . .

Brdar-Szabó and Brdar argue that this use of 'in' before the name of the place gives it a metonymic meaning which is slightly different from its English equivalent. Rather than pointing directly to the government institutions that are intended in their English-language equivalents, these metonymies have a much broader meaning in German and Hungarian. As well as referring to Government institutions, they also refer to politicians, journalists covering political issues, members of the general public who are interested in those issues, and so on. This means that, in different contexts, the same place name can be used to refer to different aspects of political life, or to the press or media in general that are connected with that particular city, as we can see here:

U Sarajevu na trgovima u sjevernom dijelu grada smatraju ovu izjavu nezgodnom.
(lit. '*in Sarajevo* in squares in northern part city consider this statement awkward.') (2012: 732)

This sentence would translate into more natural-sounding English thus:

In Sarajevo in squares and in the northern part of the city this statement is considered awkward.

To sum up, in German and Hungarian, the metonymic use of place names has a broader, more inclusive meaning than it does in English. This may lead to misunderstandings in cross-linguistic communication, particularly in the political arena.

Some cross-linguistic variation in metonymy use can be attributed to the economy with which concepts can be expressed without recourse to metonymy in some languages. For example, Ruiz de Mendoza Ibáñez (personal communication) points out that Nunberg's (1979) now famous example 'The ham sandwich is waiting for his check' does not work well in Spanish, partly because Spanish has a syntactic solution that is as economical as metonymy and that requires no extra inferential activity. He argues that, through nominalisation of the present participle, Spanish can omit as much content material as the English metonymy:

El del bocadillo de jamón
(lit. 'the (one) of the ham sandwich').

This is possible in English, but it sounds extremely clumsy and is very wordy:

The one that has ordered a ham sandwich.

The nominalised present participle is generally preferred in Spanish to its metonymic equivalent as it allows for anaphoric reference to be expressed more smoothly. Thus the following is preferred:

Ten cuidado con el/la de ese coche, que va como un loco/una loca.
(lit. 'Watch for the ($one_{MASC/FEM}$) in that car; he/she is driving recklessly')

Whereas its metonymic equivalent sounds very clumsy:

Ten cuidado con ese coche, que va como loco (*él/*ella va como loco/a).
(lit. 'Watch that car; it's driving recklessly') (he/she's driving recklessly)

The same is true for the following example, where the nominalised present participle is used:

Los/las de los autobuses están de huelga y ellos/ellas no quieren volver al trabajo.
(lit. 'The ones of the buses are on strike and they$_{\mathrm{MASC/FEM}}$ don't want to go back to work')

The nominalised present participle is much less clumsy than its metonymic equivalent:

Los autobuses están de huelga y *ellos/*ellas no quieren volver al trabajo.
(lit. 'Buses are on strike and they$_{\mathrm{MASC/FEM}}$ don't want to go back to work')

These subtle yet important differences may present a challenge to language learners and they may explain some of the 'foreign-sounding' expressions that are occasionally produced by English learners of Spanish and Spanish learners of English.

Languages also vary according to whether they conventionally attach metonymic or metaphorical meanings to certain source domains. For instance, Charteris-Black (2003) compared the ways in which three concepts – the mouth, the tongue and the lip – are used figuratively in English and Malay. He found that in English they are far more likely to be used metonymically (e.g. when someone is described as being 'tight lipped'), whereas in Malay they are far more likely to be used metaphorically. He theorises that the main reason for this is that in Malay it is more important to use face-saving strategies than in English, and the use of metaphor is more appropriate in this case as it is much less direct than metonymy. Again, these differences may lead to comprehension and production problems for non-native speakers of these languages.

There are some cases where cross-linguistic variation in metonymy is particularly likely to lead to problems in communication. For example, in the area of pragmatic inferencing, Brdar-Szabó (2009) found that the use of stand-alone conditionals to function as indirect directives is possible in English and German but not in Hungarian and Croatian. In other words, in English and German it is possible to use the words 'if you could do X. . .?' to mean 'please will you do X?', whereas in Hungarian and Croatian this sounds very strange. She argues that this relationship is based on a scenario-based illocutionary metonymy (see Chapter 3), rather than a frame-based one. Scenario-based metonymies are more universal than frame-based ones, but they are also subject to subtle forms of cross-linguistic variation such as the one identified here.

Cross-linguistic variation involving scenario-based metonymies has also been observed by Panther and Thornburg (1999), who showed how the

POTENTIALITY FOR ACTUALITY metonymy operates very differently in English and Hungarian. They were able to demonstrate that speakers of English make regular use of the POTENTIALITY FOR ACTUALITY metonymy to express sense relations, such as 'I can smell the garlic' and 'it can be seen that', whereas in Hungarian, these would be translated as 'I feel the garlic smell' and 'it is available for seeing that'. Differences such as these have the potential to create problems in cross-linguistic communication, as additional pragmatic inferencing patterns are required that are simply not present in all languages.

Finally, in their study of cross-linguistic variation in the use of metonymy in service encounters, Radden and Seto (2003) show how different languages select different instances of the 'shopping scenario' as metonymic vehicles. They contrast 'HAVE' languages, which use a PRECONDITION FOR ACTION metonymy, with 'BE' languages, which rely on an EXISTENCE FOR ACTION metonymy, to produce sentences such:

ENGLISH Do you have any 40-watt lightbulbs?
JAPANESE 40-watt no denkyu (wa) arimasuka?
(Are there any 40-watt lightbulbs?)

Here the shopping scenario itself probably provides sufficient context for the hearer to infer the intended message (i.e. that the speaker would like to purchase a 40-watt lightbulb). However, in some of the other examples listed above, the intended meaning may not be immediately obvious as there are insufficient contextual clues to allow the reader or hearer to disambiguate the possible metonymic senses.

Another way in which metonymy has the potential to give rise to cross-linguistic misunderstandings relates to the fact that metonymies can appear, at least on the surface, to be simply 'referential', while carrying subtle yet strong pragmatic overtones. In her comparison of metonymic extensions of the word 'face' in English and Persian, Shaghayegh Alirezaie (2012) found considerable variation in the way in which the word is used metonymically in both languages, which she attributed to socio-historical features of Anglo Saxon and Persian cultures. Her findings are particularly important as they show that the concept of 'face' means very different things to different people. This is significant, given the wide cross-cultural variation in terms of the importance that is attached to 'face' ('saving face' and 'loss of face') in different cultures. Her findings are also relevant to current debates about whether or not it is acceptable for women to have to cover their faces in different cultures, as the need for women to cover their faces derives from metonymic extensions of the 'meanings' of a woman's face.

There has been some exploratory work involving survey data on the extent to which different metonymy types are exploited by different languages. For example, May (2013) interviewed thirty-two speakers of thirteen typologically varied languages about the productivity of eight metonymy types in their languages. She found wide variation in the productivity of these different metonymy types across the different languages and was able to attribute her findings to both socio-economic and formal linguistic factors. For example, she found that the PRODUCER FOR PRODUCT metonymy type is highly productive in most languages, especially in those whose speakers live in countries that have a strong manufacturing base. She notes that the Chinese employ large numbers of these types of metonymy. Examples include: 'Lin ning' (a famous Chinese sports brand), 'Wahaha' and 'Jiaduobao' (beverage manufacturers) and 'Dabao' (a maker of facial cream). She contrasts this with Finland, which, with the exception of Nokia, does not have such a large manufacturing base, and notes that PRODUCER FOR PRODUCT metonymies such as these are relatively rare in Finnish. She also notes that the readiness or non-readiness of a language to absorb English PRODUCER FOR PRODUCT metonymies reflects the globalisation of English and possible levels of resistance to cultural and linguistic penetration of foreign brands. For example, in Italian, the word 'aspirapolvere' (lit. 'suck dust') is preferred to the word 'Hoover' (which was originally an American brand). Despite the fact that the American brand is very popular, Italians still prefer to use the literal term. May also observes that there are sometimes formal linguistic reasons for the use or non-use of particular PRODUCER FOR PRODUCT metonymies. For instance, in Thai, the alliterative metonymic term 'Mama' (a producer of instant noodles) is preferred to the literal Thai term: 'ba mi gueng sum sed roob', which is unwieldy.

May found the PART FOR WHOLE metonymy type to be highly productive in all the languages studied, although the actual 'parts' that were selected were not always predictable. In many cases, such as the use of 'rice' to refer to a meal by speakers of East Asian languages, salience and frequency were the overarching principles, in line with Radden and Kövecses' taxonomy. She noted that, in Indonesian, the word 'tail' is used to refer to a whole animal such as a cow or chicken, as in 'I can see three tails in that field'. This contrasts with the more common use of 'head' in English (as in 'three heads of cattle'). However, it is not completely out of line with the cognitive principles proposed by Radden and Kövecses as both the head and the tail are extreme points and a tail is a distinguishing feature of many animals, and one which sets them apart from humans. Some PART FOR WHOLE metonymies are highly culturally bound, such as the Japanese term 'nabe' (lit. 'pot') which refers to a very popular stew-type meal. 'Nabe' refers not just to the physical pot itself, which is placed in the centre of the dining table, but to all of the various stew ingredients; it is even inclusive of the stove and the characteristically convivial style of this meal. ACTION FOR COMPLEX EVENT metonymies were also fairly widely spread across all the languages in May's study. In Arabic, the term 'let's spread the books' is used to refer to studying, and in German, 'throw oneself into the keys' means to play the piano and 'to swing the ladle' refers to cooking.

May argues that a range of socio-economic, political, cultural and linguistic features works alongside the cognitive principles proposed by Kövecses and Radden to influence the extent to which these different metonymies are exploited in the different languages. These factors include the degree of openness to other cultures, the level of international brand presence in a particular culture, the diet and drinking customs of a culture, formal features of the words involved such as their degree of complexity or the presence of alliteration, the relative complexity of the original words, the landscape and distribution of the population, and preferred styles of humour, irony and euphemistic language. Thus the way in which a particular language makes use of these different metonymy types may provide insights into its culture.

Research has also shown that there is cross-cultural variation in the use of metonymic gestures. For example, in Ghana, using the left hand during communication is considered by many people to be a taboo, as it is metonymically associated with certain bodily functions that one would not wish to share with others. Kita and Essegbey (2001) investigated the effect of this taboo on the gestural practice of members of the Ghanaian society by observing gestures that are produced in naturalistic situations where participants were asked to give route directions. They found that participants tended to put their left hands on their lower backs, which at times looked like they were hiding them from their interlocutors. At times this action made it very difficult to perform certain gestures but this did not prevent them from doing it. On the rare occasions where they did use gestures involving the left hand, these gestures were significantly less expansive than those involving their right hand, which again appears to reflect the metonymically motivated taboo. Knowledge of this taboo would be useful for non-Ghanaians to prevent them from committing social faux pas when speaking to Ghanaians.

8.3 Problems caused by misunderstandings of metonymy in cross-linguistic and cross-cultural communication

In the preceding section, we looked at a number of ways in which the use of metonymy varies across languages and cultures. It was hypothesised that some of these types of variation may lead to communication difficulties, but none of these hypotheses have been actually put to the test. In this section, I introduce work that has explored the ways in which metonymy can be misunderstood by speakers of different languages, and the problems that this can cause.

One of the most dramatic examples of the negative consequences of a possible cross-cultural misunderstanding involving metonymy occurred in 1945 when the USA bombed Hiroshima and Nagasaki. In their famous 'Potsdam Declaration', the Americans gave the Japanese an ultimatum: unconditional surrender or all-out nuclear attack. Japan's response to the Potsdam Declaration was ambiguous. The

Japanese Premier, Kantarō Suzuki used the word 'mokusatsu'. The direct translation of this word into English is 'no comment' (Butow, 1954). Its meaning is very vague; it can mean 'reject', but it can also mean to 'let's not talk about it now'. It therefore involves a loosely defined SUB-EVENT FOR WHOLE EVENT metonymy and its meaning is heavily underspecified. In English, in contrast, it has a much more specific meaning of 'rejection' via ACTION FOR RESULT metonymy: when one withholds comment on a particular issue this implies that one does not agree with it, or that one does not wish to engage in dialogue. There is an element of finality in the English expression 'no comment' that is not present in the Japanese word 'mokusatsu'. The reasons for the Japanese use of the word 'mokusatsu' may have been related to embarrassment, discomfort, the desire to play for time or even simply not knowing what to say, but these cultural nuances do not translate easily. The word was translated simply as meaning 'reject' and the USA understood that Japan was unwilling to accept the Potsdam Declaration, which was a contributory factor to the subsequent bombing of Hiroshima and Nagasaki.

Clearly, most misunderstandings of metonymy are not as dramatic as this, but they can still interfere with successful communication between individuals with different linguistic and/or cultural backgrounds. It is very often difficult to tease apart the linguistic factors from the cultural factors, and indeed many have argued that the two are inseparable (Byram, 1997; Byram and Risager, 1999; Shore, 1996). Studies have therefore tended to focus on both linguistic and cultural factors. For example, Rost-Roth (2006) explored the use of language in academic counselling sessions at a German university involving lecturers and students with different linguistic backgrounds. Although she did not analyse these instances of miscommunication in terms of metonymy, metonymy is clearly involved. For example, she reports how a student from Iran talked at length about negative emotions that he was experiencing. A post hoc interview with the student revealed that he was in fact trying to refer to the fact that he was not happy with the programme and that this was the cause of his negative emotions. He was hoping that the lecturer would infer this. In the video data and in the follow-up interview with the German lecturer, it is clear that the lecturer did not know why the student was doing this, and had no idea what student was trying to say. The student was making use of an EFFECT FOR CAUSE metonymy (EMOTION FOR CAUSE OF EMOTION) to refer indirectly to aspects of the programme about which he was not happy, but this was lost on the lecturer. The EMOTION FOR CAUSE OF EMOTION metonymy may be more common in Persian than it is in German in situations such as this where there is a high power differential.

In another study, Littlemore (2001) asked a group of Bangladeshi civil servants studying a short course on public sector management at a British university to write down what they thought was meant by a series of metaphors and metonymies that had been used by their lecturers. One of the items in the study was the metonymy: '*can-do* civil servants', which according to the lecturer (who was interviewed as part of the study) meant 'enthusiastic and positive-thinking civil servants'. This interpretation was subsequently confirmed by two further informants, both of whom were native speakers of English.

A number of the participants in the study misunderstood this expression slightly. For example, one of them interpreted it as meaning 'capable, competent civil servants' (2001: 341). He then went on to say that

> The civil servants are the tools of administration. If the civil servants do their job efficiently, the wheel of the government will also run efficiently. (Littlemore, 2001: 341)

This participant appears to understand 'can-do civil servants' as meaning civil servants who are literally capable of doing their jobs and who work hard in order to perform their assigned duties properly. This interpretation is closer to the literal meaning of 'can-do' than was intended by the lecturer, and it appears to relate more to a worker's ability than to his or her attitude. This misinterpretation is likely to have been due to both linguistic and cultural factors. The participant who had presumably not come across this expression before appears to have used its literal meaning in his interpretation. In further discussion with the participants and the lecturers on the course, many of whom had spent time delivering courses in Bangladesh itself, it was revealed that the culture of the Bangladeshi civil service places more emphasis on hard work and obedience and that there is less room for innovation and entrepreneurship than in the UK. This cultural difference may also have played a part in this interpretation. Although the misinterpretation is unlikely to have had any disastrous consequences, the participant clearly missed the nuance of what the lecturer was trying to say.

Cross-cultural misunderstandings can also occur when metonymy is used in symbolic non-linguistic communication. Kotthoff (2006) discusses the differences between East and West Georgian styles of lament. In West Georgia, fainting and singing in slurred voices are seen as appropriate expressions of women's extreme grief after bereavement, whereas in East Georgia, women are simply expected to scratch their faces. All of these actions are related to sadness via a stylised, symbolic extension of the PHYSICAL EFFECT FOR EMOTION CAUSING IT metonymy. The underlying metonymic relationship is the same in both cases, but the physical manifestations are different. Kotthoff reports that both East and West Georgians find the mourning practices that are favoured by their counterparts to be artificial and melodramatic, and West Georgian women are asked to refrain from fainting at East Georgian funerals. This finding is analogous to work that has been done on metaphor in cross-cultural contexts, where two cultures share one underlying conceptual metaphor but the linguistic instantiations differ, each sounding odd to the other culture.

Metonymy does not always serve as a barrier to understanding in cross-linguistic communication. Sometimes it can facilitate understanding. As we saw in Chapter 5, it can also be used to mitigate some of the potentially face-threatening consequences of cross-cultural variation. Metonymic gestures can be used to reduce potential misunderstandings caused by the use of figurative language more generally in cross-linguistic encounters. For instance, in a study of academic tutorials between English-speaking lecturers and Spanish-speaking students, MacArthur *et al.* (2013b) found an unusually high proportion of words related to the semantic field of SIGHT, in comparison with spoken discourse more generally (the comparison was made with the British National Corpus). They found that, within these dyads, sight metonymies (and metaphors) were used significantly more frequently by the lecturers than by the students. The lecturers used them to refer metonymically to activities such as 'studying', 'focusing on', 'understanding', 'working on', 'appreciating' and 'noticing'. In contrast, the students used them with a much narrower range of meanings, most of which were literal or which referred simply to 'understanding'. The lecturers made frequent use of metonymic gesture to disambiguate the different senses. These included the removal of glasses, the pointing of hands to indicate the direction of the 'focusing', and the use of 'writing' gestures to indicate 'working on things'. These gestures often referred to related concepts, such as 'narrowing down' and 'grouping', which further clarified the sight metonymies. Judging by the responses of the students, these cultural and linguistic differences did not present comprehension problems, possibly as a result of these metonymic 'clarifying' gestures.

8.4 Metonymy and the language learner

As we have just seen, there is a wealth of literature exploring cross-linguistic variation in metonymy and its grammatical repercussions across a wide range of languages, and this variation can at times cause misunderstandings. Metonymic variation across languages presents a particular challenge to language learners. In the context of foreign language learning and teaching, the complex and content-sensitive role of metonymy tends to be ignored (Littlemore, 2009; Low, 2008). Although some strategies may help learners to understand and use metonymic expression in the target language, there have to date been no significant studies of the benefits of an explicit focus on metonymy in the language classroom. In this section, we look at the problems that metonymy presents to language learners in terms of both comprehension and production.

Metonymy comprehension by language learners

The fact that there is so much variation across languages means that metonymy comprehension may pose a challenge to language learners. The problem is likely to be exacerbated by the fact that metonymic motivations are not always predictable and the same metonymically used word can have opposite meanings in different contexts. For example, the word 'weathered' has a meaning of 'appearing to be affected by the weather' as in the following examples:

Those rich leather uppers have a warm *weathered* look. (BofE)

It is eerily *weathered* and almost featureless. (BofE)

The same word, when extended via metaphor into more abstract contexts, means almost the exact opposite, that the entity has *not* been affected by the 'weather' and is relatively unscathed:

Major changes have been *weathered* and a new balance has been achieved. (BofE)

The tenacious Ndebele people who have tenaciously *weathered* apartheid. (BofE)

One possible aid to comprehension is the fact that metaphorical uses of the word tend to appear in verb form while metonymic uses tend to appear in adjectival form. However, students may not automatically pick up on these subtle nuances and may need to be taught the different meanings (and their grammatical manifestations) more explicitly.

Despite the likelihood of difficulties inherent in metonymy comprehension, there has been very little work on metonymy comprehension by language learners, as most studies of figurative language comprehension have focused on metaphor.

One exception to this is a two-part study, conducted by Littlemore, Arizono and May (in preparation), which explored metonymy comprehension in Japanese learners of English. In the first part of the study, they took ten Japanese students, all of whom were conducting postgraduate study in the UK, and asked them to explain the meanings of twenty expressions instantiating a range of metonymy types. They were asked to indicate if they had encountered any of the items before and were already familiar with their meaning. These items were eliminated from the study. The aims of this part of the study were to establish what kinds of strategies Japanese-speaking learners of English employ in order to comprehend the metonymic expressions in context, what factors contribute to successful metonymy comprehension, what kinds of errors these learners make when they interpret the meanings of the metonymic expressions, and what factors present obstacles to successful metonymy comprehension. In order to answer these research questions, the responses given by the Japanese participants were compared to those given by two judges, both of whom were native speakers of English.

The students were found to employ the following metonymy comprehension strategies:

1. activating a particular 'metonymy type'
2. noticing the active zone/profile discrepancy (see Section 3.1)
3. using contextual clues.

Somewhat surprisingly, these students appear to have coped well with cross-linguistic differences in the syntactic patterns that accompany involve metonymy. For example, English makes extensive use of denominal verbs whose meaning is metonymically related to the corresponding nouns, such as this use of 'summered':

An injured bird also *summered* at Darwell Reservoir in 1958. (BNC)

This construction does not exist in Japanese, but it did not present significant problems to the participants in the study. There are interesting parallels between this finding and that of Piquer Píriz (2008) that syntactic form was not a distracting factor for young Spanish learners of English when accessing the figurative meaning of metonymies. Piquer Píriz found that the majority of the children who participated in her experiment had no problems comprehending metonymic multi-word expressions (e.g. 'give me a hand' and 'I didn't open my mouth') whose meanings were extended based on the salient functions of these body parts, even in cases where there was no corresponding expression in their native language. This is probably because these metonymies involve the extension of salient features and constitute well-established metonymic relationships, such as the PART FOR WHOLE and ACTION FOR RESULT relationship.

The students in the study were much more likely to work out the meaning of metonymic denominal verbs when the action they denoted reflected a central characteristic of the noun. For example, they experienced very few problems with the metonymic expressions *be garaged*, and *be mothered*, as they reflect the characteristics that are central to the corresponding nouns (i.e. garages are places where cars are kept and mothers look after children). In contrast to this, the metonymy 'to *landscape* the garden' presented far more problems. All of the participants in the study thought that this meant 'to have a view over a garden'. These participants appeared to be employing an OBJECT FOR ACTION metonymy, which is not involved in the English meaning of 'to landscape'. In English, the meaning of this expression is to change the appearance of a piece of land, and none of the participants got this. Some participants went on to infer that it meant 'to plant trees', thus evoking a RESULT FOR ACTION metonymic relationship. This is closer to the actual meaning of the expression, though the participants were a little too specific in their explanation. Landscaping a garden may well involve planting trees, but it is equally likely to involve lots of other things, such as moving earth, planting flowers and chopping down trees. In this example, the participants wrongly focused on different parts of the ICM. Because the meaning of 'to landscape' is not related to a central feature of a landscape, the participants found it harder to work out the meaning. Therefore, it appears that if the action that is being referred to is more salient in relation to the basic sense of the vehicle term, learners are more likely to interpret the item successfully. Littlemore *et al.* also investigated whether or not there was a relationship between successful interpretation and the imageability of the items. They found a significant correlation ($p < 0.05$), indicating that it is easier to work out the meaning of highly imageable metonymies.

Many of the errors that students made in trying to interpret the metonymies were similar to the types of errors identified for metaphor by Littlemore *et al.* (2011a). These included 'over-' and 'under-specification' (providing too much or too little information), focusing on the wrong part of the ICM (as we saw above), misinterpreting contextual cues and misinterpreting the syntax. Other errors related more closely to the fact that the authors were looking at metonymy, rather than metaphor. Most notably, a number of students interpreted the metonymic expressions as if they were metaphors. One example of this is:

It was obvious to everybody in Rome that he had to *marry money* → interpreted as meaning 'to earn big money'.

Here the intended metonymic component was not explained. Instead, the participant tried to interpret the word 'marry' metaphorically, in that he thought 'to marry' corresponded to 'to need something immensely'.

Another example of this phenomenon is:

his younger brother and sister, who [. . .] seemed to *depend on the bottle* → interpreted as 'to be attached to an obstacle/weak point'.

Post-task discussion with this participant revealed that he had interpreted 'depend on the bottle' as referring to 'an obstacle/weak point' because he thought that it seemed similar to the term 'bottleneck', which is motivated by metaphor in English.

Other examples of cases where students provided a metaphorical interpretation when a metonymic one was required included:

his younger brother and sister, who [. . .] seemed to *depend on the bottle* → interpreted as 'to depend on a certain group of people'.

Here the student explained that 'the bottle' was something which brought a certain group of people together. Another student interpreted the same example using a different metaphor:

his younger brother and sister, who [. . .] seemed to *depend on the bottle* → interpreted as 'to depend on their appearances'.

Here, the student explained that the bottle was a thing which hides its contents so it referred to 'appearance' which might hide human nature.

Some of the inappropriate metaphorical interpretations could be attributed to cultural transfer from Japanese, as we can see in the following example:

Whoever it is says you're still *nosing about in business* which doesn't concern you → interpreted as 'to be weary of business'.

The meaning provided by this student appears to be based on the Japanese expression hana ni tsuku ('to stick to one's nose') which metaphorically implies to 'to be weary of something'.

Other types of errors included cases where the students conducted an apparently wrong lexico-grammatical analysis of the intended metonymical component, as we can see here:

Being *mothered* by a grandparent was certainly not always a happily remembered experience → interpreted as 'becoming mother'.

Here the participant wrongly analysed this expression into the combination of gerund + adjectival.

In other cases, the students simply stayed within the vehicle subject matter and did not attempt any explanation of the metonymic component, as we can see in the following example:

Dobson and his mob just *laughed you off the street tonight* → interpreted as 'to make fun of you on the street'.

In other cases, the students accessed the wrong metonymy type in order to explain the expressions, as we can see in the following example:

a lone blues *trumpet* was improvising → interpreted as 'a lonely blues sound was improvising'.

Here the participant interpreted it as 'sound' by means of metonymy type INSTRUMENT FOR PRODUCT in English. The actual metonymy that is being evoked by this expression is INSTRUMENT FOR MUSICIAN, which is very common in English and which can be found in expressions such as:

It went with the sacking of the *first violin*, Marie-Alexandre Guenin. (BNC)

Another example of a student evoking the wrong metonymy type is:

In the garden you will see them *nosing around* trying to find a new place to dig a hole → interpreted as 'to growl'.

Here, the student explained that a nose produces a growling sound, so he wrongly understood it as an instantiation of INSTRUMENT FOR ACTION metonymy in English.

When the students were presented with the more subtle, Langacker-style 'active zone' metonymies (see Section 3.1), they tended to try and interpret them more as prototypical metonymies, as we can see in the final example:

Just as he was about to *open the beer* the doorbell rang → interpreted as 'to start a party'.

This is not the intended meaning of the sentence in this context although one could possibly see it as a plausible explanation. The participant explained that parties generally start with opening the bottle(s) of beer, thus evoking a SUB-EVENT FOR WHOLE EVENT metonymy. This participant was able to understand the metonymic meaning of 'open the beer', but he extended its metonymic meaning too far. Another way of explaining this interpretation is to see it as an instance of 'metonymic chaining' (Dirven, 2003), where one metonymy leads on to another. In other words, he identified two closely related metonymies, each of which moved the meaning further away from the 'basic senses' of the words in the sentence.

Other types of answer included those that were unclassifiable because of poor expression, as we can see here:

[...] vehicles *garaged* in a certain Rating District → interpreted as 'a certain rating garage'.

Here it was impossible to understand what the participant meant by this response.

In other cases, students simply misunderstood the meaning of the vehicle term:

When the Cordorys had finished *landscaping* their garden → interpreted as 'to dig up their garden'.

Here the student is reported to have misunderstood the basic meaning of landscape as 'landslide'.

In line with Littlemore *et al.*'s (2011a) findings for metaphor, cases were identified of both 'overspecification', where the students over-interpreted the meaning of the metonymy and provided too much information, and 'underspecification', where they under-interpreted the meaning of the metonymy, and did not provide enough information. An example of 'overspecification' is as follows:

An injured bird also *summered* at Darwell Reservoir → interpreted as 'to rest/relax at Darwell Reservoir during summer'.

The meaning of this expression is simply 'to spend summer', so the student has over-interpreted it in a way by adding the ideas about rest and relaxation. This interpretation is valid in the context, but it is more specific than 'to spend at a certain place during summer'. Like the aforementioned student who 'over-interpreted' the Langacker-style 'active zone' metonymies, this student appears to have evoked a metonymic chain and thus done more 'figurative work' than was required by the context.

An example of 'underspecification' is:

Ludens *tiptoed* into the kitchen → interpreted as 'to enter into the kitchen'.

The interpretation is valid in this context, but 'to tiptoe' conveys more meaning than simply 'to enter'.

The main differences between these findings and those made by Littlemore *et al.* (2011a) for metaphor were that in this study, students tended to interpret metonymies as if they were metaphors and carried out unnecessary metonymic chaining. These are both cases of 'over-interpretation', suggesting that students may not be primed to identify metonymy and interpret it as such. This may be a result of the fact that, of the two tropes, metaphor is far more widely known and people generally tend to know roughly what it is and how it should be dealt with. Metonymy is much more subtle and nuanced than metaphor and may thus present more problems to learners.

In the second part of the study, which also involved Japanese learners of English, Littlemore, Arizono and May focused on the functions performed by metonymy. The aim was to establish whether the function being performed by the metonymies would affect the students' ability to understand them. The participants were twenty-two intermediate-to-advanced English-speaking Japanese participants, all of whom were located in Japan. They were asked to interpret a set of twenty metonymies, each of which was presented in context. The metonymies were chosen because they served different functions, such as humour, irony, euphemism, dysphemism and so on. Again, their responses were compared with those given by two judges, both of whom were native speakers of English. A similar set of problems was found to those found in the first part of the study, which included the missing of important contextual clues, the rejection of possible meaning on account of perceptual 'strangeness', interference of linguistic equivalents in Japanese, over- and under-specification, a tendency to become distracted by contextual features, reluctance to 'make a guess', and positive and negative interference from cultural differences or preferences.

It was found that metonymies serving complex functions such as humour, irony and hyperbole were significantly more difficult to understand than ones that served more 'straightforward' functions, such as hyperbole and positive evaluation. These findings can be partially explained by the extent to which the examples violated the cognitive principles underlying 'typical' vehicle selection that were identified by Radden and Kövecses (1999). As we saw in Chapter 2, Radden and Kövecses argue that principles such as HUMAN OVER NON-HUMAN and STEREOTYPICAL OVER NON-STEREOTYPICAL are key factors in determining vehicle choice in metonymy. When these 'rules' were broken, learners found it very difficult to interpret the metonymies correctly. Some of the violations of cognitive principles were more serious than others when it came to their effect on metonymy interpretation. For example, the metonymic euphemism 'Is there somewhere where I can freshen up?' was misunderstood by 59 per cent of the participants in the study. This euphemism involves the deliberate violation of the CLEAR OVER LESS CLEAR principle, as the speaker presumably wishes to avoid saying that they need to use the toilet or wash their sweaty face – nor does the listener want to hear such candid information – and so it is socially appropriate or expected to disguise the real meaning. In contrast, the metonymic hyperbole 'all fingers and thumbs' did not present any comprehension problems to the participants. This expression does not violate any cognitive principles and in fact adheres to several, including the CONCRETE OVER ABSTRACT, INTERACTIONAL OVER NON-INTERACTIONAL and FUNCTIONAL OVER NON-FUNCTIONAL principles.

Finally, a number of cultural factors appeared to interfere, both positively and negatively, with the successful interpretation of metonymy. For instance, the sentence 'Billie's eyes popped out as she kissed Yanto' was understood by 85.2 per cent of the participants, a finding which could perhaps be attributed to the ubiquity of manga cartoons featuring exaggeratedly wide-eyed characters. Another sentence that was well understood was 'the Suits began to appear from their conferences', which was understood by 76.5 per cent of the participants. In Japan the notion of the smart-suited but somewhat conventional 'salaryman' is ubiquitous. Metonymies that were less well understood included 'Why am I such an anorak?', which was only understood by 37.5 per cent of the participants. The problem here is that understanding an anorak to mean a nerd or a geek involves detailed cultural information about anoraks and the sort of people who wear them, and the sorts of 'semi-autistic' behaviours and hobbies that these people traditionally engage in, such as train-spotting. For the average Japanese person, there is no reason why an anorak should refer to anything other than an item of outdoor clothing. If a CLOTHING FOR PERSON metonymy were involved, they might think of a mountaineer or a person who likes the outdoor life, as these could be described as central features of anorak-wearers. The meaning intended in the above example draws on a particular, highly peripheral characteristic of an anorak-wearer. Another item that was less well understood, possibly for cultural reasons, was the sentence 'all the pressures she was facing caused her to *hit the bottle* again', which was only understood by 36.4 per cent of the participants. Here the problem may lie in the fact that the protagonist in the example was female. In Japanese society, getting drunk is more socially acceptable for men than for women, and the fact that a woman is mentioned may have gone against the expectations of the participants and may therefore have been misleading for them. We can see here that a range of factors contribute to the misinterpretation of metonymy by Japanese speakers of English and that these factors combine linguistic and cultural features.

Finally, language learners have also been found to experience difficulties in the *identification* of metonymy. For example, Chen and Lai (2011), who treat metaphor and metonymy as a continuum, investigated the responses of twenty-eight Taiwanese learners of English when asked to rate forty sentences according to whether or not they saw them as 'figurative'. Their results showed that although the learners were capable of identifying figurative expressions in general, they were much more certain when judging metaphoric expressions than metonymic ones. They found that the topic of the sentences significantly affected the responses of the participants. For instance, their participants found it much easier to recognise expressions that conveyed anger than those that related to other topics. They conclude from this that learners of English are able to use their shared experiences in order to identify figurative language, and suggest that teachers make use of this fact to raise learners' awareness of figurative language. To the best of my knowledge, no attempts have yet been made to teach metonymy using these methods.

Metonymy production by language learners

As with metonymy comprehension, there is a paucity of research into the production of metonymy by second language learners. The most extensive study to date is that by Jiménez Catalán (2012), who conducted a corpus-based study of the use of metonymies by sixty Spanish learners of English as a foreign language. She compared metonymy production across three age groups: twenty 11–12-year-olds, twenty 15–16-year-olds and twenty adult learners. Jiménez Catalán was interested in assessing whether EFL learners make spontaneous use of metonymy when asked to write a letter in English, and whether there is a relationship between the age of the learners and their tendency to produce metonymy. In order to answer her research questions, she asked the students to write about themselves to a hypothetical host family in Great Britain. They were asked to do this in class and no dictionaries were allowed. Before conducting the metonymy analysis, she corrected spelling errors and removed proper names. She then identified instances of metonymy in the data using Barcelona's definition of metonymy and the metonymy typology provided by Radden and Kövecses (1999). She looked at both types and tokens of metonymy. Her main finding was that very little metonymy was used by the students in her study (around 8 per cent of the words used involved metonymy), even though she had taken a 'maximal' approach to its identification. As for the age/grade factor, she obtained somewhat contradictory results: whereas the amount of metonymy produced by the students increased between the ages of 11–12 and 15–16, it decreased in the adult students. No differences were observed in the types of metonymy used. Conventionalised metonymies such as grammatical and speech act patterns were found in the three age groups but non-conventionalised or novel metonymies were rare. The relatively small amount of metonymy identified by Jiménez Catalán in her study could be related to task type and register. The participants were asked to write about a very concrete topic, with a focus on transactional information exchange rather than relationship-building. In their study of metonymy use in text messaging, Littlemore and Tagg (in preparation) found that 22 per cent of the texts contained one or more metonymies, with some containing up to three. Although these figures are not exactly comparable (Littlemore and Tagg did not calculate the exact percentage of metonymically used words in their data, as many of the metonymies operated at the level of the phrase rather than the word), they do suggest a slightly higher level of metonymy use in this register. Reasons for this could include the need for rapid communication involving shorthand in text messaging (which contrasts with the time for reflection that Jiménez Catalán's participants had); the equal, intimate relationships between the writers of the text messages (which can be contrasted with the fact that Jiménez Catalán's participants were writing for an imaginary audience, and were in fact writing for their teacher, thus involving a significant power differential); the fact that texting is a much less formal register than essay writing; the fact that text-messaging itself has been found to be characterised by high levels of language play, humour and creativity (Tagg, 2013); and the fact that Jiménez Catalán's students were writing in their second language.

Indirect evidence for the avoidance of metonymy by language learners also comes from studies of phrasal verb use, although the focus of such studies is not necessarily on metonymy. For example, in her study of phrasal and prepositional verbs in a corpus of writing produced by Malay learners of English, Kamarudin (2013) was puzzled by her finding that although these learners regularly wrote about 'putting down' everyday objects – such as cups, books and toys – they virtually never wrote about 'putting down' the phone, despite the fact that this term is frequently used by native speakers of English and they would have been exposed to it fairly regularly. One reason for her finding could be that 'putting the phone down' involves a WHOLE FOR PART metonymy (it is in fact the receiver that one puts down on a traditional phone, rather than the phone itself). This may account for the apparent mismatch between the learners' frequency of exposure to this language item and their apparent failure to reproduce it in their own writing. It would be interesting to conduct a study of the role of metonymy as a possible explanatory factor in the underuse of phrasal verbs by learners of English.

In a recent study, Littlemore, Krennmayr, Turner and Turner (2011b, 2014) explored how second language learners make use of metaphor in their writing across different levels of proficiency. We found that metaphor use makes a significant contribution to a learner's performance at different levels of written language, and that the nature of its contribution varies substantially depending on their proficiency. As part of this study, in order to establish the percentage of errors that involved metaphor and to assess the role of L1 influence in these errors, we coded a number of the essays for error according to two marking criteria: a 'strict' criterion, under which non-native-like phraseology (e.g. 'all the world' instead of 'the whole world') was counted as wrong, and a 'generous' criterion, under which non-native-like phraseology was counted as correct. We then had native speakers of German and Greek (which were the two first languages of the students in our study) go through all the errors and mark them up for possible first language influence. We found that many of the instances of 'metaphor' that were coded as 'not necessarily wrong, but somehow marked' in fact involved metonymy. As the focus of the study was on metaphor rather than metonymy, we did not report our metonymy-related findings in the published paper. However, they are of interest to the current discussion so I will briefly mention some of them here. Some of the errors that contained metonymy did not appear to involve any cross-linguistic transfer. Here are two examples:

There are special traffic lights which *prefer* trams if they approach (German-speaking student; proficiency level: C1[1]).

I agree with every star who wants to protect *himself* (German-speaking student; proficiency level: B2).

The first of these examples appears to involve a SUB-EVENT FOR WHOLE EVENT metonymy combined with personification; if the traffic lights 'prefer' trams, they are more likely to go green when a tram approaches than when another sort of vehicle approaches. The second example involves a MEMBER FOR CATEGORY metonymy in which men stand for both men and women (see Chapter 5 for a discussion of the implicit sexism behind the generic use of masculine pronouns).

Many of the uses of metonymy that resulted in non-native-like phraseology appeared to involve influence from the learner's first language. In each case, the metonymy used is unmarked in the learner's first language, but sounds slightly odd in English. We can see this in the following examples:

A reason for going by bicycle is *the health* (German-speaking student; proficiency level: B2).

Because of a hill between your home and *the company* (German-speaking student; proficiency level: B2).

I wanted to go somewhere with my friends but I had to *follow* my parents (Greek-speaking student; proficiency level: B1).

The first example involves a RESULT FOR ACTION metonymy that is possible in German but which does not work in English. The second example involves an ORGANISATION FOR LOCATION metonymy that is possible in German but not in

[1] In this study we focused on five levels of proficiency within the Common European Union Framework of Reference for Languages (A2–C2). A2 was the lowest level ('false beginner') and C2 was the highest ('proficient language user').

English. The third example is a direct transfer from Greek[2] and it simply means 'go with' my parents. The word 'follow' contains a degree of passivity in English that it does not necessarily have in Greek, and therefore it sounds slightly marked in this example. In both English and Greek a MANNER FOR ACTION relationship is involved in the word 'follow'. In English, the focus is more on the manner, whereas in Greek, the focus is more on the action.

In some cases, simple grammatical mistakes were made (possibly as a result of transfer from their first language), which resulted in sentences whose meaning is different in English from what was perhaps intended by the students. We can see this in the following example:

He started as *nobody* from Austria (German-speaking student; proficiency level: B2).

Here, presumably the learner meant to say 'a nobody', which via an ATTRIBUTE FOR PERSON metonymy means an unimportant person. However, by missing out the indefinite article, he or she has inadvertently made the sentence more literal, and the person is actually 'nobody', which does not make sense.[3]

In some cases, grammatical mistakes resulted in sentences whose meaning is much more specific in English than was perhaps intended by the students. In the following example, the student inadvertently produces a word whose reading would nearly always be metonymic for a native speaker of English:

The rising costs of healthcare cause *troubles* in almost every European country (German-speaking student; level of proficiency: B2).

The 's' on the end of the word 'troubles' gives it a rather specific meaning in English. The word 'troubles' (as opposed to 'trouble') does refer to problems, but for most British speakers of English, it refers specifically to the civil war which took place in Northern Ireland between 1968 and 1998, which was referred to as 'the Troubles' (with a capital 'T'). In the Bank of English, 'the', 'in', 'Northern' and 'Ireland' are top collocates of the word 'troubles' when we look at words to the left and to the right of the search term. When the word 'troubles' is not used to refer to events in Northern Ireland, it is usually preceded by a qualifier, such as 'financial', 'economic' or ' teething' (according to the Bank of English), which explains why it sounds somewhat odd in the above example. In all of these cases, the word 'troubles' is a euphemism based on an

[2] Daphne Papadoudi, personal communication.

[3] Although German usually requires an indefinite article here too, it is possible to use the English term 'Nobody' in the same way as it is used in English. When it is used in this way, no article is needed (see www.duden.de/rechtschreibung/nobody). We can see an example of this German use of 'Nobody' in this extract from an online article about Arnold Schwarzenegger: 'Arnie-Kinderfotos und Interviews mit dem gebürtigen Steiermarker gibt dieses Porträt einen kurzweiligen, interessanten Einblick in das Leben eines Superstars, *der einmal als Nobody anefangen hat*' (Childhood photos of Arnie and interviews with the native Styrian give this portrait an entertaining, interesting view into the life of a superstar, *who started out as a nobody*).

EFFECT FOR CAUSE metonymy. We can be almost certain that the student was unaware of this very restricted sense when he or she wrote this word. Thus, he or she used a word whose meaning is narrower in English than he or she may have thought it was. In our data, metonymy was found to underlie many errors such as this, where students produced language that was not necessarily 'wrong' but was somehow 'unidiomatic'. The role of metonymy in some of these errors was very subtle indeed.

The literature on language pedagogy contains numerous examples of learner errors that appear to involve metonymy although they have not been labelled as such. For instance, Ringbom (2001: 64) refers to a phenomenon known as the 'semantic extension of single lexical unit' to fill a lexical gap in one's own language. This can lead to problems when the target language uses two words rather than one. Inaccuracies in lexical choices arise from semantically transferred errors which reflect an awareness of an existing target language form, but not of its restrictions. An example of this is the sentence uttered by a Finnish learner of English: 'He bit himself in the language.' This results from the fact that the Finnish word for both language and tongue is 'kieli' (Ringbom, 2001: 64). What Ringbom does not point out here is the fact that the use of 'kieli' to mean 'language' is a metonymic extension from its more basic meaning of 'tongue'. This metonymic extension does not work in quite the same way in English. It is possible to use the word 'tongue' to mean 'language' but it is only appropriate to do so in certain contexts, and the words 'tongue' and 'language' are by no means synonymous.

Can metonymy be 'taught' to language learners?

In stark contrast to the growing number of studies investigating the ways in which metaphor can be taught to foreign language learners, there have been no investigations thus far into whether or not language learners can be taught to understand and use metonymy. Barcelona (2010: 147–8) suggests that an explicit focus on metonymy could be beneficial to foreign language learners, and proposes the following four strategies:

1. raising learners' awareness of ubiquity of metonymy through the use of examples;
2. discussing with learners how contextual cues can be used to understand metonymy;
3. outlining and discussing language- or culture-specific barriers to metonymy comprehension; and
4. stimulating metonymy-guided reasoning.

It would be interesting to test whether these strategies actually work. Although the design of such a study would be complex, it would be worth conducting as the appropriate use of metonymy in the target language is likely to make a significant contribution to one's communicative competence. Other research indicates that getting students to act out metonymy-based expressions may lead to better retention of these expressions. For example, Lindstromberg and Boers (2005) have shown that 'manner of movement' verbs, such as 'crawl', 'leap' and 'slither', are more likely to be understood and remembered if they are physically acted out by the language learner. Although Lindstromberg and Boers did not focus on metonymy in their study, many manner-of-movement verbs involve metonymy, as we can see:

Yes I did in fact *sneeze my glasses off.* (Webcorp)

People were boarding and I *elbowed my way into line.* (BNC)

The first of these involves a CAUSE FOR EFFECT metonymy and the second involves a BODY PART INVOLVED IN ACTION FOR ACTION metonymy. No one has looked at whether sentences such as these could be usefully taught via physical movement, but one would hypothesise that they could be, as they are easy to visualise, and this would be a logical extension of Boers and Lindstromberg's findings.

Although there are no studies that have focused explicitly on the teaching of metonymy to second language learners, metonymy does occasionally surface in studies that are designed primarily to look at metaphor. The only study that puts metonymy on an equal footing with metaphor is one by MacArthur and Littlemore (2008) in which Spanish-speaking learners of English and English-speaking learners of Spanish were exposed to sets of corpus lines reflecting different figurative senses of a single word. The aim of this study was to establish whether students would develop an awareness of a 'figurative continuum' of word senses using these corpus lines. As we saw in Chapter 7, the idea of a 'figurative continuum' is that a word's senses range from the purely 'literal' through to the purely 'metaphorical', along a continuum which has metonymic senses in the middle (Dirven, 2003). So, for example, one of the words in MacArthur and Littlemore's study was 'agostado', which literally translates as 'augusted'. This word can be used metonymically to refer to the way in which the Spanish countryside looks in August (dry and yellow, parched by the sun), an expression which relies largely on a CAUSE FOR EFFECT metonymy. It can also be metaphorically extended to talk about relationships, which can also be 'agostado' (i.e. dried up and withered and on their last legs). By exposing students to sets of corpus lines that reflected different figurative senses of the same word all at the same time, MacArthur and Littlemore hoped to establish whether or not language learners would be able to use the corpus line to explore the figurative extensions of target language vocabulary, what they would do when faced with such a corpus, and whether the approach would help them learn metonymic and metaphorical extensions of word meaning.

They found the learners to be responsive to this mode of teaching but there was considerable variation across both learners and items as to how successful the method was. Alliteration and salient phraseological patterns appeared to help the students to notice and learn the meanings of the items, as did the use of gesture. They also found that those items whose *central* features were extended metonymically and metaphorically were more easily learned than those items that involved the metonymic and metaphorical extension of *peripheral* features that were extended. This meant that students experienced difficulties with items such as 'pencil in', 'table a motion' and 'mushroom' as they tried to work out their meanings by referring to central features such as the flatness of the table, the long, thin nature of a pencil and the shape of a mushroom. These features are of course not involved in the figurative extension processes of these items. This finding is in line with Littlemore, Arizono and May's (in preparation) finding mentioned above: learners expect central features to be extended rather than peripheral ones when searching for metonymic meaning, and when this is not the case it can lead to problems. Other findings made by MacArthur and Littlemore that correspond to those made by Littlemore, Arizono and May include the fact that students were able to use several different strategies in their search for meaning, such as the use of context, reference to the basic sense, and transfer, but that these strategies were rarely used in combination, and like Littlemore, Arizono and May's students, they sometimes got 'stuck' at the metaphorical end of the continuum and had difficulties understanding some of the items simply as metonymy. For example, they were unhappy with the idea that 'aletear' (to wing) simply means 'to flap', and continued to search for metaphorical interpretations for some of the items, despite having been told by the teacher that they had reached the appropriate level of understanding. To be fair, this finding could have been a reflection of the nature of the test, which focused on both metaphor and metonymy, but it is an interesting observation nonetheless.

We can thus see that there is still work to be done on the teaching of metonymy. It may be appropriate to cover it in the context of phraseology and collocation, as it does underlie a large number of fixed expressions (Hilpert, 2006). A focus on metonymy in these cases would give the learner a glimpse of the motivation behind the fixed phrase and the processes involved in its formation, which may lead to deeper and longer-lasting learning. Whether this is in fact true needs to be the subject of future studies.

8.5 Metonymy and translation

The fact that metonymy use varies so significantly from language to language suggests that it may present a challenge to translators. When faced with a metonymy in the source language, a translator can either translate it directly into the target language or find a corresponding target language expression (which may or may not involve metonymy) that is more culturally appropriate. For example, in English we can talk about a 'white table cloth restaurant', to mean a good-quality, expensive restaurant, as we can see in the following examples:

Firefly is Panama City Beach's only five star, *white table cloth restaurant.* (Webcorp)

A casual, *white table cloth restaurant* serving authentic northern Italian cuisine. (Webcorp)

the next time I have the means to go to a *white table cloth restaurant* [. . .] (Webcorp)

This involves a SALIENT PROPERTY FOR CATEGORY metonymy. If a translator were translating this into Japanese, where good restaurants do not necessarily have white table cloths, he or she could choose to keep the original term (which would involve cultural transfer and may make the reader think of European restaurants rather than Japanese restaurants) or he or she could find an equivalent Japanese term in Japanese, such as 'Kaiseki ryori', which refers to a restaurant serving traditional Japanese haute cuisine. Kaiseki ryori restaurants are expensive, but apart from that they have nothing in common with 'white table cloth' restaurants. Each of these two strategies involves the retention of part of the meaning and a loss of part of the meaning of the original message.

Jakobson (1971a and 1971b) refers to these two strategies as 'interlingual' and 'intersemiotic'. Interlingual translation involves the replacement of a verbal sign with another sign belonging to the target language. In intersemiotic translation, on the other hand, rather than focusing on the words, the translator needs to emphasise the overall message that needs to be conveyed. Thus the translator, instead of paying attention to the verbal signs, concentrates more on the information that is to be delivered. This distinction between tight 'literal' translation and a looser form of translation that focuses on the overall meaning rather than the words themselves runs through translation studies as a discipline. As with all types of language, one would expect different strategies to be appropriate in different contexts of use. In other words, one would also expect strategies to vary according to the type of metonymy involved, the function that it is performing, and the genre and register features of the text within which it is found. As we will see below, metonymies that draw on specific cultural references probably need to be translated loosely with the use of target language equivalents, whereas more direct translations can be found for the less culturally bound examples. The syntactic and illocutionary differences that are found between languages leave the translators with choices as to how close to the original text they want to sound.

Denroche (2012, 2013) looks at the issue of metonymy in translation from a different perspective. Rather than talking about the translation of metonymy, he sees metonymy itself as a translation strategy. In line with what we've seen in other chapters in this book, he believes metonymy to be a fundamental principle in conceptualisation and is thus interested in metonymy as a processing skill. He argues that the ability to 'think metonymically' is a skill that translators frequently draw upon, allowing them to make sense of the indeterminate nature of language, allowing for subtlety of expression, and changes in focus within a given schema. He goes on to discuss the 'principle of indeterminacy' (see Sections 3.2 and 5.5 of this volume), and argues that because languages are deliberately designed to under-refer, relatively small sets of words can be used flexibly and creatively to refer to an infinite number of ideas and concepts. This indeterminacy is the reason why translators need to look for partial matches rather than direct correspondences across languages, and metonymic processing is the enabler to interpretation.

He criticises much of the current literature on translation for focusing on 'literal' language and 'idioms', which he argues artificially polarises language into 'literal plateaus' and 'metaphorical spikes'. As all language is metonymic to some extent, he argues that traditional views of 'shift theory' (see Munday, 2008), which focus on the adjustments that are made by translators to express things differently in the target language, should be expanded to include the idea of 'metonymic' shifts. Because he takes a maximalist, Langacker-style approach to metonymy, he sees virtually every instance of translation as involving some kind of metonymic shift. To illustrate his ideas, he discusses the decision made by a German–English translator when translating the German term 'Feiner Papierwaren'. The translator goes through five different possibilities: 'fine paperware', 'fine paper goods', 'fine paper products', 'fine stationery' and 'quality stationery' before finally settling on 'fine paper goods'. By making this decision, the translator is therefore putting his or her own metonymic slant on the information by choosing to highlight certain features of the phenomenon while downplaying others. Searching for direct equivalents becomes no longer desirable. Denroche believes that, in translation, it is metonymic processing that turns indeterminacy and fuzziness into a virtue: 'metonymy provides the key to translation because fuzziness is what metonymy does best' (Denroche, personal communication). Denroche's ideas suggest that it would be worth focusing on metonymy in translator training programmes. Not only could such programmes focus on the explanatory role that metonymy can play in language errors and mistranslations, they might also evaluate the more positive contribution that metonymy can potentially play in increasing translator awareness, which would lead to a concomitant improvement in translation skills.

Another challenge for the translator derives from the role played by metonymy in linguistic humour. We saw in Chapter 5 that metonymy is often exploited for humorous purposes and, as one might expect, this sort of humour does not translate easily across languages. In line with Denroche's proposal,

Rojo López (2009) discusses the challenges that metonymy-based humour presents to translators, and suggests that translators make use of metonymy as an inferential process involving frame semantics and ICMs when attempting to translate this sort of humour. She illustrates her ideas with examples from three British novels and their translations into Spanish: *Small World* by David Lodge, *Money* by Martin Amis and *The Buddha of Suburbia* by Hanif Kureishi. In these novels, she finds four examples of the most productive types of metonymic mappings: PART FOR WHOLE, MATERIAL FOR OBJECT, CAUSE FOR EFFECT and PRODUCER FOR PRODUCT. She follows Peirsman and Geeraerts' (2006a) prototypical organisation of conceptual contiguity, which was discussed in Chapter 3, and classifies these mappings into two different domains: contiguity in the spatial and material domain and contiguity in the domain of actions, events and processes. For reasons of space, we will discuss just one of her examples here. In the *Buddha of Suburbia*, two characters are having a racist conversation about their Indian neighbour:

And has he got his camel parked outside?
No, he came on a magic carpet
Cyril Lord or *Debenhams*? (Kureishi, 1990: 12)

The references to 'Cyril Lord' and 'Debenhams' involve a PRODUCER FOR PRODUCT metonymy and they represent 'upmarket' and 'everyday' carpets respectively. Rojo López points out that a direct translation into Spanish would simply not work here as these two shops are not known in Spain and it would be difficult to think of two equivalent shops in Spain. Moreover, as the action takes place in the UK it would be very odd to mention Spanish shops. She therefore suggests that translators employ a different metonymic relationship, the TRAIT FOR PRODUCT relationship, when translating this into Spanish, to produce the sentence: artesana o sintetica? Being explicit about the role of metonymy in examples such as this and deliberately looking for alternative metonymic relationships is likely to prove a useful strategy for translators.

8.6 Conclusion

In this chapter, we have seen that metonymy presents both challenges and opportunities in cross-linguistic and cross-cultural communication. It can be difficult for language learners to understand, with these difficulties stemming from several sources, such as misleading contextual clues, interference from one's first language, over- and under-specification and a general fear of the unknown. Metonymy also lies behind many uses of the target language that appear 'marked' if not necessarily 'wrong'. An explicit focus on metonymy in the language classroom may therefore bring considerable benefits to learners and would reveal the mechanisms that lie behind different forms of expression and help explain why languages vary in terms of the perspective that they take. For translators, too, metonymy has the potential to serve as a powerful tool for expression, and the presentation of different perspectives allows for creativity in the translation process. In inter-cultural communication we know relatively little about the extent to which, or the ways in which, metonymy contributes to misunderstanding or increases shared knowledge between speakers, as it is such an elusive concept, and speakers will rarely be aware of its presence. However, as we saw above, a failure to grasp the intended metonymic meaning of an utterance can have significant consequences. It would therefore be worthwhile conducting more thorough investigations of the use of metonymy in cross-linguistic and cross-cultural communication.

9 'These huts did absolutely unbelievable work'

What do we now know about metonymy?

9.1 Introduction

In this book, we have seen that metonymic thinking is an everyday process which plays a key role in helping us make sense of the world. Because of this, metonymy features in all forms of communication, where it performs a wide range of functions. We have also seen that a focus on metonymy has the potential to provide new insights into the ways in which we communicate in language as well as in other modes of communication. In this chapter, I sum up what we now know about metonymy, showing how this knowledge takes us well beyond 'traditional' views. I then briefly outline a few things that we still do not know about metonymy, and suggest new avenues for research, with a focus on real-world applications.

9.2 What do we now know about metonymy?

Traditional accounts of metonymy have focused mainly on its referential function and have looked at how it works in language, mainly relying on examples where the metonymy is in the noun group. In this book, we have seen that it is more appropriate to adopt a broader definition of metonymy than this, move beyond its referential functions and explore the role that it plays in real-world communication. When we look at metonymy in this way, we can see that it has a number of characteristics that show it to be a far more interesting and unpredictable phenomenon than one might think. Taken together, these characteristics show that metonymy works just as hard as metaphor and that it does just as many things as metaphor. Some of the main characteristics of metonymy follow.

Metonymy is not just found in language

Although it is often described as a 'figure of speech', metonymy does not just exist in language. It is a key component of our thinking processes and therefore finds outlets in many different forms of expression, including film, art, music, dance, sign language and gesture. By studying the ways in which it operates in these different modes of expression, we have been able to witness different features of metonymy from those that have traditionally been explored in linguistic accounts.

Metonymy serves a wide range of rhetorical functions

We have seen that metonymy serves an array of functions, such as persuasion, relationship-building, evaluation, euphemism and the expression of irony. Metonymy can also contribute to the cohesiveness of texts because of the 'Domain Availability Principle' and the existence of broad matrix domains. Metonymy serves subtle illocutionary functions, many of which do not transfer seamlessly across languages. There are numerous discourse-community-specific uses of metonymy, such as the dentist's receptionist who calls to the dentist 'your 3.30 toothache is here', or the father on the touchline at the children's football match who shouts to his son 'stand on it'. The meanings of these metonymies may not always be apparent to people outside those particular discourse communities, or even people, such as the young football players, who are still in the process of being initiated into the discourse communities. We have also seen metonymy being used in the service of euphemism and dysphemism, hyperbole, creative language play and humour. It plays a key role in vague language and all the subtle nuances that vague language is used to perform. Finally, we have seen examples of metonymy being used for ideology and positioning, particularly by politicians, but also in other contexts, such as everyday communication and even literature. In addition to performing all of these functions, metonymy serves as a key device in meaning extension in both spoken and sign language as well as in other modes of artistic expression.

Metonymy is often used playfully and creatively and for humorous effect

We have seen in this volume that metonymy plays a key role in creative expression in forms of expression including language, art, film and music, and as such, serves as a useful, but perhaps unexpected device for creating new meaning. It has the potential to be involved in the creation of new relationships, especially in art where items are unexpectedly juxtaposed to create new meaning and to help us see things in radically different ways, and to question our assumptions about the world. Metonymy is often involved in 'playful' activity, not just in language but in all forms of expression. The contrast between the literal and metonymic meanings of words and concepts is often used as a creative and/or humorous device. Another feature of metonymy which allows it to be involved in creative language play and humour is the fact that, like metaphor, it can involve multiple mappings between the source and target domain, and these mappings can be very complex. This complexity means that people play with metonymy at least as much as they play with metaphor.

Metonymy can be found in many different parts of speech

When we look at traditional accounts of metonymy in the literature, we see that the examples used are nearly always nouns, and that they nearly always occur in head position, such as the now-famous 'ham sandwich on Table 6' example. However, when we look at metonymy in real-world data, we see that it appears in a wide range of parts of speech besides the noun. Metonymy allows people to have 'round table' discussions, 'walk up the aisle', 'hoover up' and have 'healthy diets'. As we can see in these examples, metonymies are by no means always the nouns, although the artificially created examples that are discussed in the literature often are.

Metonymy extends beyond the level of the word

Metonymy can operate well beyond the level of the individual word. It is often very difficult to say where exactly the metonymy sits in a sentence, and metonymic meaning is rarely attached to just one particular word. Rather, metonymic meaning tends to hover over a sentence or a phrase. Metonymy can also serve as an important form of cohesion across a whole text or speech or even a whole book. This is also true of metonymy in other forms of communication. In music, brief metonymic episodes can refer to entire musical genres, and in film and theatre a whole scene can operate as a single metonymy.

Metonymy is subtle and flexible

The final important thing to say about metonymy is that its meanings can be extremely flexible and open to interpretation. Metonymic meaning relies very heavily on context and shared experience. The subtle nature of metonymy means that it provides a useful tool to speakers who may not want to be entirely specific about exactly what it is that they are talking about, as we saw in Chapter 5, where the speaker referred to 'Longfield Terrace' to refer obliquely to a series of the traumatic events that took place there during his childhood. This flexibility, combined with the fact that shared background knowledge is often required to access the intended meaning, explains why metonymy plays such a key role in the building and negotiating of relationships.

9.3 What do we still not know about metonymy and how might metonymy research continue to be used in the 'real world'?

Despite these gains in our knowledge about metonymy, there are still a number of unanswered questions. Moreover, we have seen that metonymy has a large number of potential real-world applications – particularly in the areas of psychological counselling, education, translation studies, advertising and inter-cultural communication – but there have to date been no studies of the actual contribution that an awareness of metonymy might make in these areas. In this section, I outline those areas where more research into metonymy could usefully be conducted, beginning with theoretical issues and then moving out towards more practical applications.

On a theoretical level, a first concern is that we are still not very good at defining and identifying it. Much of the difficulty here derives from the similarity between metonymy and metaphor. Although much has been written on the similarities and differences between metonymy and metaphor and the relationship between them, close examination of the phenomena in real-life communication reveals a very messy situation. Because of the substantial amount of overlap between them, the clear-cut examples that are often discussed in the literature cannot be said to be representative of the phenomena as a whole, and the claims that are made about these examples may not be applicable to other less prototypical instances of metonymy, or indeed metaphor. The fact that it is often difficult to disambiguate metonymy from metaphor therefore makes it difficult to identify in language and in other forms of expression. It is also difficult to see where an instance of metonymy begins and ends, particularly in forms of expression such as music, dance and sign language, but also in language, where, as we have just seen, it operates at the level of the phrase or even of the entire text, not just at the level of the word.

A second area where theoretical knowledge is lacking is the issue of 'novel' versus 'conventional' metonymy. Many uses of metonymy are so conventional that people may not even see them as metonymy, which makes them very different from some of the highly original and creative uses of metonymy that we have seen in this book. We have seen, for example, that creative and conventional uses of metonymy are processed very differently in the mind, regardless of the mode in which they are presented, with conventional metonymy being processed in much the same way as literal language. More work needs to be done to see how these differences relate to the clines from prototypical to less prototypical metonymy that were discussed in Chapter 3. Particular attention needs to be paid to instances of metonymy that lie in the middle of the continuum. Although they may look conventional and thus be processed as such, they may well encode a particular perspective or evaluative slant that is so subtle that it will be taken at face value and not questioned by the interlocutor. Such uses of metonymy are likely to be among the most powerful forms of persuasive language.

A third under-explored theoretical issue that would benefit from more research concerns the roles played by metonymy in other modes of expression besides language. In this book, we have only really focused on a small number of modes of expression; it would be interesting to examine the ways in which metonymy operates in others, such as mime, dance and religious ritual. This last area would be particularly interesting as it would allow for a focus on the role of metonymy in the meaning-making process and in helping people address fundamental questions concerning life and death.

Metonymy research has a great many potential practical applications. The most socially relevant is the role that it plays in the development of delusions in patients with schizophrenia and related disorders. Because of the way it blends fantasy and reality metonymic thinking is a particularly pernicious phenomenon in this context. This is because it sits half way between 'literal' thinking and 'metaphorical' thinking. Although people may be used to the idea of metaphor and the fact that it is used to describe one thing in terms of another, there is much less awareness of metonymy outside the field of linguistics. Even if people have heard of it, they are often unsure as to exactly what it is. This means that they are unlikely to be aware of the role that it plays in their own thinking processes, and they may at times conflate it with 'literal' thinking. In psychology this is likely to be true of both patients and counsellors, making metonymy-based delusions much more difficult to identify than ones that are based on metaphor. It would therefore be helpful to make the role of metonymic thinking more explicit during counselling sessions, thus helping patients to address and confront the exact nature of some of their delusions. More research is therefore needed to explore the benefits or otherwise of focusing explicitly on metonymy during psychological counselling, and of including it in training programmes for counsellors.

Metonymy research also has the potential to contribute to the field of education. A more overt focus on metonymy would be particularly beneficial for students of language (be it their own language, or a foreign language), as it could help them to develop a clearer understanding of how language works. It could also help them to speak and write more effectively by using metonymy to perform functions such as persuasion, relationship-building, and the expression of humour and irony. We have seen that metonymy can present serious comprehension difficulties to second language learners; what we do not yet know is the extent to which learners are aware of these difficulties, and how they might be helped to overcome them. It might also be useful to focus on metonymy in subjects such as art, music, design and media studies. We have seen that many of the creative processes underlying these disciplines rely on metonymy. Even the so-called 'hard sciences' contain theoretical concepts that have a strong metonymic basis, and this is reflected in the terminology that is used in those disciplines. If the metonymic basis of some of this terminology were explained to students, it might improve their understanding of the concepts themselves. All academic disciplines employ metonymy to some extent in their construction of their world view, and metonymic thinking guides and influences reasoning processes in all walks of life. Nevertheless there have been very few attempts to analyse this and its implications for epistemology and interdisciplinary communication. A heightened awareness of the role played by metonymic thinking in theory construction, and of the different ways in which this process operates across disciplines could lead to improvements in communication and understanding between researchers from different disciplinary backgrounds.

The work on the role of metonymy in advertising that we saw in Chapter 5 suggests that there may be a place for a more explicit, systematic focus on multimodal metonymy by those working in advertising. At present, much of the creative work that is done in advertising is carried out in an intuitive manner, and a more systematic analysis of the metonymic thinking processes that underlie the decision-making processes employed by both advertisers and consumers could prove beneficial. Empirical studies involving informants could usefully test out the impact of metonymy on consumers' attitudes towards the products being advertised. The findings from such research could then be used to make advertisements more effective and more targeted, and to make them work better on a psychological level.

Metonymy has the potential to make a significant contribution to intercultural communication and understanding. We saw in Chapter 4 how metonymy is used to create 'in-groups' and 'out-groups', and to refer to 'others' in less than complimentary ways. This is sometimes done inadvertently, and when this is the case it may contribute to increased levels of antagonism. As with the counselling contexts discussed above, people may be aware of metaphor and of the ways in which it is used to make sense of abstract concepts, but they are often much less aware of metonymy and the role that it plays in the development and expression of ideas. As a result, the metonymic nature of some widely discussed ideas may not be fully acknowledged. For example, in British school history lessons, children learn about the way 'Germany' behaved in the Second World War and the fact that 'we' fought the 'Japanese', who had a reputation for being 'indomitable'. There is often little consideration of the metonymic basis of such claims and the fact that they are not literally true. In contemporary politics, we rarely see discussions of exactly what politicians mean when they talk about 'the European Union', or even 'the economy'. Terms such as these are used as metonymic shorthand to refer to different aspects of highly complex entities. In order for any successful communication to take place, there needs to be a tacit agreement between speakers that they are being used to talk about the same thing. However, this is unlikely to be the case, particularly when the speakers have different linguistic, cultural or political backgrounds. An increased awareness of the nature, extent and power of metonymy among politicians, diplomats, businessmen and -women, translators, and others that are involved in cross-linguistic or cross-cultural communication could go some way towards improving international understanding.

Finally, we saw in Chapter 6 how important accurate metonymy resolution can be for human–computer interaction. Work on the grammatical forms of metonymy and the functions that it performs could contribute to the endeavour of metonymy recognition by machines. If computers are to interpret human language properly, then they need to be programmed to 'understand' that human language and communication in general is often not literal, and that perspective is always encoded in language. We have already seen that an ability to detect and comprehend metonymy improves the success rate of language 'comprehension' by computers, but, as with all the areas listed above, there is still much more to be done.

9.4 Conclusion

Metonymy is everywhere. It shapes the way we think and the way we influence the thoughts of others. Meaning is underspecified in all forms of communication, leaving much of the interpretative work to the reader, viewer or listener. Metonymic thinking forms the core of this interpretative work and is something that we engage in all the time in order to extract meaning from language and other forms of communication. On a recent tour of the work huts in the grounds of Bletchley Park in the UK, where the Nazi 'enigma code' was broken in 1941, the tour guide uttered the metonymy 'these huts did unbelievable work' to refer to the contribution that the (mainly female) decoders working inside those huts had made to the war effort. This relatively innocuous use of metonymy went largely unnoticed by the tour group, but the guide was able to use these six words to express a large amount of information concisely and elegantly. What the tour guide was saying about those women working in those huts in Bletchley Park is also true of metonymy. It does 'absolutely unbelievable work' but it tends to do so behind the scenes; it is a modest trope, and more often than not we do not even notice it. But we should.

References

Abbott, C., and Forceville, C. (2011). Visual representation of emotion in manga: loss of control is loss of hands in Azumanga Daioh, volume 4. *Language and Literature, 20* (19): 91–112.

Alač, M., and Coulson, S. (2004). The man, the key or the car: who or what is parked out back? *Cognitive Science Online*, 2: 21–34. Available at: http://cogscionline.ucsd.edu/2/vol2_issue1.pdf.

Alexander, R. (1997). *Aspects of Verbal Humour in English*. Tübingen: Gunter Narr.

Allan, K., and Burridge, K. (1991). *Euphemism and Dysphemism*. Oxford University Press.

Al-Sharafi, A. (2004). *Textual Metonymy: A Semiotic Approach*, Basingstoke: Palgrave Macmillan.

Annaz, D., Van Herwegen, J., Thomas, M. S. C., Fishman, R., Karmiloff-Smith, A., and Rundblad, G. (2008). The comprehension of metaphor and metonymy in children with Williams syndrome. *International Journal of Language and Communication Disorders, 44* (6): 962–78.

Attardo, S. (2006). Cognitive linguistics and humor. *Humor: International Journal of Humor Research, 19* (3): 341–362.

Attardo, S., and Raskin, V. (1991). Script theory revis(it)ed: joke similarity and joke representational model. *Humor: International Journal of Humor Research, 4* (3): 293–347.

Barcelona, A. (ed.) (2003a). *Metaphor and Metonymy at the Crossroads: A Cognitive Perspective*. Berlin and New York: Mouton de Gruyter.

Barcelona, A. (2003b). Metonymy in cognitive linguistics: an analysis and a few modest proposals. In H. Cuyckens, Th. Berg, R. Dirven and K.-U. Panther (eds.) *Motivation in Language. Studies in Honour of Gunter Radden*. Amsterdam: Benjamins, 223–55.

Barcelona, A. (2003c). Names: a metonymic 'return ticket' in five languages. *Jezikoslovlje, 4*: 11–41.

Barcelona, A. (2003d). The case for a metonymic basis of pragmatic inferencing: evidence from jokes and funny anecdotes. In K.-U. Panther and L. Thornburg (eds.) *Metonymy and Pragmatic Inferencing*. Amsterdam: John Benjamins, 81–102.

Barcelona, A. (2004). Metonymy behind grammar: the motivation of the seemingly 'irregular' grammatical behaviour of English paragon names. In G. Radden and K.-U. Panther (eds.) *Studies in Linguistic Motivation*. Berlin: Mouton de Gruyter, 357–74.

Barcelona, A. (2010). Metonymic inferencing and second language acquisition. *AILA Review, 23*: 134–55.

Barcelona, A. (2011). Reviewing the properties and prototype structure of metonymy. In R. Benczes, A. Barcelona and F. J. Ruiz de Mendoza Ibáñez, (eds.) *Defining Metonymy in Cognitive Linguistics: Towards a Consensus View*. Amsterdam: John Benjamins, 7–57.

Barcelona, A. (2012). Metonymy-guided inferences in creative thinking (humour, theology and art). Paper presented at the 9th Conference of the International Association Researching and Applying Metaphor, Lancaster, United Kingdom.

Barker, P. (1993). *The Eye in the Door*. London: Penguin Books.

Barker, P. (1996). *Liza's England*. London: Virago Press.

Barnbrook, G., Mason, O., and Krishnamurthy, R. (2013). *Collocation: Implications and Applications*. Basingstoke: Palgrave Macmillan.

Barnden J. (2010). Metaphor and metonymy: making their connections more slippery. *Cognitive Linguistics, 21* (1), 1–34.

Barnden, J. (2013). Hyperbole, metaphor, simile and irony: a constellation of connections. Paper presented at the Stockholm Metaphor Festival, Stockholm, Sweden.

Barnes, J. (2009). *Staring at the Sun*. London: Vintage Books.

Barthes, R. (1972). *Mythologies*. New York: Hill and Wang.

Barthes, R. (1993). *Œuvres complètes*. Paris: Éditions du Seuil.

Bartsch, R. (2002). Generating polysemy: metaphor and metonymy. In R. Dirven and R. Pörings (eds.) *Metaphor and Metonymy in Comparison and Contrast*. Berlin and New York: Mouton de Gruyter, 49–74.

BBC (n.d.). Listening Project website, www.bbc.co.uk/radio4/features/the-listening-project.

Bede (731). *An Ecclesiastical History of the English People*. Oxford World Classics.

Benczes, R. (2013). The role of alliteration and rhyme in novel metaphorical and metonymical compounds. *Metaphor and Symbol, 28*: 167–84.

Biernacka, E. (2013). 'The role of metonymy in political discourse. Unpublished PhD thesis, Milton Keynes: The Open University.

Blank, A. (1999). Co-presence and succession: a cognitive typology of metonymy. In K.-U. Panther and G. Radden (eds.) *Metonymy in Language and Thought*. Amsterdam: John Benjamins, 169–91.

Bräm, P. B., and Bräm, T. (2004). Expressive gestures used by classical orchestra conductors. In C. Müller and R. Posner (eds.) *The Semantics and Pragmatics of Everyday Gestures: Proceedings of the Berlin Conference April 1998*. Berlin: Weidler Buchverlag.

Brdar, M. (2007). *Metonymy in Grammar: Towards Motivating Extensions of Grammatical Categories and Constructions*. Osijek: Faculty of Philosophy, Josip Juraj Strossmayer University.

Brdar, M., and Brdar-Szabó, R. (2003). Metonymic coding of linguistic action in English, Croatian and Hungarian. In K.-U. Panther and L. Thornburg (eds.) *Metonymy and Pragmatic Inferencing*. Amsterdam: John Benjamins, 241–66.

Brdar, M., and Brdar-Szabó, R. (2009). The (non) metonymic use of place names in English, German, Hungarian and Croatian. In K.-U. Panther, L. Thornburg and A. Barcelona (eds.) *Metonymy and Metaphor in Grammar*. Amsterdam: John Benjamins, 229–57.

Brdar-Szabó, R. (2009). Metonymy in indirect directives: stand-alone conditionals in English, German, Hungarian, and Croatian. In K.-U. Panther, L. Thornburg and A. Barcelona (eds.) *Metonymy and Metaphor in Grammar*. Amsterdam: John Benjamins, 323–36.

Brdar-Szabó, R., and Brdar, M. (2004). Predicate adjectives and grammatical-relational polysemy: the role of metonymic processes in motivating cross-linguistic differences. In G. Radden and K.-U. Panther (eds.) *Studies in Linguistic Motivation*. Berlin: Mouton de Gruyter, 321–55.
Brdar-Szabó, R., and Brdar, M. (2011). What do metonymic chains reveal about the nature of metonymy? In R. Benczes, A. Barcelona and F. J. Ruiz de Mendoza Ibáñez (eds.) *Defining Metonymy in Cognitive Linguistics: Towards a Consensus View*. Amsterdam: John Benjamins, 217–48.
Brdar-Szabó, R., and Brdar, M. (2012). The problem of data in cross-linguistic research on metonymy. *Language Sciences*, *34*, 728–45.
Brône, G., and Feyaerts, K. (2003). The cognitive linguistics of incongruity resolution. Unpublished manuscript, University of Leuven.
Bührig, K., and ten Thije, J. D. (eds.) (2006). *Beyond Misunderstanding: Linguistic Analyses of Intercultural Communication*. Amsterdam: Philadelphia.
Butow, R. (1954). *Japan's Decision to Surrender*. Stanford University Press.
Byram, M. (1997). *Teaching and Assessing Intercultural Communicative Competence*. Clevedon: Multilingual Matters.
Byram, M., and Risager, K. (1999). *Language Teachers, Politics and Cultures*. Clevedon: Multilingual Matters.
Cameron, L. (2003). *Metaphor in Educational Discourse*. London: Continuum Press.
Cameron, L., and Deignan, A. (2003). Combining large and small corpora to investigate tuning devices around metaphor in spoken discourse. *Metaphor and Symbol*, *18* (3): 149–60.
Cameron, L., and Deignan, A. (2006). The emergence of metaphor in discourse. *Applied Linguistics*, *27* (4): 671–90.
Carston, R. (1997). Enrichment and loosening: complementary processes in deriving the proposition expressed? *Linguitische Berichte*, *8*, 103–27.
Carter, R. (2004). *Language and Creativity: The Art of Common Talk*. London: Routledge.
Channell, J. (1994). *Vague Language*. Oxford University Press.
Charteris-Black, J. (2003). Speaking with forked tongue: a comparative study of metaphor and metonymy in English and Malay phraseology. *Metaphor and Symbol*, *18* (4): 289–310.
Charteris-Black, J. (2012). Shattering the bell jar: metaphor, gender and depression. *Metaphor and Symbol*, *27* (3): 199–216.
Chen, Y., and Lai, H. (2011). EFL learners' awareness of the metonymy-metaphor continuum in figurative expressions. *Language Awareness*, *21* (3): 235–48.
Chenard, M. M. (2005). King Oswald's holy hands: metonymy and the making of a saint in Bede's Ecclesiastical History. *Exemplaria*, *17* (1): 33–56.
Chuang, Y.-C. (2010). Metaphors and gestures in music teaching: an examination of junior high schools in Taiwan. Unpublished PhD dissertation, University of York, UK.
Cienki, A., and Mittelberg, I. (in preparation). Creativity in the forms and functions of spontaneous gesture. Draft paper received through personal communication.
Cockroft, R., and Cockroft, S. (2005). *Persuading People: The Art of Rhetoric*. Basingstoke: Palgrave Macmillan.
Collins COBUILD English Grammar (2011). Glasgow: Harper Collins.
Corbett, E. P. J. (1990). *Classical Rhetoric for the Modern Student*. New York: Oxford University Press.

Coulson, S., and Oakley, T. (2003). Metonymy and conceptual blending. In K.-U. Panther and L. Thornburg (eds.) *Metonymy and Pragmatic Inferencing*. Amsterdam: John Benjamins, 51–79.

Croft, W. (2002). The role of domains in the interpretation of metaphors and metonymies. In R. Dirven and R. Porings (eds.) *Metaphor and Metonymy in Comparison and Contrast*. Cognitive Linguistics Research 20. Berlin and New York: Mouton de Gruyter, 161–205.

Croft, W., and Cruse, A. (2004). *Cognitive Linguistics*. Cambridge University Press.

Cutting, J. (2007). Introduction. In J. Cutting (ed.) *Vague Language Explored*. Basingstoke: Palgrave Macmillan, 3–19.

Deignan, A. (2005a). *Metaphor and Corpus Linguistics*. Amsterdam: John Benjamins.

Deignan, A. (2005b). A corpus linguistic perspective on the relationship between metonymy and metaphor. *Style, 39* (1): 72–91.

Deignan, A., and Armstrong, S. (forthcoming, 2015). Payback and punishment: figurative language in Scottish penal policy. In B. Herrmann and T. B. Sardinha (eds.) *Metaphor in Specialist Discourse: Investigating Metaphor Use in Specific and Popularized Discourse Contexts*. Amsterdam: John Benjamins.

Deignan, A., Littlemore, J., and Semino, E. (2013). *Figurative Language, Genre and Register*. Cambridge University Press.

Denroche, C. (2012). Metonymic processing: a cognitive ability relevant to translators, editors and language teachers. In G. Mininni and A. Manuti (eds.) *Applied Psycholinguistics: Positive Effects and Ethical Perspectives*. Milan: FrancoAngeli, 69–74.

Denroche, C. (2013). A metonymic theory of translation. Paper presented at the 3rd International Conference on Meaning Construction, Meaning Interpretation: Applications and Implications (CRAL, 2013), University of La Rioja, Logrono, Spain.

Dickens, C. (2004). *The Pickwick Papers*. London: Penguin Classics.

Dirven, R. (1999). Conversion as a conceptual metonymy of an event structure. In R. Dirven, and R. Pörings (eds.) *Metaphor and Metonymy in Comparison and Contrast*. Berlin and New York: Mouton de Gruyter, 275–87.

Dirven, R. (2003). Metonymy and metaphor: different mental strategies of conceptualisation [1993]. In R. Dirven, and R. Pörings (eds.) *Metaphor and Metonymy in Comparison and Contrast*. Berlin and New York: Mouton de Gruyter, 75–112.

Durán Escribano, P., and Roldan Riejos, A. (2008). The role of context in the interpretation of academic and professional communication. In T. Gibert Maceda and L. Alba Juez (eds.) *Estudios de Filología Inglesa: Homenaje a la Dra Asunción Alba Pelayo*. Madrid: Universidad Nacional de Educación a Distancia, 81–94.

Earles, J. L., and Kersten, A. W. (2000). Adult age differences in memory for verbs and nouns. *Aging, Neuropsychology, and Cognition Neuropsychology, Development and Cognition, 7* (2): 130–9.

Evans, V. (2007). *A Glossary of Cognitive Linguistics*. Edinburgh University Press.

Evans, V., and Green, M. (2006). *Cognitive Linguistics: An Introduction*. Edinburgh University Press.

Fass, D. (1991). Met*: a method for discriminating metonymy and metaphor by computer. *Computational Linguistics, 17* (1): 49–90.

Fass, D. (1997). *Processing Metonymy and Metaphor: Contemporary Studies in Cognitive Science and Technology*, Vol. I, Westport, CT: Ablex Publishing.

Fauconnier, G., and Turner, M. (1999). Metonymy and conceptual integration. In K.-U. Panther and G. Radden (eds.) *Metonymy in Language and Thought*. Amsterdam: John Benjamins, 77–90.

Faulks, S. (2010). *A Week in December*. London: Vintage Books.

Faulks, S. (2012). *A Possible Life: Part V 'You Next Time'*. London: Hutchinson.

Fellbaum, C. (ed.) (1998). *Wordnet: An Electronic Lexical Database*. Cambridge, MA: MIT Press.

Ferrari, F. (2007). Metaphor at work in the analysis of political discourse: investigating a 'preventive war' persuasion strategy. *Discourse and Society*, *18* (5): 603–25.

Fillmore, C. (1982). Frame semantics. In The Linguistic Society of Korea (eds.) *Linguistics in the Morning Calm*. Seoul: Hanshin. 111–37.

Forceville, C. (2008). Pictorial and multimodal metaphor in commercials. In E. F. McQuarrie and B. J. Phillips (eds.) *Go Figure! New Directions in Advertising Rhetoric*, Armonk, NY: ME Sharpe, 272–310.

Forceville, C. (2009). Metonymy in visual and audiovisual discourse. In E. Ventola and A. J. Moya Guijarro (eds.) *The World Told and the World Shown: Multisemiotic Issues*. Basingstoke: Palgrave Macmillan, 56–74.

Forceville, C. (2012). Creative metaphors, metonymies, blends? Music & sound in documentary film. Paper presented at the 9th Conference of the International Association Researching and Applying Metaphor, Lancaster, United Kingdom.

Friedman, J. (2012). Cézanne and the poetics of metonymy. *Word and Image: A Journal of Verbal and Visual Enquiry*, *23* (3): 327–36.

Frischberg, N. (1979). Historical change: from iconic to arbitrary. In E. Klima and U. Bellugi (eds.) *The Signs of Language*. Harvard University Press.

Frisson, S. (2009). Semantic underspecification in language processing. *Language and Linguistics Compass*, *3* (1): 111–27.

Frisson, S., and Pickering, M. J. (1999). The processing of metonymy: evidence from eye movements. *Journal of Experimental Psychology: Learning, Memory, and Cognition*, *25*: 1366–83.

Gallese, V. (2009). Mirror neurons, embodied simulation, and the neural basis of social identification. *Psychoanalytic Dialogues*, *19* (5): 519–36.

Gallese, V., and Lakoff, G. (2005). The brain's concepts: the role of the sensory-motor system in conceptual knowledge. *Cognitive Neuropsychology*, *22* (3/4): 455–79.

Gavilán, J. M., and García-Albea, J. E. (2011). Theory of mind and language comprehension in schizophrenia: poor mindreading affects figurative language comprehension beyond intelligence deficits. *Journal of Neurolinguistics*, *24*: 54–69.

Geeraerts, D. (2003). The interaction of metaphor and metonymy in composite expressions. In R. Dirven and R. Pörings (eds.) *Metaphor and Metonymy in Comparison and Contrast*. Berlin: Mouton de Gruyter, 435–65.

Gibbs, R. (1994). *The Poetics of Mind: Figurative Thought, Language, and Understanding*. Cambridge University Press.

Gibbs, R. (1999). Speaking and thinking with metonymy. In K.-U. Panther and G. Radden (eds.) *Metonymy in Language and Thought*. Amsterdam: John Benjamins, 61–76.

Gibbs, R. (2000). Making good psychology out of blending theory. *Cognitive Linguistics*, *11*, 3–4: 347–58.

Gibbs, R. (2007). Experiential tests of figurative meaning construction. In G. Radden, K. M. Köpcke, T. Berg and P. Siemund (eds.) *Aspects of Meaning Construction*. Amsterdam: John Benjamins, 19–32.

Gibbs, R. (2013). Metaphoric cognition as social activity: dissolving the divide between metaphor in thought and communication. *Metaphor and the Social World, 3* (1): 54–75.

Gibbs, R., and Santa Cruz, M. (2012). The unfolding of conceptual metaphors. *Metaphor and Symbol, 27* (4): 299–311.

Giora, R., and Fein, O. (1999). On understanding familiar and less-familiar figurative language. *Journal of Pragmatics, 31* (12): 1601–18.

Goldberg, A. (1995). *A Construction Grammar Approach to Argument Structure*. University of Chicago Press.

Goldberg, A. (2006). *Constructions at Work*. Oxford University Press.

Goossens, L. (1990). Metaphtonymy: the interaction of metaphor and metonymy in expressions for linguistic action. *Cognitive Linguistics*, 1 (3): 323–40.

Goossens, L. (2003). Metaphtonymy: the interaction of metaphor and metonymy in expressions for linguistic action [revised version]. In R. Dirven and R. Pörings (eds.) *Metaphor and Metonymy in Comparison and Contrast*. Berlin and New York: Mouton de Gruyter, 349–78.

Gradečak-Erdeljić, T. (2004). Euphemisms in the language of politics or how metonymy opens one door but closes the other. In P. Cap (ed.) *New Developments in Linguistic Pragmatics*. Department of English Language, University of Łódź, 27.

Grady, J. (1997). Theories are buildings revisited. *Cognitive Linguistics, 8* (4): 267–90.

Green, D. (2005). *Metonymy in Contemporary Art: A New Paradigm*. Minneapolis: University of Minnesota Press.

Gries, S. Th. (2011). Phonological similarity in multi-word units. *Cognitive Linguistics, 22* (3): 491–511.

Halliday, M. A. K. (1994). *An Introduction to Functional Grammar*. London: Edward Arnold.

Halliday, M. A. K. (2004). *An Introduction to Functional Grammar* (3rd edn.) London: Edward Arnold.

Halverson, S., and Engene, O. (2010). Domains and dimensions in metonymy: a corpus-based study of Schengen and Maastricht. *Metaphor and Symbol, 25*: 1–18.

Hamilton, C. (2012). New directions in rhetoric. Presentation given at the Centre for Advanced Research in English (CARE), University of Birmingham.

Hamilton, M. (1988). Using masculine generics: does generic *he* increase male bias in the user's imagery? *Sex Roles, 19* (11/12): 785–99.

Handl, S. (2011). *The Conventionality of Figurative Language: A Usage-Based Study*. Tubingen: Narr Verlag.

Handl, S. (2012). From FOR to AND: metonymic underspecification as a test case for linguistic theory. Paper presented at the 9th conference of the International Association Researching and Applying Metaphor, Lancaster, United Kingdom.

Harabagiu, S. (1998). Deriving metonymic coercions from Wordnet. In *The Proceedings of the COLING ACL Workshop 'Usage of Wordnet in Natural Language Processing Systems', Montreal, Quebec*. New Brunswick, NJ: Association for Computational Linguistics, 142–8.

Harrison, S. (forthcoming, 2015). The production line as a context for low metaphoricity: exploring links between gestures, iconicity, and artefacts on a factory shop floor. In B. Herrmann and T. Berber Sardinha (eds.) *Metaphor in Specialist Discourse: Investigating Metaphor Use in Technical, Scientific and Popularized Discourse Contexts*. Amsterdam: John Benjamins.

Herrero Ruiz, J. (2011). The role of metonymy in complex tropes: cognitive operations and pragmatic implications. In R. Benczes, A. Barcelona and F. J. Ruiz de Mendoza Ibáñez (eds.) *Defining Metonymy in Cognitive Linguistics: Towards a Consensus View*. Amsterdam: John Benjamins, 167–93.

Hilpert, M. (2006). Keeping an eye on the data: metonymies and their patterns. In A. Stefanowitsch and S. Gries (eds.) *Corpus-based Approaches to Metaphor and Metonymy*. Berlin: Mouton de Gruyter, 123–52.

Hilpert, M. (2007). Chained metonymies in lexicon and grammar: a cross-linguistic perspective on body part terms. In G. Radden, K.-M. Köpcke, T. Berg, and P. Siemund (eds.) *Aspects of Meaning Construction*. Amsterdam: John Benjamins, 77–98.

Holliday, A. (1999). Small cultures. *Applied Linguistics*, *20* (2): 237–64.

Hopper, P., and Traugott, E. (1993). *Grammaticalization* (2nd edn) Cambridge University Press.

Humphrey, H., Kemper, S., and Radel, J. (2004). The time course of metonymic language text processing by older and younger adults. *Experimental Aging Research: An International Journal Devoted to the Scientific Study of the Aging Process*, *30* (1): 75–94.

Hyland, K. (1998). *Hedging in Scientific Research Articles*. Amsterdam: John Benjamins.

Jäkel, O. (1999). Metonymy in onomastics. In K.-U. Panther and G. Radden (eds.) *Metonymy in Language and Thought*. Amsterdam: John Benjamins, 211–29.

Jakobson, R. (1956). Two aspects of language and two types of aphasic disturbances. Reproduced in L. Waugh and M. Monvill-Burston (eds.) (1990) *On Language: Roman Jakobson*. Cambridge, MA: Harvard University Press, 115–33.

Jakobson, R. (1971a). On linguistic aspects of translation. In R. Jakobson, *Selected Writings 2: Word and Language*. The Hague: Mouton de Gruyter, 260–6.

Jakobson, R. (1971b). The metaphoric and metonymic poles. In R. Jakobson and M. Halle (eds.) *Fundamentals of Language*. The Hague and Paris: Mouton de Gruyter, pp. 90–6.

Jiménez Catalán, R. M. (2012). Exploring the age factor in the production of metonymies by EFL learners. Paper presented at the seventh conference of the International Association, Researching and Applying Metaphor, Lancaster, UK.

Johnson, M., and Larson, S. (2009). Something in the way she moves: metaphors of musical motion. *Metaphor and Symbol*, *18* (2), 63–84.

Joue, G., Mittelberg, I., Evola, L., Boven, K., Willmes, F., and Schneider, U. (2012). Mono-modal metaphors in speech and co-verbal gestures: an fMRI study. Paper presented at the 9th Annual Conference of the International Organisation of Researching and Applying Metaphor, Lancaster, UK.

Kamarudin, R. B. (2013). A study on the use of phrasal verbs by Malaysian learners of English. Unpublished PhD Dissertation submitted to the University of Birmingham.

Kamei, S., and Wakao, T. (1992). Metonymy: reassessment, survey of acceptability, and its treatment in a machine translation system. In *The Proceedings of the 30th Annual Meeting of the Association for Computational Linguistics*, Newark, DE: ACL, 309–11.

Kaneko, M., and Sutton-Spence, R. L. (2012). Iconicity and metaphor in sign language poetry. *Metaphor and Symbol*, *27*: 107–30.

Kauschke, C., and Stenneken, P. (2008). Differences in noun and verb processing in lexical decision cannot be due to word form and morphological complexity alone. *Journal of Psychological Research*, *37*: 443–52.

Kimbara, I. (2006). On gestural mimicry. *Gesture, 6* (1): 39–61.

Kita, S., and Essegbey, J. (2001). Pointing left in Ghana: how a taboo on the use of the left hand influences gestural practice. *Gesture, 1* (1): 73–94.

Klepousniotou, E., and Baum, S. R. (2007). Clarifying further the ambiguity advantage effect in word recognition: effects of aging and left-hemisphere damage on the processing of homonymy and polysemy. *Brain and Language, 103*: 148–9.

Knapton, O., and Rundblad, G. (2012). Metaphor, metonymy and agency in obsessive-compulsive disorder. *Paper presented at the 4th UK Cognitive Linguistics Conference*, London, United Kingdom.

Koller, V. (2013). Cognitive linguistics and ideology. In J. Taylor and J. Littlemore (eds.) *Companion to Cognitive Linguistics*. London: Continuum, 234–52.

Kotthoff, H. (2006). Communicating affect in intercultural lamentations. In K. Bührig and J. D. ten Thije (eds.) *Beyond Misunderstanding: Linguistic Analyses of Intercultural Communication*. Amsterdam: Philadelphia, 289–312.

Kövecses, Z. (2006). *Language, Mind and Culture: A Practical Introduction*. Oxford University Press.

Kövecses, Z. (2010). *Metaphor: A Practical Introduction*. Oxford University Press.

Kövecses, Z. (2013). The metaphor–metonymy relationship: correlation metaphors are based on metonymy. *Metaphor and Symbol, 28*: 75–88.

Kövecses, Z., Palmer, G., and Dirven, R. (2002). Language and emotion: the interplay of conceptualisation with physiology and culture. In R. Dirven and R. Pörings (eds.) *Metaphor and Metonymy in Comparison and Contrast*. Berlin: Mouton de Gruyter, 133–60.

Kress, G., and van Leeuwen, T. (1996). *Reading Images: The Grammar of Visual Design*. London: Routledge.

Kristiansen, G. (2008). Style-shifting and shifting styles: a socio-cognitive approach to lectal variation. In G. Kristiansen and R. Dirven (eds.) *Cognitive Sociolinguistics: Language Variation, Cultural Models, Social Systems*. Berlin: Mouton de Gruyter, 45–88.

Kristiansen, G., and Geeraerts, D. (2013). Contexts and usage in cognitive sociolinguistics. *Journal of Pragmatics, 52*: 1–4.

Krott, A. (2012). The role of metonymy and reference point phenomena in children's interpretation of novel noun–noun compounds. Paper presented at the University of Birmingham Psychology Department seminar series.

Kureishi, H. (1990). *The Buddha of Suburbia*. London: Faber and Faber.

Ladewig, S., and Tessendorf, S. (2008). Interactive metonymy: co-constructing meaning and reference in gesture, Paper presented at the 2nd Annual Conference of the UK Cognitive Linguistics Association, University of Brighton, United Kingdom.

Lakoff, G. (1987). *Women, Fire and Dangerous Things: What Categories Reveal about the Mind*. University of Chicago Press.

Lakoff, G., and Johnson, M. (1980/2003). *Metaphors We Live By*. University of Chicago Press.

Langacker, R. W. (1987). *Foundations of Cognitive Grammar*, Vol. I: *Theoretical Prerequisites*. Stanford University Press.

Langacker, R. W. (1993). Reference-point constructions. *Cognitive Linguistics 4*: 1–38.

Langacker, R. (1999). *Grammar and Conceptualization*. Berlin: Mouton de Gruyter.

Langacker, R. W. (2008). *Cognitive Grammar: A Basic Introduction*. Oxford University Press.

Langacker, R. W. (2009). Metonymic grammar. In K.-U. Panther, L. Thornburg and A. Barcelona (eds.) *Metonymy and Metaphor in Grammar.* Amsterdam: John Benjamins, 45–71.

Larsen-Freeman, D., and Cameron, L. (2008). *Complex Systems and Applied Linguistics.* Oxford University Press.

Lee, J., and Collins, P. (2008). Gender voices in Hong Kong English textbooks: some past and current practices. *Sex Roles, 59* (1/2): 127–37.

Lee, K. Y. (2013). A genre analysis of written academic feedback. Unpublished PhD dissertation, University of Birmingham.

Leveling, J., and Hartrumpf, S. (2008). On metonymy recognition for geographic information retrieval. *International Journal of Geographical Information Science, 22* (3): 289–99.

Levin, M. (2008). 'Hitting the back of the net just before the final whistle': high-frequency phrase in football reporting. In E. Lavric and G. Pisek (eds.) *The Linguistics of Football.* Tubingen: Gunter Narr Verlag: 143–55.

Levin, M., and Lindquist, H. (2007). Sticking one's nose in the data: evaluation in phraseological sequences with nose. *ICAME Journal, 31,* 87–110.

Levinson, S. C. (2000). *Presumptive Meanings: The Theory of Generalized Conversational Implicature.* Cambridge, MA: MIT Press.

Liebscher, G. (2006). Perspectives in conflict: an analysis of German–German conversations. In K. Bührig and J. D. ten Thije (eds.) *Beyond Misunderstanding: Linguistic Analyses of Intercultural Communication.* Amsterdam: Philadelphia: 155–74.

Lindstromberg, S., and Boers, F. (2005). 'From movement to metaphor with manner-of-movement verbs. *Applied Linguistics, 26* (2): 241–61.

Litman, P. (2010). The relationship between gesture and sound: a pilot study of choral conducting behaviour in two related settings. Unpublished MA dissertation, Institute of Education, London.

Littlemore, J. (2001). The use of metaphor in university lectures and the problems that it causes for overseas students. *Teaching in Higher Education 6*: 333–51.

Littlemore, J. (2008). The relationship between associative thinking, analogical reasoning, image formation and metaphoric extension strategies. In M. S. Zanotto, L. Cameron and M. C. Cavalcanti (eds.) *Confronting Metaphor in Use: An Applied Linguistic Approach.* Amsterdam: John Benjamins: 199–222.

Littlemore, J. (2009). *Applying Cognitive Linguistics to Second Language Learning and Teaching.* Basingstoke: Palgrave Macmillan.

Littlemore, J., and Tagg, C. (in preparation). A framework for understanding creative metonymies in a corpus of SMS text messages.

Littlemore, J., Chen, P. T., Koester A., and Barnden, J. (2011a). Difficulties in metaphoric comprehension faced by international students whose first language is not English. *Applied Linguistics, 23* (1): 1–23.

Littlemore, J., Krennmayr, T., Turner, J., and Turner, S. (2011b). Investigating figurative proficiency at different levels of second language writing. Cambridge ESOL Final Project Report.

Littlemore, J., Krennmayr, T., Turner, J., and Turner, S. (2014). Investigating figurative proficiency at different levels of second language writing. *Applied Linguistics,* 35 (2): 117–44.

Littlemore, J., Arizono, S., and May, A. (in preparation). The comprehension of metonymy by Japanese learners of English: the influence of form and function.

Lodge, D. (1977). *The Modes of Modern Writing: Metaphor, Metonymy and the Typology of Modern Literature*. London: Arnold.

Louw, W. E. (1993). Irony in the text or insincerity in the writer? The diagnostic potential of semantic prosodies. In M. Baker, G. Francis and E. Tognini-Bonelli (eds.) *Text and Technology: In Honour of John Sinclair*. Amsterdam: John Benjamins, 157–76.

Low, G. (2008). Metaphor and education. In R. Gibbs (ed.) *The Cambridge Handbook of Metaphor*. Cambridge University Press.

Lowder, M. W., and Gordon, P. C. (2013). It's hard to offend the college: effects of sentence structure on figurative-language processing, *Journal of Experimental Psychology: Learning, Memory and Cognition*, *39* (4): 993–1011.

MacArthur, F., and Littlemore, J. (2008). A discovery approach using corpora in the foreign language classroom. In F. Boers and S. Lindstromberg (eds.) *Cognitive Linguistic Approaches to Teaching Vocabulary and Phraseology*. Amsterdam: Mouton de Gruyter, 159–88.

MacArthur, F. *et al.* (2013a). Metaphor-use in one-to-one academic consultations in English: implications for Spanish mobility in Europe. Project funded by the Spanish Ministry of Education.

MacArthur, F., Littlemore, J., and Krennmayr, T. (2013b). SEEING is not just UNDERSTANDING: sight metaphors in undergraduate office hours consultations. Paper presented at the Third International Conference on Meaning Construction and Meaning Interpretation: Applications and Implications, University of Rioja at Logroño, Spain.

Magorian, M. (1983). *Goodnight Mr Tom*. London: Puffin Books.

Mandel, M. (1977). Iconic devices in American sign language. In L. A. Freedman (ed.) *On the Other Hand*. London: Academic Press, 57–107.

Markert, K., and Hahn, U. (2002). Understanding metonymies in discourse. *Artificial Intelligence*, *135* (1–2): 145–98.

Markert, K., and Nissim, M. (2009a). Corpus-based metonymy analysis. *Metaphor and Symbol*, *18* (3): 175–88.

Markert, K., and Nissim, M. (2009b). Data and models for metonymy resolution. *Language Resources and Evaluation*, *43*: 123–38.

May, A. (2013). To what extent and why are the following conceptual metonymies exploited across thirteen typologically varied languages? PRODUCER FOR PRODUCT; AGENT FOR ACTION; PART FOR WHOLE; WHOLE FOR PART; ACTION FOR COMPLEX EVENT; CATEGORY FOR MEMBER; MEMBER FOR CATEGORY; OBJECT FOR ACTION. Unpublished MA project, University of Birmingham, UK.

McNeill, D., Quek, F., McCullough, K.-E., Duncan, S., Furuyama, N., Bryll, R., Maand, X.-F., and Ansari, R. (2001). Catchments, prosody and discourse. *Gesture*, *1* (1): 9–33.

Meadows, B. (2006). Distancing and showing solidarity via metaphor and metonymy in political discourse: a critical study of American statements on Iraq during the years 2004–2005. *Critical Approaches to Discourse Analysis across Disciplines*, *1* (2): 1–17.

Miller, A. (1995). *A View from the Bridge*. Harlow: Heinemann.

Mittelberg, I., and Waugh, L. (2009). Metonymy first, metaphor second: a cognitive semiotic approach to multimodal figures of thought in co-speech gesture. In C. Forceville and E. Urios-Aparisi (eds.) *Multimodal Metaphor*. Amsterdam: Mouton de Gruyter, 330–56.

Moscovici, S. (2001). The history and actuality of social representations. In G. Duveen (ed.) *Social Representations: Explorations in Social Psychology*. New York University Press, 120–55.

Müller, C. (2008). *Metaphors, Dead and Alive, Sleeping and Waking: A Dynamic View*. University of Chicago Press.

Müller, C., and Cienki, A. (2009). Words, gestures, and beyond: forms of multimodal metaphor in the use of spoken language. In C. Forceville and E. Urios-Aparisi (eds.) *Multimodal Metaphor*. Amsterdam: Mouton de Gruyter, 297–327.

Munday, J. (2008). *Introducing Translation Studies: Theories and Applications*. London: Routledge.

Nerlich, B., and Clarke, D. (2001). Serial metonymy: a study of reference-based polysemisation. *Journal of Historical Pragmatics*, 2 (2): 245–72.

Nerlich, B., Clarke, D., and Todd, Z. (1999). 'Mummy, I like being a sandwich': metonymy in language acquisition. In K.-U. Panther and G. Radden (eds.) *Metonymy in Language and Thought*. Amsterdam: John Benjamins, 361–84.

Norrick, N. (1981). *Semiotic Principles in Semantic Theory*. Amsterdam: John Benjamins.

Norton, P. (1990). The lady's not for turning. But what about the rest? Margaret Thatcher and the Conservative Party. *Parliamentary Affairs*, *43* (3): 41–58.

Nunberg, G. (1979). The non-uniqueness of semantic solutions: polysemy. *Linguistics and Philosophy*, *3*, 143–84.

Nunberg, G. (1995). Transfers of meaning. *Journal of Semantics*, *12*: 109–32.

O'Flynn, C. (2010). *The News Where You Are*. London: Penguin.

Onysko, A., and Degani, M. (2012). The interplay of metaphor and metonymy in the interpretation of novel English compounds. Paper presented at the UK Cognitive Linguistics Association, Biennial Conference, London, UK.

Ortiz, M. J. (2011). Primary metaphors and monomodal visual metaphors. *Journal of Pragmatics*, *43*: 1568–80.

Pankhurst, A. (1999). Recontextualization of metonymy in narrative and the case of Morrison's Song of Solomon. In K.-U. Panther and G. Radden (eds.) *Metonymy in Language and Thought*. Amsterdam: John Benjamins, 385–400.

Panther, K.-U., and Thornburg, L. (1998). A cognitive approach to inferencing in conversation. *Journal of Pragmatics*, *30*: 755–69.

Panther, K.-U., and Thornburg, L. (1999). The potentiality for actuality metonymy in English and Hungarian. In K.-U. Panther and G. Radden (eds.) *Metonymy in Language and Thought*. Amsterdam: John Benjamins, 333–57.

Panther, K.-U., and Thornburg, L. (2002). The roles of metaphor and metonymy in English –er nominals. In R. Dirven and R. Porings (eds.) *Metaphor and Metonymy in Comparison and Contrast*. Berlin and New York: Mouton de Gruyter, 279–322.

Panther, K.-U., and Thornburg, L. (eds.) (2003). *Metonymy and Pragmatic Inferencing*. Amsterdam and Philadelphia: John Benjamins.

Panther, K.-U., and Thornburg, L. (2007). Metonymy. In D. Geeraerts and H. Cuyckens (eds.) *The Oxford Handbook of Cognitive Linguistics*. Oxford University Press, 236–62.

Panther, K.-U., and Thornburg, L. (2009). On figurative in grammar. In K.-U. Panther, L. Thornburg and A. Barcelona (eds.) *Metonymy and Metaphor in Grammar*. Amsterdam: John Benjamins, 1–44.

Panther, K.-U., and Thornburg, L. (2012). Antonymy in language structure and use. In M. Brdar, I. Raffaelli and M. Žic Fuchs (eds.) *Cognitive Linguistics between*

Universality and Variation. Newcastle upon Tyne: Cambridge Scholars Publishing, 161–88.

Panther, K.-U., Thornburg, L., and Barcelona, A. (eds.) (2009). *Metonymy and Metaphor in Grammar*. Amsterdam: John Benjamins.

Papafragou, A. (1996). On metonymy. *Lingua*, *99*, 169–95.

Peirce, C. S. (1966). *Selected Writings*. New York: Dover.

Peirsman, Y., and Geeraerts, D. (2006a). Metonymy as a prototypical category. *Cognitive Linguistics*, *17* (3): 269–316.

Peirsman, Y., and Geeraerts, D. (2006b). Don't let metonymy be misunderstood: an answer to Croft. *Cognitive Linguistics*, *17* (3): 327–35.

Pérez-Sobrino, P. (2011). Don't be so green: analysis of the interaction between multimodal metaphor in greenwashing advertisements. 2nd Conference of Young Researchers on Anglophone Studies. University of Salamanca, Spain.

Pérez-Sobrino, P. (2013a). Metaphor use in advertising: analysis of the interaction between multimodal metaphor and metonymy in a greenwashing advertisement. In E. Gola and F. Ervas (eds.) *Metaphor in Focus: Philosophical Perspectives on Metaphor Use*. Newcastle upon Tyne: Cambridge Scholars Publishing, 67–82.

Pérez-Sobrino, P. (2013b). Metonymic reasoning in musical understanding. Paper presented at the 3rd International Conference on Meaning Construction, Meaning Interpretation: Applications and Implications (CRAL, 2013), University of La Rioja, Logrono, Spain.

Pfaff, K., Gibbs, R., and Johnson, M. (1997). Metaphor in using and understanding euphemism and dysphemism. *Applied Psycholinguistics*, *18* (1): 59–83.

Pinelli, E. (2012). Framing identities in media discourse: the role of metonymy and metaphor. Paper presented at the UK Cognitive Linguistics Association, Biennial Conference, London, UK.

Piquer Píriz, A. M. (2008). Reasoning figuratively in early EFL: some implications for the development of vocabulary. In F. Boers and S. Lindstromberg (eds.) *Cognitive Linguistic Approaches to Teaching Vocabulary and Phraseology*. Berlin and New York: Mouton de Gruyter, 219–40.

Pragglejaz Group (2007). MIP: A method for identifying metaphorically used words in discourse. *Metaphor and Symbol*, *22* (1), 1–40.

Pramling, N., and Pramling-Samuelsson, I. (2009). The prosaics of figurative language in preschool: some observations and suggestions for research. *Early Child Development and Care*, *179* (30): 329–38.

Quirk, R., Greenbaum, S., Leech, G., and Svartvik, J. (1985). *A Comprehensive Grammar of the English Language*. Harlow: Longman.

Radden, G. (2000). How metonymic are metaphors? In A. Barcelona (ed.) *Metaphor and Metonymy at the Crossroads*. Berlin and New York: Mouton de Gruyter, 93–108.

Radden, G. (2005). The ubiquity of metonymy. In J.-L. Otal Campo, I. Ferrando and B. Belles Fortuno (eds.) *Cognitive and Discourse Approaches to Metaphor and Metonymy*. Castellón de la Plana: Universitat Jaume I, 11–28.

Radden, G., and Kövecses, Z. (1999). Towards a theory of metonymy. In K.-U. Panther and G. Radden (eds.) *Metonymy in Language and Thought*. Amsterdam: John Benjamins, 17–59.

Radden, G., and Seto, K. I. (2003). Metonymic construals of shopping requests in HAVE and BE languages. In K.-U. Panther and L. Thornburg (eds.) *Metonymy and Pragmatic Inferencing*. Amsterdam and Philadelphia: John Benjamins, 223–39.

Radden, G., Köpcke, K.-M., Berg, T., and Siemund, P. (2007). The construction of meaning in language. In G. Radden, K.-M. Köpcke, T. Berg and P. Siemund (eds.) *Aspects of Meaning Construction*. Amsterdam: John Benjamins, 1–15.

Rapp, A. M., Erb M., Grodd, W., Bartels, M., and Markert, K. (2011). Neurological correlates of metonymy resolution. *Brain and Language*, *119* (3): 196–205.

Rapp, A. M., Mutschler, D. E., and Erb, M. (2012). Where in the brain is nonliteral language? A coordinate-based meta-analysis of functional magnetic resonance imaging studies. *Neuroimage*, *63*: 600–10.

Raskin, V. (1985). *Semantic Mechanisms of Humor*. Dordrecht: D. Reidel.

Rhodes, J. E., and Jakes, S. (2004). The contribution of metaphor and metonymy to delusions. *Psychology and Psychotherapy: Theory, Research and Practice*, *77*: 1–17.

Richardson, P. (2013). Exploring certainty in religious discourse. Unpublished PhD dissertation, University of Birmingham.

Ringbom, H. (2001). Lexical transfer in L3 production. In J. Cenoz, B. Hufeisen and U. Jessner (eds.) *Cross-Linguistics in Third Language Acquisition: A Psycholinguistic Perspective*. Clevedon: Multilingual Matters, 29–68.

Rojo López, A. M. (2009). A cognitive approach to the translation of metonymy-based humor. *Across Languages and Cultures*, *10* (1): 63–83.

Rost-Roth, M. (2006). Intercultural communication in institutional counselling sessions. In K. Bührig and J. D. ten Thije (eds.). *Beyond Misunderstanding: Linguistic Analyses of Intercultural Communication*, Amsterdam: Philadelphia, pp. 189–216.

Rudicell, R. (1992). Using metonymy and myth to teach film, *The English Journal*, *81* (7): 78–81.

Ruiz de Mendoza Ibáñez, F. J. (1998). On the nature of blending as a cognitive phenomenon. *Journal of Pragmatics*, *30*: 259–74.

Ruiz de Mendoza Ibáñez, F. J., and Diez Velasco, O. I. (2002). Patterns of conceptual interaction. In R. Dirven and R. Porings (eds.) (2003). *Metaphor and Metonymy in Comparison and Contrast*. Berlin and New York: Mouton de Gruyter, 489–532.

Ruiz de Mendoza Ibáñez, F., and Diez Velasco, O. I. (2004). Metonymic motivation in anaphoric reference. In G. Radden and K.-U. Panther (eds.) *Studies in Linguistic Motivation*. Berlin: Mouton de Gruyter, 293–320.

Ruiz de Mendoza Ibáñez, F. J., and Mairal Uson, R. (2007). High level metaphor and metonymy in meaning construction. In G. Radden, K.-M. Köpcke, T. Berg and P. Siemund (eds.) *Aspects of Meaning Construction*. Amsterdam: John Benjamins, 33–49.

Ruiz de Mendoza Ibáñez, F. J., and Otal Campo, J. L. (2002). *Metonymy, Grammar and Communication*. Granada: Comares.

Ruiz de Mendoza Ibáñez, F. J., and Pérez Hernández, L. (2001). Metonymy and grammar: motivation, constraints, and interaction. *Language and Communication*, *21*: 321–57.

Ruiz de Mendoza Ibáñez, F. and Pérez Hernández, L. (2003). Cognitive operations and pragmatic implication. In K.-U. Panther and L. Thornburg (eds.) *Metonymy and Pragmatic Inferencing*. Amsterdam: John Benjamins, 23–50.

Rundblad, G., and Annaz, D. (2010a). Metaphor and metonymy comprehension: receptive vocabulary and conceptual knowledge. *British Journal of Developmental Psychology*, *28*: 547–63.

Rundblad, G., and Annaz, D. (2010b). The atypical development of metaphor and metonymy comprehension in children with autism. *Autism*, *14* (1): 29–46.

Ryland, S. (2011). Resisting metaphors: a metonymic approach to the study of creativity in art analysis and practice. Unpublished PhD dissertation, University of Brighton, UK.

Sappan, R. (1987). *The Rhetorical-Logical Classification of Semantic Changes*. Braunton: Merlin Books.

Saussure, F. de (1915). *Course in General Linguistics*, trans. R. Harris, ed. C. Bally, A. Sechehaye and A. Reidlinger. London: Duckworth.

Serrano Losado, M. (2013). Pictorial metaphor and metonymy at work: the case of painkiller advertising. Paper presented at the 3rd International Conference on Meaning Construction, Meaning Interpretation: Applications and Implications (CRAL, 2013), University of La Rioja, Logrono, Spain.

Seto, K.-I. (1999). Distinguishing metonymy from synecdoche. In K.-U. Panther and G. Radden (eds.) *Metonymy in Language and Thought*. Amsterdam: John Benjamins, 91–120.

Shaghayegh Alirezaie, M. (2012). Preserving the water of one's face: socio-cultural foundations of metonymic and metaphorical conceptualizations of the face in Farsi. Paper presented at the UK Cognitive Linguistics Association Annual Conference, King's College London, July.

Shore, B. (1996). *Culture in Mind*. Oxford University Press.

Slobin, D. I. (2000). Verbalized events: a dynamic approach to linguistic relativity and determinism. In S. Niemeier and R. Dirven (eds.) *Evidence for Linguistic Relativity*. Amsterdam: John Benjamins, 108–38.

Soukup, B. (2013). Austrian dialect as a metonymic device: a cognitive sociolinguistic investigation of Speaker Design and its perceptual implications. *Journal of Pragmatics*, *53*: 72–82.

Spenney, M. J., and Haynes, O. H. (1989). Semantic and phonological performance in adults learning novel object and action words. *Journal of Psycholinguistic Research*, *18*: 341–52.

Sperber, D., and Wilson, D. (1987). Precis of relevance: communication and cognition. *Behavioral and Brain Sciences*, *10*, 697–754.

Sperber, D., and Wilson, D. (2004). Relevance theory. In G. Ward and L. Horn (eds.) *Handbook of Pragmatics*. Oxford: Blackwell, 607–32.

Stallard, D. (1993). Two kinds of metonymy. In *The Proceedings of the 31st annual meeting on Association for Computational Linguistics*, Columbus, OH: ACL, 87–94.

Steen, G. (1999). From linguistic to conceptual metaphor in five steps. In R. Gibbs and G. Steen (eds.) *Metaphor in Cognitive Linguistics*. Amsterdam: John Benjamins, 57–97.

Stefanowitsch, A. (2003). A construction-based approach to indirect speech acts. In K.-U. Panther and L. Thornburg (eds.) *Metonymy and Pragmatic Inferencing*. Amsterdam: John Benjamins, 105–26.

Stvan, L. S. (2007). Lexical conflation and edible iconicity: two sources of ambiguity in American vernacular health terminology. *Communication and Medicine*, *4* (2): 189–99.

Stvan, L. S. (2012). Metonymy-driven polysemy in health discourse. Paper presented at the 9th Conference of the International Association, Researching and Applying Metaphor, Lancaster, United Kingdom.

Sutton-Spence, R., and Coates, R. (2011). Football crazy? Place-names and football club-names in British Sign Language. *Nomina*, 34: 5–25.

Sutton-Spence, R., Kaneko, M., and West, D. (2012). Mode-specific metaphors in creative sign language. Paper presented at the 9th Conference on Researching and Applying Metaphor, Lancaster, UK.

Tagg, C. (2012). *The Discourse of Text Messaging*. London: Continuum.

Tagg, C. (2013). Scraping the barrel with a shower of social misfits, *Applied Linguistics*, *34* (4): 480–500.

Talmy, L. (1985). Lexicalisation patterns semantic structure in lexical forms. In T. Shopen (ed.) *Language Typology and Syntactic Description,* Vol. III: *Grammatical Categories and the Lexicon*. Cambridge University Press, 93–121.

Tang, L. (2007). Figurative language in a nursery setting and a non-native speaker's perspective on this discourse community. Unpublished MA dissertation, University of Birmingham.

Taub, S. (2004). *Language from the Body: Iconicity and Metaphor in American Sign Language*. Cambridge University Press.

Tay, D. (2011). Discourse markers as metaphor signalling devices in psychotherapeutic talk. *Language and Communication*, *31*: 310–17.

Tay, D. (2012). Applying the notion of metaphor types to enhance counselling protocols. *Journal of Counselling and Development*, *90* (2), 142–9.

Taylor, J. R. (2002). Category extension by metonymy and metaphor. In R. Dirven and R. Porings (eds.) *Metaphor and Metonymy in Comparison and Contrast*. Berlin and New York: Mouton de Gruyter, 323–34.

Taylor, J. R. (2003). *Linguistic Categorization*. Oxford University Press.

ten Thije, J. D. (2006). Notions of perspective and perspectivising in intercultural communication research. In K. Bührig and J. D. ten Thije (eds.) *Beyond Misunderstanding: Linguistic Analyses of Intercultural Communication*. Amsterdam: Philadelphia, 97–153.

Tomasello, M. (2003). *Constructing a Language: A Usage-Based Theory of Language Acquisition*. Cambridge, MA: Harvard University Press.

Traugott, E., and Dasher, R. (2002). *Regularity in Semantic Change*. Cambridge University Press.

Tsujimora, N., and Davis, S. (2011). A construction approach to innovative verbs in Japanese. *Cognitive Linguistics*, *22* (4): 799–825.

Ullmann, S. (1951). *The Principles of Semantics*. Oxford: Blackwell Publishing.

Urios-Aparisi, E. (2009). Interaction of multimodal metaphor and metonymy in TV commercials: four case studies. In C. Forceville and E. Urios-Aparisi (eds.) *Multimodal Metaphor*. Berlin and New York: Mouton de Gruyter, 95–117.

van Dijk, T. (1998). *Ideology: A Multidisciplinary Approach*. London: Sage.

Van Herwegen, J., Dimitrious, D. and Rundblad, G. (2013). Development of novel metaphor and metonymy comprehension in typically developing children and Williams syndrome. *Research in Developmental Disabilities*, 34 (4): 1300–11.

Veale, T., Feyaerts, K., and Brône, G. (2006). The cognitive mechanisms of adversarial humor. *International Journal of Humor*, *19*: 305–40.

Villicañas, N., and White, M. (2013). Pictorial metonymy as a creativity source in Purificacīōn Garcīa advertising campaigns. *Metaphor in the Social World*, 3 (2): 220–39.

Vosshagen, C. (1999). Opposition as a metonymic principle. In K.-U. Panther and G. Radden (eds.) *Metonymy in Language and Thought*. Amsterdam: John Benjamins, 289–308.

Warren, B. (1999). Aspects of referential metonymy. In K.-U. Panther and G. Radden (eds.) *Metonymy in Language and Thought*. Amsterdam: John Benjamins, 121–37.

Warren, B. (2003). An alternative account of the interpretation of referential metonymy and metaphor. In R. Dirven and R. Porings (eds.) *Metaphor and Metonymy in Comparison and Contrast*. Berlin and New York: Mouton de Gruyter, 113–130.

Warren, B. (2006). *Referential Metonymy*. Scripta Minora, 2003–4. Royal Society of Letters at Lund, Sweden.

Whalen, Z. N. (2004). Play along: video game music and metaphor and metonymy. Unpublished MA thesis, University of Florida.

Wilcox, P. (2004). A cognitive key: metonymic and metaphorical mappings in ASL. *Cognitive Linguistics*, *15* (2): 197–222.

Wilcox, S. (2007). Signed languages. In D. Geeraerts and H. Cuyckens (eds.) *The Oxford Handbook of Cognitive Linguistics*. Oxford University Press, 1113–36.

Wilcox, S., Wilcox, P., and Jarque, M. J. (2003). Mappings in conceptual space: metonymy, metaphor, and iconicity in two signed languages. *Jezikoslovlje*, *4* (1): 139–222.

Wojciechowska, S., and Szczepaniak, R. (2013). Modified idioms with HAND: a corpus-based study of the metaphor-metonymy interplay. Paper presented at the Annual Conference of the UK Cognitive Linguistics Association, King's College London.

Wolk, C., Bresnan J., Rosenbach A., and Szmrecsanyi B. (2013). Dative and genitive variability in Late Modern English: exploring cross-constructional variation and change. *Diachronica*, *30* (3): 382–419.

Yamanashi, M.-A. (1987). Metonymic interpretation and associative processes in natural language. In M. Naga (ed.) *Language and Artificial Intelligence, International Symposium on Language and Artificial Intelligence* (16th–21st March 1986, Kyoto, Japan). Amsterdam: Elsevier Science Publishers, 77–86.

Yu, N. (2000). Figurative uses of finger and palm in Chinese and English. *Metaphor and Symbol*, *15* (3): 159–75.

Yu, N. (2009). Nonverbal and multimodal manifestations of metaphors and metonymies: a case study. In C. Forceville and E. Urios-Aparisi (eds.) *Multimodal Metaphor*. Berlin and New York: Mouton de Gruyter, 119–43.

Zaidel, E., Kasher, A., Soroker, N., and Batori, G. (2002). Effects of right and left hemisphere damage on performance on the 'Right Hemisphere Communication Battery'. *Brain and Language*, *80* (3): 510–35.

Zhang, W., Speelman, D., and Geeraerts, D. (2011). Variation in the (non)metonymic capital names in mainland Chinese and Taiwanese Chinese. *Metaphor and the Social World*, *1* (1): 90–112.

Index